The Church and Indigenous Peoples in the Americas

✝

STUDIES IN WORLD CATHOLICISM

Michael L. Budde and William T. Cavanaugh, *Series Editors*

Karen M. Kraft, *Managing Editor*

Other Titles in This Series

Beyond the Borders of Baptism: Catholicity, Allegiances, and Lived Identities. Edited by Michael L. Budde. Vol. 1, 2016. ISBN 9781498204736.

New World Pope: Pope Francis and the Future of the Church. Edited by Michael L. Budde. Vol. 2, 2017. ISBN 9781498283717.

Scattered and Gathered: Catholics in Diaspora. Edited by Michael L. Budde. Vol. 3, 2017. ISBN 9781532607097.

Fragile World: Ecology and the Church. Edited by William T. Cavanaugh. Vol. 4, 2018. ISBN 9781498283403.

A Living Tradition: The Holy See, Catholic Social Doctrine, and Global Politics 1965–2000. By A. Alexander Stummvoll. Vol. 5, 2018. ISBN 9781532605116.

Love, Joy, and Sex: African Conversation on Pope Francis's Amoris Laetitia and the Gospel of Family in a Divided World. Edited by Stan Ilo. Vol. 6, 2018. ISBN 9781532618956.

The Church and Indigenous Peoples in the Americas

In Between Reconciliation and Decolonization

EDITED BY

Michel Andraos

FOREWORD BY

William T. Cavanaugh

CONTRIBUTORS

Jaime C. Bascuñán
Marie Battiste
Joanne Doi, MM
Pedro Gutiérrez Jiménez
Stephen P. Judd, MM
Sylvain Lavoie, OMI
Brian McDonough

Rosa Isolde Reuque Paillalef
J. Jorge Santiago Santiago
Robert J. Schreiter, CPPS
Roger Schroeder, SVD
Eva Solomon, CSJ
Roberto Tomichá Charupá, OFM Conv.
Francis White Lance

CASCADE *Books* • Eugene, Oregon

THE CHURCH AND INDIGENOUS PEOPLES IN THE AMERICAS
In Between Reconciliation and Decolonization

Studies in World Catholicism 7

Cascade Books
An Imprint of Wipf and Stock Publishers
199 W. 8th Ave., Suite 3
Eugene, OR 97401

www.wipfandstock.com

PAPERBACK ISBN: 978-1-5326-3111-5
HARDCOVER ISBN: 978-1-5326-3113-9
EBOOK ISBN: 978-1-5326-3112-2

Cataloguing-in-Publication data:

Names: Andraos, Michel, editor. | Cavanaugh, William T., 1962–, foreword.

Title: The church and indigenous peoples in the Americas : in between reconciliation and decolonization / edited by Michel Andraos ; foreword by William T. Cavanaugh.

Description: Eugene, OR : Cascade Books, 2019 | Series: Studies in World Catholicism 7 | Includes bibliographical references and index.

Identifiers: ISBN 978-1-5326-3111-5 (paperback) | ISBN 978-1-5326-3113-9 (hardcover) | ISBN 978-1-5326-3112-2 (ebook)

Subjects: LCSH: Catholic Church—Missions. | Americas. | Indigenous peoples—Religion. | Christianity and culture.

Classification: BV2180 .C56 2019 (print) | BV2180 .C56 (ebook)

To the *Pueblo Creyente* of the Diocese of San Cristóbal de las Casas, Chiapas, Mexico, in honor of its twenty-fifth anniversary, and in solidarity with its long resistance and journey of hope for *otra iglesia y otro mundo posibles*: another possible church and world.

Contents

Contributors | ix

Foreword by William T. Cavanaugh | 1
Introduction by Michel Andraos | 3

PART ONE: Regional Indigenous Theological Voices
                     and Responses

A: Bolivia

1: Toward a Church with an Indigenous Face: Some Premises
   and Urgent Challenges | 13
   ROBERTO TOMICHÁ CHARUPÁ, OFM CONV.

2: Beyond the Colonial Wound: The Emergence of the Indigenous
   Theological Movement in Latin America | 30
   STEPHEN P. JUDD, MM

B: Canada

3: My Experience Working as an Indigenous Person with
   Indigenous People | 45
   EVA SOLOMON, CSJ

4: The Truth and Reconciliation Commission of Canada | 56
   BRIAN McDONOUGH

5: Walking a New Path: A Harvest of Reconciliation—Forging a Renewed
   Relationship between the Church and the Indigenous Peoples | 78
   SYLVAIN LAVOIE, OMI

C: *Chile*

6: My Experience as a Mapuche Christian | 101
ROSA ISOLDE REUQUE PAILLALEF

7: Christian and Mapuche Dialogue: A Theological Reflection Toward
Mutual Understanding | 107
JAIME C. BASCUÑÁN

D: *Mexico*

8: Mayan Indian Theology: A Journey of Decolonizing the Heart | 121
PEDRO GUTIÉRREZ JIMÉNEZ

9: Accompaniment in the Process of Dialogue-Encounter with the
Indigenous Peoples from the Diocese of San Cristóbal de las Casas,
Chiapas, Mexico: 1969–2019 | 135
J. JORGE SANTIAGO SANTIAGO

E: *The United States of America*

10: Lakota-Christian Dialogue | 151
FRANCIS WHITE LANCE

11: Steps Toward Reconciliation: The CTU-Lakota Relationship | 160
ROGER SCHROEDER, SVD

PART TWO: Reflections and Future Perspectives

12: Reconciling Truths and Decolonizing Practices for the Head,
Heart, and Hands | 177
MARIE BATTISTE

13: Witness and Practice of Living Memory | 193
JOANNE DOI, MM

14: Horizons of Memory and Hope: Some Concluding Reflections | 203
ROBERT J. SCHREITER, CPPS

Bibliography | 215
Index | 229

Contributors

Jaime C. Bascuñán is assistant professor in the Faculty of Religious Studies and Philosophy at the Catholic University of Temuco in Chile's southern Araucanía Region. In his work, he has also coordinated a project of inter-cultural-interreligious, Christian-Mapuche dialogue. He holds a doctorate of ministry from Catholic Theological Union (Chicago) and worked for a time in ministry formation in the Archdiocese of Chicago.

Marie Battiste is a Mi'kmaw educator, a member of the Potlotek First Nations, Nova Scotia, and professor of educational foundations at the University of Saskatchewan in Canada. She holds graduate degrees from Harvard and Stanford and is an elected fellow of the Royal Society of Canada. She is widely published, and her recent books include *Living Treaties: Narrating Mi'kmaw Treaty Relations* (CBU Press, 2016) and *Decolonizing Education: Nourishing the Learning Spirit* (Purich Press, 2013).

Joanne Doi, MM, is professor of intercultural studies and ministry at Catholic Theological Union (Chicago). A Maryknoll sister, she has served in the southern Andes Mountains of Peru doing pastoral work and economic development projects among Indigenous people. She holds a doctorate in interdisciplinary studies from the Graduate Theological Union (Berkeley).

Pedro (jPetul) Gutiérrez Jiménez, of Mayan-Tzeltal heritage, is coordinator of indigenous theology at the Institute for Intercultural Studies and Research in San Cristóbal de las Casas, Chiapas, Mexico. Previously, he served on the Mesoamerican Commission for Indian/Indigenous Theology and also as an advisor to both the Mexico Bishops' Commission for Indigenous Pastoral Ministry and to CONAI, the National Commission of Intermediation, during the peace talks between the Zapatista National Liberation Army and the Mexican government.

Stephen P. Judd, MM, is a Maryknoll missionary who served for decades in southern Peru and Bolivia, working in pastoral ministries among the Aymara and Quechua Indigenous peoples, as director of the Andean Pastoral Institute in Cuzco, Peru, and of the Maryknoll Mission Center and Language Institute in Cochabamba, Bolivia. He holds a PhD in the sociology of religion from the Graduate Theological Union (Berkeley); he has published the memoirs of his years in Peru as *De Apacheta en Apacheta: Testimonio de Fe en el Sur Andino Peruano* (Verbo Divino, 2015).

Sylvain Lavoie, OMI, is archbishop emeritus of Keewatin–The Pas in Manitoba, Canada, and has spent over thirty years ministering among the Indigenous peoples of north and central Saskatchewan. Currently, he serves as chaplain and spiritual director at Star of the North Retreat Centre in St. Albert, Alberta, where his ministry includes offering workshops and retreats on Indigenous ministry, biblical spirituality, addictions awareness, the twelve-step program, forgiveness, and healing. He is the author of *Drumming from Within: Tales of Hope and Faith from Canada's North* (Novalis, 2009).

Brian McDonough is a lecturer in theological studies at Concordia University (Montreal) and previous director of the Office of Social Action in the Roman Catholic Archdiocese of Montreal. His archdiocesan work involved promoting human rights, working with community organizations, assisting refugee claimants and asylum seekers, and accompanying prisoners in a perspective of restorative justice. He holds an MA in theology from Concordia and a law degree from McGill University (Montreal). His teaching interests include social ethics, faith, culture and media, cosmology, and eco-justice.

Rosa Isolde Reuque Paillalef is a Mapuche feminist, political and human rights activist, and has been a leader within the Mapuche Indigenous rights movement in Chile for over thirty years. Currently, she is executive secretary of the Office of Mapuche Pastoral Ministry in the Diocese of San José in Temuco, Chile. She is the author of *When a Flower is Reborn: The Life and Times of a Mapuche Feminist* (Duke University Press, 2002).

J. Jorge Santiago Santiago is a current board member and past director of the community-based nonprofit, DESMI (Social and Economic Development for Indigenous Mexicans) in San Cristóbal de las Casas, Chiapas, Mexico. He has a degree in theology from Rome's Pontifical Gregorian University and is coauthor of a book on economic solidarity, *Si Uno Come que Coman Todos: Economía Solidaria* (DESMI, 2001); his 1996 and 1999 interviews with Bishop Samuel Ruiz have been published, respectively, as *Seeking Freedom* and *La Pasión de Servir al Pueblo*.

Robert J. Schreiter, CPPS, is the Vatican Council II Professor of Theology at Catholic Theological Union (Chicago). He holds a doctorate in theology from the University of Nijmegen (The Netherlands), and his many books include *Constructing Local Theologies* (Orbis, 1985) and *The Ministry of Reconciliation: Spirituality and Strategies* (Orbis, 1998). Past president of the American Society of Missiology and of the Catholic University of America, he has also been working with Church leaders worldwide for twenty-five years in the area of reconciliation.

Roger Schroeder, SVD, is the Louis J. Luzbetak, SVD Professor of Mission and Culture and professor of Intercultural Studies and Ministry at Catholic Theological Union (Chicago). A priest and member of the Divine Word Missionaries, he holds a doctorate in missiology from the Pontifical Gregorian University in Rome. His experience with indigenous peoples includes six years of life and work in Papa New Guinea and almost yearly visits since 1991 to the Lakota reservations in South Dakota. His publications include *What is the Mission of the Church? A Guide for Catholics* (Orbis, 2008).

Eva Solomon, CSJ, is executive director of the Building Bridges Project in Winnipeg, Manitoba, for Canada's Assembly of Western Catholic Bishops's Standing Committee on Aboriginal Affairs. An Anishinaabe and member of Henvey Inlet First Nation, she has been a Sister of St. Joseph of Sault Ste. Marie for fifty-five years and holds a DMin in cross-cultural ministry. She received the 1999 Christian Culture Gold Medal Award from Assumption University in Windsor, Ontario, for her work among Aboriginal people and in reconciling Anishinaabe spiritual traditions with Christianity.

Roberto Tomichá Charupá, OFM Conv., is director of the Latin American Institute of Missiology at the Catholic University of Bolivia (Cochabamba) and a visiting professor at the Pontifical University of St. Bonaventure (Rome). Since 2006, he has also served as an advisor to the Conference of

Latin American Bishops (CELAM) on issues related to missions and Indigenous theology. Born into an Indigenous Chiquitano family in Bolivia,
he is a priest of the Conventual Franciscan order and holds a doctorate in
missiology; he has published a variety of books and journal articles in Latin
America and Europe.

Francis White Lance, a member of the Oglala Sioux Tribe of the Pine Ridge
Reservation in South Dakota, is a Sundance leader and Yuwipi man. He is
also an ordained priest of the Anglican Catholic Church in America; he holds
an MA in theological studies from Seabury-Western Theological Seminary
(now Bexley-Seabury in Chicago) and an honorary PhD from Winona State
University (Minnesota). A descendant of the legendary Oglala Sioux chief,
Tasunke Witko (Crazy Horse), he has published two books on the Lakota
way of life: *Why the Black Hills are Sacred* and *Tasunke Witko Woihanble*.

Foreword

The goal of this volume—and the conference from which it came—is to allow Indigenous[1] voices to be heard, voices too long silenced within the church. The conversations represented in the volume are much too rare. In recent decades, progress has been made in the official recognition of the many sins and crimes committed against Indigenous peoples by representatives of the church over the centuries. Formal apologies are good and necessary for going forward in a spirit of repair and reconciliation. But apologies are not enough. After the wrongs—many ongoing—have been recognized, what can we do concretely to take positive steps toward the full incorporation of Indigenous gifts in the body of Christ? What is God doing among Indigenous peoples from which the rest of us need to learn? The contributors to this volume, both Indigenous and non-Indigenous, offer compelling reflections on what works and what does not.

There is an ancient Christian principle known in Latin as *preparatio evangelica* that expresses some of the ambivalence of the encounter of European and Euro-American missionaries with Indigenous peoples. The basic idea is that God was already at work among the peoples of the world, preparing the way for the gospel, long before the arrival of the missionaries. In the hands of a writer like Eusebius, *preparatio evangelica* indicates the superiority of Christianity over pagan belief systems, whose insights were superseded and absorbed by the coming of the gospel. *Preparatio evangelica* in this sense can be a tool used by the colonizers to assimilate other cultures. But in a more positive sense, the principle can be a recognition that God has long been at work in Indigenous cultures before the advent of the colonizers and that, in

---

1. Editor's note: I opted for capitalizing "Indigenous" throughout the book. Most Indigenous academics are capitalizing the word because it is used as a proper noun referring to specific peoples and not in a generic sense; this is now becoming a common practice in academic publications.

fact, the good news in some way was already there, before the missionaries came with their version of it. The gospel is not something simply brought by the missionaries, but rather something that can happen in the gifts of God that Indigenous and non-Indigenous people can offer to one another. The church is a *tertium quid*, something built anew in this encounter, expressing the genius of every culture but the sole possession of none. I think this is the hope that animates the contributions to this volume.

The conference out of which this volume grew was a collaboration between the Catholic Theological Union (CTU) in Chicago and the Center for World Catholicism and Intercultural Theology at DePaul University. Michel Andraos of CTU was the driving force behind this initiative, and I am grateful for his hard work and generous spirit. There was a beautiful spirit at the conference; as people told their stories and listened to one another, one could not help but see seeds being planted for a new intercultural church. I trust that some of that spirit shows through in the pages that follow.

William T. Cavanaugh
Director of the Center for World Catholicism and Intercultural Theology
DePaul University, Chicago

Introduction

MICHEL ANDRAOS

The title of this volume, *The Church and Indigenous Peoples in the Americas*, takes its name from the international conference jointly organized in November 2016 by the Center for World Catholicism and Intercultural Theology (CWCIT) at DePaul University and Catholic Theological Union (CTU).

The relationship between Christianity and the Indigenous peoples of America has received a lot of attention over the past few decades. The commemoration of the five-hundredth anniversary of the beginning of the conquest of Indigenous America was a moment of reflection for the churches on their involvement in this violent history. Since the 1990s, in many parts of the Americas, churches have been issuing apologies to the Indigenous peoples for European Christianity's role in the conquest and subsequent colonization. Unfortunately, the violence of the prior five centuries has not disappeared. Rather, it continues to be the reality that Indigenous peoples of America, from northern Canada to southern Chile, experience in their daily lives and in their relationships with the states, churches, and society at large. As Mohawk scholar, activist, and public intellectual Taiaiake Alfred argues, Indigenous peoples continue to have only one of two options in their relationship with the dominant societies: exclusion or forced assimilation. He writes: "In this spiritual and psychological war of genocide and survival, immersed in colonial cultures, surrounded by Settlers, and falsely labeled as citizens of the states which have forcibly integrated them, Onkwehonwe [original or indigenous people] are offered only two choices on the question of culture and identity within the aboriginal paradigm: accept being excluded—and the alienation, loss, and frustration that that situation implies—or choose to become assimilated."[1] This argument is asserted by Indigenous voices across the Americas and beyond.

The relationship with the churches has not been radically different from that of the states, as most authors in this book attest. While several movements in the churches over the past few decades have been proactive in supporting and defending Indigenous peoples' rights, and overall many non-Indigenous church missionaries, ministers, and activists paid with their lives for this cause, the situation still requires radical structural transformation and the courage to take institutional actions that are consistent with the churches' public statements. Noted Indigenous Zapoteco theologian Eleazar López Hernández says that, in this regard, "The contradictions between official statements and ecclesial realities are well known."[2] Reflecting on this necessary and urgent transformation from a theological and pastoral perspective was the main purpose of the 2016 conference entitled "The Church and Indigenous Peoples in the Americas." As clearly articulated throughout the book, there is a need for new and different pastoral and theological ways of thinking and acting. The contributions in this book point toward these new ways.

Another important aspect that the contributors in this volume address is intercultural, interreligious, and theological dialogue with Indigenous peoples. What several contributors make clear is that, while church leaders in the Americas, and most recently Pope Francis, have been apologizing for the mistakes that have occurred since the conquest of Indigenous America, not much serious dialogue has taken place yet about what a new relationship with the Indigenous peoples would look like, especially in relation to rethinking the old theology. In his apologies, Pope Francis specifically mentioned the church's involvement in colonization, and other recent popes—in particular John Paul II—have also apologized.[3] Yet, there remains much resistance to structural changes from the ecclesial hierarchy. Despite the advances of the Indigenous theology movements discussed by several authors in this book, we are still a long way from the transformations required in mainstream theology and pastoral practices to make them truly intercultural. One key question is left without a satisfying answer: Why are the desired dialogues and transformations not advancing seriously and rapidly enough, given the acknowledged significance and urgency of this task? Advancing this conversation by doing historical, social, and theological analyses for

1. Alfred, *Wasáse,* 128. Thomas King's book *The Inconvenient Indian* provides a good historical summary of this relationship.

2. López Hernández, "Teologías Indígenas en las Iglesias Cristianas," 294.

3. For comments on Pope Francis' apologies, see Andraos, "Church and the Indigenous Peoples," 42–45, and "Pope Francis and the Indigenous Peoples," 1–5.

tackling this and other such questions is precisely the area in which this volume hopes to make a contribution.

A group of Indigenous and non-Indigenous theologians, pastoral leaders, and scholars from different parts of the Americas came together to discuss the future of this dialogue in relation to decolonization and reconciliation, focusing primarily on the theological and pastoral perspectives. The driving question of both the 2016 conference and this publication is this: How can theology and the churches contribute to moving forward the processes of intercultural dialogue with Indigenous peoples and become active, responsible actors in the processes of decolonization and reconciliation? Indigenous theologians generally contest reconciliation without a clear and concrete commitment to ongoing decolonization of theology and pastoral ministry. However, as several authors in this volume note, there is not yet theoretical clarity in the churches about what a decolonial theology and pastoral ministry would look like. It remains to be seen how the church structures and ministry that have been heavily shaped by the colonial experience could truly become part of a "decolonial turn."[4] The contributions in this volume, it is our hope, help us to start imagining this new theology.

Pope Francis's recent address during his January 2018 meeting with the peoples of Amazonia strongly urges the Catholic Church to make taking sides with the Indigenous peoples and advocating for their concerns central to the church and its institutions. As he told the peoples of Amazonia, "I wanted to come to visit you and listen to you, so that we can stand together, in the heart of the church, and share your challenges and reaffirm with you a heartfelt option for the defense of life, the defense of the earth and the defense of cultures." In the same address, Francis advocates for a truly intercultural dialogue where Indigenous peoples, their traditions, wisdom, cultures, and spiritualities are the main partners. He concludes his address with a plea for Indigenous peoples to shape the culture of the church and contribute to building "a Church with an Amazonian face, a Church with a native face."[5]

This is a big and challenging agenda for the church, and this volume does not pretend to offer a comprehensive discussion of such a complex and critical topic. The contributors offer focused analyses and reflections on certain instances of the relationship between the church and the Indigenous peoples of America. They highlight processes where this relationship is advancing, as well as the challenges, obstacles, and setbacks on this journey. A

---

4. For an introduction to the concept of "decolonial turn," see Medina, "Decolonial Primer," 281–83; Grosfoguel, "Epistemic Decolonial Turn"; and Cormie, "Another Theology Is Possible," 266.

5. Francis, "Meeting with Indigenous Peoples."

limitation of the book is that it primarily focuses on these processes within the Roman Catholic context. It is important to note that discussions on this topic are taking place in all the Christian churches and from a variety of perspectives. This book's primary focus on the Catholic context is simply due to the limited scope of the conference; the discussion in this book is only one part of a much larger conversation and one more step of a long journey.

The book has two main parts. In Part One, "Indigenous Theological Voices and Responses," Indigenous authors from five different geographical regions represented at the conference—Canada, the United States, Mexico, Bolivia, and Chile—open the conversation and are followed by a non-Indigenous contributor from the same region broadly responding to their presentation. As the conference did, the book privileges the Indigenous voice in these conversations. The non-Indigenous respondents from each region are all pastoral leaders and/or theologians who have been working in solidarity with Indigenous peoples, in most cases for several decades. The stories told in this book are still evolving. The contributors are all key actors in these stories and represent processes of theological and pastoral praxis in their own contexts. They do not represent a geographical region but rather an important praxis in that region that they were invited to discuss, and they speak about their personal stories and their concrete experiences and involvement.

I would like here to briefly highlight the contributions, the authors, and their contexts in order to give the reader some background; I follow the regional alphabetical order, as in the table of contents. Speaking from the Bolivian context, Roberto Tomichá and Stephen Judd tell the story of the recent emergence of *teología india*, the Indigenous theology movement in the church and the contribution of this theology to imagining an "Indigenous autochthonous church." Tomichá, himself an Indigenous Chiquitano Aymara theologian, does this from the two perspectives of Indigenous memory and the current Indigenous theological proposals for imagining a truly intercultural theology in the church. Judd, a Maryknoll missioner in the Aymara region for most of his life, tells the story of the encounter between the Maryknoll and the Indigenous worlds and how *teología india* has challenged and transformed mission theology—and continues to do so.

The reader will note more contributions from Canada than the other regions, and this is primarily because of the importance of the Indigenous resurgence movements that have been taking place in that country over the past decades; additionally, most people outside the Canadian context know very little about these movements. This new resurgence is a *kairos* moment and could potentially, in the years to come, make a significant contribution to transform the relationships between the churches and Indigenous peoples, with implications beyond Canada.[6] Eva Solomon, Indigenous Sister of Saint Joseph, and Sylvain Lavoie, archbishop emeritus of the Diocese of Keewatin-The Pas and an Oblate of Mary Immaculate missionary, are the pioneers who started the Building Bridges organization for promoting ministry from an Indigenous perspective. This organization has been working for over a decade under the umbrella of the Catholic Bishops of Western Canada. Solomon and Lavoie present their insights on the reality of the relationship between the Catholic Church of Canada and the Indigenous peoples, and the current challenges of that reality in light of the findings and final report of the Truth and Reconciliation Commission of Canada (TRC) on the Indigenous Residential Schools. Solomon shares her story, personal experience, and theological reflection on reconciliation, offering a unique understanding of this context. Lavoie also shares his personal story, experience, and reflections on the current challenges and hopes of pastoral ministry in Western Canada and beyond. Brian McDonough's chapter provides background and an in-depth overview on the TRC, as well as a reflection on the responses of different entities, focusing primarily on the Catholic perspectives. McDonough, well-positioned for this task, concludes his chapter with a profound and hopeful theological reflection.

The two contributors from Chile—Rosa Isolde Reuque Paillalef and Jaime Bascuñán—make a particular contribution from the southernmost part of the continent. A lifelong Mapuche leader, diplomat for a short period of time, and now pastoral leader at the Diocese of Temuco, Reuque tells the story of her long journey of trying to reconcile her multiple experiences of being a Mapuche, a Christian, a Catholic, and a woman. Reuque collaborates with the Institute of Theological Studies at the Catholic University of Temuco to develop a program of intercultural and interreligious dialogue with the Mapuche people. Bascuñán describes and reflects on this in his chapter. Even in a region with a Mapuche majority such as Araucanía, where the Catholic University of Temuco is located, intercultural and interreligious dialogue continues to be a challenge today. And it is this challenge and process of dialogue that is Bascuñán's main focus.

Pedro Gutiérrez Jiménez—or jPetul, his Tzeltal name that he prefers to use—and Jorge Santiago Santiago from the Diocese of San Cristóbal de las Casas, in Chiapas, Mexico, share the unique story of a local church that has been intentional for many decades about forging a new decolonial relationship with the Indigenous peoples of the region. Promoting a local

6. For a good introduction to the roots and vision of the Indigenous political, cultural, and spiritual resurgence in Canada, see the excellent works of Simpson, *Dancing On Our Turtle's Back* and *As We Have Always Done*. See also the important recent work by Asch, *Resurgence and Reconciliation*.

Indigenous theology known as *teología india maya* and a decolonial ecclesiology, *iglesia autoctona*, have been the two axes of building a local Catholic church with an Indigenous face and leadership. Through telling his story of "decolonizing the heart," jPetul gives us an extensive presentation on the emergence of the Mayan *teología india* and its contribution to strengthening the Indigenous peoples of the diocese and beyond in their journey of self-determination and liberation. JPetul outlines this theology's basic concepts and methods, weaving these into his personal journey of decolonization. Santiago tells the story of accompaniment to a pastoral process in its social and political contexts as well as the story of the emergence of a *Pueblo Creyente*, a people of faith and hope in the diocese. A new subject of its own history, *Pueblo Creyente* is committed to working for peace with justice and dignity in the midst of a prolonged conflict. Santiago's chapter focuses on the theology of accompaniment. He reflects on the ways that a local church accompanies Indigenous peoples in their struggles for self-determination, liberation, and the defense of life and Mother Earth. This is the same challenge to the church that Pope Francis raised in his above-mentioned address in Amazonia. Both of these authors from Chiapas have accompanied the Indigenous movements they discuss since their beginnings, and they speak to us as key actors with profound experience and knowledge.

The two chapters from the United States center on the relationship of CTU (which cosponsored the original conference) with two Native American Lakota communities in South Dakota. Francis White Lance, a Lakota and Christian medicine man, and Roger Schroeder, an SVD missionary and professor of missiology at CTU, speak of an evolving relationship of healing and reconciliation and how, in the process, CTU's theological curriculum in relation to mission has been significantly transformed. White Lance gives his own account of transformation, explaining what it means for him now to be both Lakota and Christian. These accounts of a growing mutual relationship of trust, which are part of a bigger story, show us how this relationship of learning and solidarity has influenced and transformed hundreds of missionaries and theologians over the past few decades. As Schroeder says, this relationship is "mission in reverse."

Part Two of the book, "Reflections and Future Perspectives," includes Marie Battiste, an Indigenous scholar and member of the Mi'kmaw nation, renowned for her scholarship on Indigenous knowledge and decolonizing education. By incorporating insights from other disciplines and perspectives, Battiste's contribution helps the reader reflect on decolonizing theology and pastoral ministry. The chapter Battiste contributed is an expanded version of her presentation. Joanne Jaruko Doi and Robert Schreiter, two theologians at CTU with particular experience in this area, provide concluding reflections in their chapters. Doi writes from her many years of ministry as a Maryknoll missioner in the Andean Indigenous world and reflects from that perspective. Renowned in the fields of intercultural theology and reconciliation, among other things, Schreiter gives us—as he did at the 2016 conference—a succinct summary of some key points from each contribution and presenting an overall reflection.

The conference took place during the same time that the Indigenous resistance at Standing Rock in North Dakota was reaching a critical moment. What happened at Standing Rock is significant for theology and the relationship between the churches and Indigenous peoples. Part of the broader Indigenous resurgence in the Americas, Standing Rock was on everyone's minds throughout the conference, and as it came to a close, the participants published the following statement as a gesture of solidarity:[7]

> Gathered on the campuses of DePaul University and Catholic Theological Union, situated on traditional Potawatomi Territory, we, participants at the conference "The Church and Indigenous Peoples in the Americas," hereby express our support and our solidarity with the Lakota water-protectors of Standing Rock—as well as with their allies, both Indigenous and non-Indigenous—in their ongoing, nonviolent resistance to the construction of the pipeline encroaching upon their sacred sites and potentially endangering their clean water supplies.

My collaboration on this project—both organizing the conference and editing this book—with CWCIT's director, William Cavanaugh, and its staff, Karen Kraft and Francis Salinel, has been a great pleasure. Their highly professional and friendly support made this task not only possible but pleasant. Organizing an international conference and editing a book written by fifteen contributors from five different countries in two languages and different styles, including translation and cross-language editing, is a daunting task. In particular, without Karen Kraft's dedication, efficiency, and high-quality editorial skills, this book could not have become a reality.

The translations from the Spanish of the original conference presentations and the final versions published here were the collaborative effort of Paloma Cabetas, Karen Kraft, and Michel Andraos. Specific credits are given in each chapter. The final version, however, was done by the editor, and I take full responsibility for any mistakes. Translating theological Spanish

7. Thanks to Brian McDonough, contributor to this volume, and Sr. Dawn Nothwehr, professor of ethics at CTU, for drafting this statement, which was endorsed by all participants present at the conference and made public. The statement was sent to Chief David Archambault and Bishop David Dennis Kagan of the Diocese of Bismarck, North Dakota, on behalf of the conference participants.

with all the nuances of this subject is a delicate task. I did this to the best of my ability, while trying to be faithful to the intent of the authors as I understand it. To make the translation and editing as accurate as possible, I was in conversation back and forth with the authors as needed. The comments in the footnotes entitled "editor's notes" are Karen Kraft's contributions, intended to add clarity and provide helpful information to the English reader about unfamiliar concepts and terms.

A project like this requires several hundred hours to put together, and it was a great pleasure for me to do that. My great debt of gratitude goes primarily to the authors with whom I communicated over the past two and half years. I thank them deeply for the long hours they put into preparing their talks for the conference, traveling to Chicago, and then editing their papers for publication in this book. I thank them for trusting me with their valuable contributions and stories. Editing this book has only been possible for me because of the long-term relationship I have with most of the authors as well as their trust and interest in our common project and cause. It has been an honor and a privilege to be entrusted with this task, and I have been deeply inspired and nourished by this work over the past two years.

Finally, on a personal note, my relationship with the Diocese of San Cristóbal de las Casas in Chiapas, Mexico goes back to the mid-1990s. The theology and pastoral work of this diocese, and of Samuel Ruiz (its bishop from 1960–2000), were the main theological "school" where I began to learn about the important topic of the church and Indigenous peoples of the Americas, and this eventually became the topic of my doctoral dissertation and continues to be central to my theological research to the present day. The relationship of learning and solidarity that started in the 1990s continues today in a variety of forms: ongoing solidarity visits, nearly-annual traveling seminars with my CTU students, and occasional collaborative publications. I owe the diocese of San Cristóbal, its people, and movements a great debt of gratitude for the deep theological learning and personal transformation I have experienced over the years. My participation in the march of the Pueblo Creyente in San Cristóbal in January of 2015 is what inspired the idea of the conference.[8] This movement has inspired my theology of hope and continues to do so.[9] For this reason, I dedicate this book to the *Pueblo Creyente* of the Diocese of San Cristóbal.

---

8. For a short video documentary on the march, see Andraos, "March of the Pueblo Creyente."

9. The Pueblo Creyente has recently published its story of the twenty-five years since it began. See Comisión de Pueblo Creyente, *Veinticinco Años del Pueblo Creyente.*

PART ONE

Regional Indigenous Theological Voices and Responses

A: Bolivia

1

Toward a Church with an Indigenous Face: Some Premises and Urgent Challenges[1]

ROBERTO TOMICHÁ CHARUPÁ, OFM CONV.

Pope Francis, in his first apostolic exhortation, *Evangelii Gaudium*, clearly highlighted the transcultural character of the Christian message and, consequently, the urgency of a Christianity which is also transcultural, capable of assuming in its expressions the plurality of ancestral and emerging cultures, which are always in a process of transformation. In fact, "we would not do justice to the logic of the incarnation if we thought of Christianity as mono-cultural and monotonous. While it is true that some cultures have been closely associated with the preaching of the gospel and the development of Christian thought, the revealed message is not identified with any of them; its content is transcultural."[2] Such an affirmation allows us to better understand what John Paul II expresses in his encyclical, *Fides et Ratio*, when he refers to the second criterion of discernment of the relationship between faith and cultures—a criterion valid for all times, according to which "the Church cannot abandon what she has gained from her inculturation in the world of Greco-Latin thought. To reject this heritage would be to deny the providential plan of God who guides his Church down the paths of time and history."[3] Therefore, Christian memory and transculturality represent two interrelated theological moments whose continuous deepening and re-reading allow us to live and express a Christianity that has an Indigenous face, mind, and heart.

1. Translated by Michel Andraos and Paloma Cabetas.
2. Francis, *Evangelii Gaudium*, 117; hereafter, *EG*.
3. John Paul II, *Fides et Ratio*, 72.

In the case of the Latin America and Caribbean peoples, the Christian process that they lived was, as expressed by bishop Toribio de Mogrovejo (1573), a "new *Christianity of the Indies*," or rather, a Christianity that was colonial, dependent, and peripheral, and in which the religious-Christian elements merged with the political and economic interests of the Spanish and Portuguese kingdoms of the times.[4] In this context of colonial Christendom which included and controlled Christianity, we need to understand the emergence and consolidation of the Latin American and Caribbean Church. It not only subordinated but also (except in some cases) displaced—and even destroyed—Indigenous religious expressions. We must say that some missionaries spoke out and even gave their own lives in defense of justice for the Indigenous and black people; as Pope John Paul II remarks,

> they chose to live among the Indigenous peoples from the beginning, in order to learn their language and adapt to their customs. Others promoted the formation of catechists and collaborators who acted as interpreters . . . In this living together with the Indigenous peoples, many missionaries became farmers, carpenters, builders of houses and temples, school teachers and apprentices of the autochthonous culture.[5]

It is precisely this living together (*convivencia*) of the missionaries among the Indigenous people that allowed the church to begin to glimpse some alternative traits of what the Second Vatican Council would later define as an "autochthonous church."[6]

This paper intends to summarize some characteristics, or theological-cultural features, of what is an "Indigenous autochthonous church" from two perspectives: (1) the Latin American Indigenous memory and (2) current Indigenous theological proposals.

A Theological Presupposition: "The Revealed Message . . . Has a Transcultural Content"

In order to approach, get to know, understand, and learn from Indigenous wisdom, an important premise is the attitude of listening, respecting, and being open to otherness and diversity. Our way of seeing, thinking, and responding to a specific reality is always conditioned by a certain context (geographical, domestic, familiar, cultural, social, etc.) and, therefore, the

4. Dussel, *Desintegración de la Cristiandad*, 52.

5. John Paul II, "Carta Apostólica a los Religiosos," 7.

6. Second Vatican Council, *Ad Gentes*, 6; hereafter, *AG.*

same happens to our way of thinking, our way of living Christianity, and our way of being the church. Every human experience—and consequently, every Christian experience—is always contextual and, therefore, accentuates certain features, moving others into the background. For this reason, "Christianity will have to respond ever more effectively to this need for inculturation. Christianity, 'while remaining completely true to itself, with unswerving fidelity to the proclamation of the Gospel and the tradition of the Church, will also reflect the different faces of the cultures and peoples in which it is received and takes root.'"[7] In other words, from the point of view of personal experience, "the expression of truth can take different forms. The renewal of these forms of expression becomes necessary for the sake of transmitting to the people of today the Gospel message in its unchanging meaning."[8] From there comes the urgent need for today's men and women in the church to incorporate *other* ways of knowledge and *other* logics as integral parts of living an authentic Christianity. These wisdoms—which are living experiences of faith and theological truths elaborated from other norms and languages and are generally more narrative, more symbolic, and celebratory—need to be incorporated into the ecclesial tradition of the Americas today.

Through this attitude of listening, encountering, and possibly *convivencia* (living together) with those who are different—as the Indigenous world could be—and with everything that represents diversity (like other living beings, the cosmos), the gestation of a Christian church, which is by nature missionary and has its origin in the Trinity itself,[9] is made possible. As noted before, it is a local church that lives and reflects on Christian faith from its own context in a continuous transformation, and therefore its theology will always be open, itinerant, and nomadic, but with deep roots that converge precisely in the Christic-Trinitarian mystery which is present in all that exists.[10] This position, in fact, is founded on the same principle of the incarnation, because the Son of God assumed the *whole* of human reality, with its peculiar distinctive traits, in order to elevate it to communion with the Father, according to his salvific design.[11] For that reason, "we would not do justice to the logic of the incarnation if we thought of Christianity as

7. John Paul II, *Novo Millennio Ineunte*, 40; Francis, *EG*, 116.

8. John Paul II, *Ut Unum Sint*, 19; Francis, *EG*, 41.

9. Second Vatican Council, *AG*, 2.

10. Francis, *EG*, 29.

11. "What has not been taken up by Christ is not made whole; what is united to God is redeemed": St. Gregory Nazianzen, Letter 101 (Migne, *Patrologiae Cursus Completus*, 181; hereafter *PG*). See also *AG*, 3: "what has not been taken up by Christ is not made whole."

monocultural and monotonous," because the content of the revealed message "is transcultural."[12] Moreover, the Word placed his dwelling (John 1:14) in the world, and the Holy Spirit is present in the whole of creation, which is aspiring to its redemption and full harmony (Rom 8:22). Therefore, creation has a cosmic dimension in close harmony with our surroundings. Or, as the Vatican II document, *Gaudium et Spes,* expresses, "by His incarnation, the Son of God has united Himself in some fashion with every man," and later on, "the Holy Spirit in a manner known only to God offers to every man the possibility of being associated with this paschal mystery."[13]

From these theological principles, well-founded on Scripture, the ecclesial tradition, and the current ordinary and extraordinary magisterium, the cultural and religious expression of different peoples manifest not only the "seeds of the Word" and the "seminal Logos,"[14] but also the Paschal Mystery itself, which is welcomed, expressed, and celebrated through their own symbols. These expressions reveal the One-Triune Mystery, and, as Pope Francis declares, following Saint Bonaventure, "the Trinity has left its mark on all creation . . . *each creature bears in itself a specifically Trinitarian structure,* so real that it could be readily contemplated if only the human gaze were not so partial, dark, and fragile."[15] In reality, today's challenge is precisely "trying to read reality through a Trinitarian lens."[16] In other words, we need to revisit the Christian tradition through the lens of relationships, connection, and interpenetration, or, as expressed in classical terms, we need to recover the theological dimension of *perichoresis* in all the spheres of human and ecclesial life. This perception of reality is precisely one of the contributions of the Amerindian peoples.

A Vital Principle: "In the World, Everything is Connected"

From the beginning of time, many Amerindian peoples have lived and conceived reality as eminently relational. Everything has life, and everything is connected—human beings as well as other living beings and the cosmic-creational surroundings. This relational disposition or attitude is expressed in different cultural forms of daily life such as images, symbols, representations, dreams, comparisons, narratives, myths, celebrations, and also in the very *philosophies, theologies,* and *spiritualities* of the Indigenous peoples. In

12. Francis, *EG,* 117.
13. Paul VI, *Gaudium et Spes,* 22.
14. See Gorski and Tomichá, *Semillas del Verbo.*
15. Francis, *Laudato Si',* 239; hereafter, *LS.*
16. Francis, *LS,* 239.

this regard, and as an example, in Náhuatl philosophy, "the universe is a *system of symbols* that reflect one another: colors, time, oriented spaces, asters, gods, and historic phenomena are in correspondence one with another,"[17] which would lead to the formulation of three principles of life: symbolic representation, mutual inclusion, and reciprocity at every level. For the Mayas, cosmic symmetry and mathematical structure—in addition to symbolic representation—are fundamental principles of reality.

In South America, and more precisely in the Andean world, the principle, trait, or fundamental and determining style of living and conceiving the cosmos is "the relatedness of everything," that is, "each element, being, and person is related to all the other elements, beings, and persons . . . Everything is in some way related (linked, connected) with everything else."[18] The basic Andean entity in relating to the cosmos is not the substantial "being," but the relationship whose primordial structure of relationship allows the formation of the particular beings and not vice versa: "the 'reality' (as a holistic 'all') 'is' (exists) as a *set of 'beings' and events that are interrelated*."[19] In other words, while a certain "Western" philosophy centers on a "logical exclusivity" based on three principles—non-contradiction, identity, and excluded middle—the Andean peoples live instead the "non-duality" of reality:[20] they value relationships rather than being, celebrations rather than discourses, practical expressions rather than theoretical content, poetry rather than prose, orthopraxis rather than orthodoxy. They try to integrate, balance, and harmonize contraries in a spacial-temporal process marked by periods and cycles in a reality conceived as undulatory. These strongly relational principles are lived at the personal, communitarian, and cosmic levels. At the personal level, for example, the human being (*jaqi* in the Aymara language) is understood as eminently relational. Calixto Quispe explains: "We Aymaras are *Jaqi,* and we become fully *Jaqi,* when we form a couple and a unity, in harmony with nature and with the guarding spirits. Therefore, a *Jaqi* is instituted by the community and for the community."[21] From there, the human being's task is

---

17. Estermann, *Compendio de la Filosofía,* 4:199.

18. Estermann, *Compendio de la Filosofía,* 4:201, 1:289–90.

19. In other words, "the 'principle of relatedness' tells us that each 'being,' event, status of conscience, feeling, fact and possibility is immersed in multiple relationships with other 'beings,' events, status of conscience, feelings, facts and possibilities" (Estermann, *Compendio de la Filosofía,* 1:290). This connecting principle is made explicit in at least five life principles which characterize Andean daily life: complementarity, reciprocity, correspondence, integrality, and cyclicity.

20. See Estermann, *Si el Sur fuera el Norte,* 30–31.

21. Bernabé and Huanca, *Pacha-Jaqi-Runa,* 38.

to strive to be better *Jaqi* in his or her interpersonal relationships: the couple, family, community, and cosmos.

In the same vein, according to another Aymara, Fernando Huanacuni, relatedness is not exclusive to human beings but comprises everything that exists: "Our grandparents have bequeathed us these generational experiences, these ways of wisdom, because they learned what life is about; life where everything is interrelated, everything is interdependent. Therefore, they wisely took care of everything."[22] He then adds that the foundation of such a relationship is the fact that all that exists is full of and inspires life: "everything lives: our mountains live, the water lives, the tree lives. In the same way that we feel and think, they also feel and think . . . everything is important, there is no small thing, there is no big thing."[23] Therefore, for the Indigenous peoples, relatedness is communitarian-cosmic, and the human being lives and is understood from the viewpoint of that reciprocity.

This relational and connective characteristic of the reality in which we live was also affirmed by Pope Francis himself in his encyclical, *Laudato Si'*, when he affirms that "everything is connected,"[24] and "everything is related"[25] or even "closely interrelated."[26] Obviously, "the conviction that everything in the world is connected"[27] represents a key for *spiritual interpretation* for "all the aspects of the global crisis"[28] and all that is happening around us. In this way, relatedness acquires its ultimate meaning in the personal-communitarian experience of encounter with that ultimate source which allows every connection—in Christian terms, the Trinitarian Mystery, a Mystery that has various names according to specific Indigenous peoples. The Indigenous criticism and *self*-criticism of a certain individualism and inherited colonial ethnocentrism, which is very androcentric and patriarchal, and is present in the Latin American and Caribbean society and church, is done with the hope of returning to the Indigenous spiritual roots.

---

22. Huanacuni, "Buen Vivir-Vivir Bien," 00:43–1:11.

23. Huanacuni, "Buen Vivir-Vivir Bien," 10:56–11:13.

24. Francis, *LS*, 16, 91, 117, 138, 240.

25. Francis, *LS*, 70, 120, 142.

26. Francis, *LS*, 137, 213.

27. Francis, *LS*, 16.

28. Francis, *LS*, 137.

Creative and Cosmic Spirituality: "Let Us Thank the Most High and Supreme Eternal God, Trinity and Unity"

Relatedness, connection, reciprocity—these are the Indigenous peoples' everyday experience of life in the personal, communitarian, and cosmic spheres. In reality, it is about a true living out of the Mystery. In this regard, the Aymara scholar, Sofía Chipana Quispe, reminds us of the urgency of sharing "from the Indigenous spiritualities . . . our cosmic visions, which perceive reality as lived in a way that is inter-connected and inter-related. This gives a holistic vision that is plural, centered on life and on the earth, and that brings us to a commitment and to deconstruct theological principles that try to present themselves as the only theological way to reflect."[29] Therefore, the Indigenous spiritualities challenge Christianity and the way it is practiced in the local churches, and they ask Christianity to open its horizons to the whole living reality without exclusion, overcoming, for example, communitarian reductionism (both organizational and ministerial) that ultimately expresses a reductionist vision of the divine Symbol. In other words, the Indigenous spiritualities express a partial understanding of the Trinitarian Mystery. There is, then, an urgency to move from religious monoculturality to spiritual transculturality, which tries to gather the spiritual experiences of Indigenous peoples as riches that manifest the same divine reality.

In other words, in Christian theological terms, the foundation and meaning of all reality is the God Mystery—eternal, sublime, supreme interrelation, who is beyond our reflections and formulations; the ultimate and definitive one; the absolute; the Sacred par excellence who attracts, seduces, and at the same time awakens reverence and fear; the *tremendum et fascinans*.[30] Mystery who gathers and integrates the whole of human life and experience, both relational and cosmic. How do we live this mystery in our daily experience? In this regard, one of the spiritual traits of the Mystery in the Indigenous world is the experience of the *nurturing* God, a God who takes care of and accompanies creation, particularly God's sons and daughters: a

> God who follows his work closely; who continues to nurture life and asks us to nurture life. God asks the caring spirits to nurture (to take care of)—the protecting spirits (of the hills, the food, the house, the lakes . . .), and of course, the *Pachamama*, the great sister-mother or providence of God. The Aymara insist:

29. Chipana Quispe, "Desafíos y Tareas," para. 18.
30. Otto, *Lo Santo.*

we are co-nurturers (co-creators): we have been charged with the task of continuing to nurture, with great love, what God has given us.[31]

In the traditional Christian vision, which is more theoretical and speculative, that Mystery is called the Triune God: *perichoresis*,[32] *circumincession* (interpenetration of one person in the other), or *circuminsession* (the static and ecstatic being of the persons in one another), communion of three divine beings, family; the absolute Mystery, fathomless, ineffable;[33] the "permanent interpenetration . . . eternal co-relatedness, self-surrender"[34] among divine persons; cosmotheandric or interdependence of God-being human-world; the "ultimate structure of reality . . . constitutively relational among three distinct but inseparable poles."[35]

Those who have been able to deeply connect with the Uni-Triune Mystery in order to live an experience of relational spiritual wholeness are, of course, the saints. For example, according to Francis of Assisi, *all* that is created are living creatures, plural and biodiverse, called to coexist as *sisters* who obey and praise the only Most High Creator. Consequently, human beings must be "subject to every human creature out of love for God," that is, "to all the beasts and the wild animals,"[36] including *all* that exists in the heavens and on earth. We are talking about an obedience (*ob-audire*) understood as a profound listening, an inner listening that is critical, joyful, and ardently seeks a full and authentic harmony with *all* its surroundings by means of *each one* of the creatures, which are also *rational* and, therefore, *subjects* before the Creator. In effect, Francis of Assisi "preached [to the flowers], inviting them to praise the Lord, as if they enjoyed the gift of reason";[37] "he greeted [creatures] as if they possessed reason . . . He preached to the flowers, to the woods, to the trees and the rocks, as if they were gifted with

---

31. Jordá, "Aporte Región Andina," 93.

32. This Greek term has two meanings: "one thing being contained in another, dwelling in, being in another—a situation of fact" and also "interpenetration or interweaving of one person with the others and in the others." It is a process of "active reciprocity, a clasping of two hands: the Persons interpenetrate one another and this process of communing forms their very nature" (Boff, *Trinity and Society*, 135–36).

33. See Zarazaga, *Dios es Comunión*, 52.

34. Boff, *Trinity and Society*, 5.

35. Panikkar, *Ecosofía*, 28. The Trinity "is a culmination of a truth that penetrates all the domains of Being and the conscience, and this vision unites us as humans" (Panikkar et al., *La Trinidad y la Experiencia Religiosa*, 22).

36. Francis of Assisi, *Scritti*, 278, 212.

37. Celano, "Vita Prima," 356–57.

reason";[38] "he conversed with them [with fire and with other creatures] with inner and outer joy, as if they were rational beings."[39]

Such profound communication was ultimately founded in the mystical-spiritual experience of an encounter with a common principle, consistent and convergent, a *Father* who made it possible to acknowledge creatures as fraternal: "He called all creatures by the name of brother or sister, recognizing a single principle."[40] And thus, his Trinitarian praise: "let us honor, praise, serve, sing, and bless, glorify, and greatly exalt, magnify, and thank the Most High and supreme eternal God—Trinity and Unity—Father, Son, and Holy Spirit, creator of all things and savior of all those who believe and hope in him and love him."[41] In his contemplative praise, Francis experienced the Mystery of God present in creation.

From Latin America, Mother Laura Montoya Upegui (1874–1949) is certainly the one who most fully lived and celebrated with intensity the presence of God together with the Indigenous people in the midst of the forest. In this regard, she states, "They don't have a tabernacle, but they have nature! Here, I really hit the nail on the head, I told myself. But it would be necessary to teach our sisters to look for God in nature the way they look for him in the tabernacle, because even if His presence is different, in both places He is present, and love must learn to seek Him and find Him wherever He is."[42] This Colombian saint, founder of a religious congregation dedicated to working among the Indigenous peoples, teaches the whole church through her example that it is possible to live a eucharistic and Trinitarian spirituality in harmony with all that is created. In this sense, we have an urgent need to know and recover the ancestral memory of the Indigenous peoples.

A Self-Critical Urgency: "Decolonize Minds, Recuperate Historical Memory"

Wise people who transcend time and space are such because, somehow, they gathered and nourished themselves from deep ancestral memory that, for centuries, has continued to forge "together-living well," or a full and authentic life (John 10:10). In the words of Chipana Quispe, ancestrality is expressed in "myths and legends, stories still told, songs still sung,

38. Dalarun, "Thome Celanensis," 48 and 57; Dalarun, *La Vita Ritrovata*, 66, 88.

39. *Speculum Perfectionis*, 115, in Menesto and Brufani, *Fontes Franciscani*, 2040.

40. Dalarun, "Thome Celanensis," 57.

41. Francis of Assisi, *Primera Regla*, §23.

42. Montoya Upegui, *Autobiografía*, 647. Laura Montoya was canonized at the Vatican on May 12, 2013.

folklore, dance expressions, proverbs, taboos, laments, ethical norms, allegories, metaphors, imagination, maps, codes that all reflect a new vision of life."[43] Therefore, through attentive and deep listening, it will be possible to recreate or revisit those ways of wisdom of our grandparents, so they can be recognized and lived in all spaces of everyday life and become sources and inspirations for elaborating Amerindian theologies that are in harmony with the project of "living well."[44]

As a believing community, the church must remember and make present its plural character, assuming its concrete history with all its ups and downs of lights, shadows, and contradictions, always ready to purify its memory, "through a renewed historical and theological evaluation that should lead—if done correctly—to a corresponding recognition of its guilt and contribute to the true path of reconciliation."[45] Without this process of healing and personal and collective harmonization, the church will not be able to authentically begin to live its new reality, much less envision itself for the future with creativity. Therefore, it must be very attentive to listening and discerning "what the Spirit is saying to the churches" (Rev 2:7), allowing itself to be challenged by the "signs of the times."[46] The Holy Spirit, as the "living memory of the Church," is precisely the one who allows every disciple to remember and remain faithful to the love of Jesus Christ and to His plan for the Reign of God, or the "together-living well," avoiding in this way every kind of social, cultural, or ecclesial forgetfulness. In this regard, Pope Francis affirms that "The apostles never forgot the moment when Jesus touched their hearts: 'It was about four o'clock in the afternoon' (John 1:39)."[47] He also said this in Paraguay: "A people which forgets its own past, its history, and its roots, has no future; it is a dull people. Memory, if it is firmly based on justice and rejects hatred and all desire for revenge, makes the past a source of inspiration for the building of a future of serene coexistence."[48]

Gathered in Aparecida on the occasion of the Fifth General Conference, the Latin American and Caribbean bishops commented on this topic: "In some cases, there still exists a mindset and a certain way of looking down on Indigenous and Afro-Americans. Hence, the decolonizing of minds and

43. Chipana Quispe, "Desafíos y Tareas," para. 16.

44. For more details, see issue 6.8 of the journal *Diálogos: Revista de Culturas, Espiritualidades y Desarrollo Andino-Amazónica.*

45. International Theological Commission, *Memory and Reconciliation*, 10.

46. Paul VI, *Gaudium et Spes,* 4.

47. Francis, *EG,* 13.

48. Francis, "Meeting with Government Authorities," para. 4.

knowledge, recovery of historic memory, and enhancement of intercultural spaces and relationships are conditions for affirming the full citizenship of these peoples."[49] In other words, we are talking about overcoming an internalized colonialism in the mentality, attitude, and ecclesial structures which affirm the supremacy of a dominant Western vision, which is embodied, for example, in a precise style of organization (power, government) and a unique epistemic model (knowledge, theology), therefore dismissing *other* visions and styles, *other* epistemologies and ways of knowledge, *other* religious experiences, and *other* spiritualities. From the Indigenous point of view, such an ecclesial paradigm, which is monocultural and monotheological, prevents in fact a fraternal presence that is active, positive, and creative in Christian communities. For the Indigenous peoples who are conscious of their own identity, for example, entering and staying in ecclesial structures continues to mean abandoning their own cultural and religious traditions. In this regard, Eleazar López rightly noted that "living the Gospel, with a double belonging faithfully, has been the cause of many problems in relating to non-Indigenous members of the Church."[50]

In fact, we ourselves "have been born from that particular experience of memory,"[51] a memory which is "essential for Christian thinking, and like all memory it is particular and privileges certain moments and events in the Christian past, certain books and ideas, certain terms, and most of all certain persons."[52] Therefore, in front of a diversified and plural Christian experience—one which is at the same time human and divine, transparent and ambiguous, with its flowers and its thorns, full of life and richness—we need options, risks, and free decision in order to walk the paths of this life. In summary, we need a leap of faith, a leap in the darkness, like Abraham himself who, out of faith, "*set out,* not knowing where he was going" (Heb 11:8). And the one who walks opens up the spaces, the horizons, the feelings, the visions; the one who walks does not stay still but runs, like Mary Magdalene, who went to the tomb very early, "when it was still dark" (John 20:1), without looking at her own defects, but seized by the desire to meet the One who gave meaning to her life, because he was Life in fullness. This is a model of discipleship for all times: to be attracted, beguiled by the Risen Lord.

49. Conferencia General del Episcopado Latinoamericano y del Caribe, *Concluding Document,* 96. In the official version (the fourth draft, approved on May 31, 2007) the original "colonial mindset" was changed to a "certain way of looking down on Indigenous and Afro-Americans."

50. López Hernández, "América: Diálogo de la Iglesia," 61.

51. Potente, *Una Vita Religiosa per Tutti,* 133.

52. Wilken, *Spirit of Early Christian Thought,* 145.

For the Indigenous peoples, and more specifically for the Aymara women, there is a spiritual memory, a thread that supports their lives and expresses itself—for example, in the *ajayu* (spirit, soul) and the *qamasa* (courage, self-esteem)—and is capable of transforming their own inner-relational life in order to "achieve the utmost *qamaña* in body and soul."[53] This memory has a feminine face, as the Ruah (Spirit) is feminine, not so much because of its gender, but because of the readiness to take risks and to defend life. For this reason, the "living well" is an invitation to each person—independently of their position, class, age, or religious belief—to dialogue with their own roots, to know how to dive into their own depth, their own history, to fulfill those dreams, desires, utopias, or projects inherited from their ancestors, such as taking care of the cosmos, generating life, overcoming many difficulties, and transmitting ways of wisdom to new generations. Such experiences of harmony and reencounter with one's own roots acquire daily expression in our own familiar space which, in the Indigenous world, has communitarian and also cosmic dimensions.

A Communitarian Space: "Vital Nest that Welcomes Humanity, Nature, and its Spirits"

The Indigenous family, from the sociocultural point of view, acquires unity and cohesion in the extended family with all the relatives, with its diversity of rules, customs, prohibitions, preferences, according to each context: "the units of kinship constitute the social organization and the basis of the social structure . . . They have a much wider range of roles—such as forming the basic unit of production, and of political and religious representation."[54] When we speak about extended family, we mean the cohesion or unit of people belonging to a group who are linked not only biologically by blood or even by community, but also by the "incorporation" or "inclusion" of someone who, although belonging to another community or people, becomes a member of the group. In this last case, there are many examples of Christian missionaries who inserted themselves in the Indigenous peoples' world to the point of being profoundly transformed by their traditions, customs, mentalities, and very different spiritualities. Among other examples, we can talk of the Capuchin bishop, Alejandro Labaka, who lived among the Indigenous Huaorani of Ecuador. Not only was he adopted by them, but

---

53. Bernabé, *Identidad y Espiritualidad*, 139, and also 124, 135, 137.
54. Oyarce and Popolo, "Hogar y Familia Indígenas," 125.

he also became part of the Indigenous family itself: a true son with a father (*Inihua*), a mother (*Pahua*), and Huaorani siblings.[55]

In the Andean Quechua-Aymara world, the extended family lives in close connection with the local community to which one belongs, traditionally called *ayllu*, where the people practice mutual help and socioeconomic redistribution called *ayni*. This practice is better known as *reciprocity*, a central trait of the Andean ethic, which is defined as "a social relationship which links a person with others, with social groups, and with communities; it also links groups with groups, communities with communities, producers with producers, and producers with consumers, through the flow of goods and services among the interrelated parts."[56] *Ayllu* and *ayni* reciprocally complement each other and are communitarian mediations of life. In the words of Calixto Quispe, *ayllu* is "the vital nest of the different cultures . . . nest for the different communities, and in the communities also exist homes that are themselves nests . . . The community institutes the house as a vital nest to welcome humanity, nature, and its spirits . . . The home knows how to get angry when human beings think of themselves as all powerful."[57] The Aymara people live out this relational-communitarian-reciprocal principle even outside of their communities of origin, not without the tensions, negotiations, adaptations, and transformations that are proper to new contexts. In this regard, Julio Pérez Quispe explains that "the Aymaras in the city and urban society have always to exist in two different ways of being, like *two personalities*: one, destined to face and accommodate the modern urban society, with an attitude of subordination . . . and another, destined to relate to their country people, to the other Aymaras whom they find in the cities."[58] This attitude, necessary to survive, does not stop the Aymaras from continuing their way of being and of living in community, beyond their own place of origin when living in more urban and westernized milieus, even in those environments permeated by the digital culture. In effect, wherever they live, the Aymaras share their effort, their work, their austerity, their capabilities, their discipline or orderly living, their sense of responsibility, their reciprocity, their mutual respect (which does not distinguish social rank or financial power), their lack of idleness (*ama qhella*: do not be idle), and their community loyalty, among other things.

55. Labaca Ugarte, *Crónica Huaorani*, 37; see Tomichá, "Inculturación e Interculturalidad."

56. Mayer, "Las Reglas de Juego," 37. The author closely follows the work of Marcel Mauss.

57. Bernabé et al., *Pacha, Suma Qamaña*, 32–33.

58. Bernabé et al., *Pacha, Jiwasan QWamawisa*, 29; see Bernabé, *Mujer Aymara Migrante*.

Efraín Cáceres Chalco, from the south of Peru, highlights the enduring values in the Quechua communities, especially the act of forgiveness or
pampachanakuy, which is of great importance for the life of a people. Similarly, the Andean *runa* must cultivate serenity, regularity, sincerity, simplicity,
truthfulness (*ama llulla*: do not be a liar), humility, equanimity, and concen-
tration.[59] This last value reminds us how Andean ethics are supported by a
contemplative and symbolic vision of reality. In fact, "the earth does not give
just like that"—it requires attention and spiritual dedication, religious affec-
tion, and ultimately a permanent connection with the Sacred that sustains the
world, which the Quechua and Aymara call *Pacha*. This *Pacha* is the Andean
converging symbol par excellence, a window or a door not only for understanding, but also for knowing oneself and coexisting with the Mystery that
sustains the Life of all that exists. From the viewpoint of Christian tradition,
such consistency is found in the Uni-Trinitarian and Triune God—Father,
Son, and Holy Spirit—source and origin of everything, the ultimate Symbol
of expansive convergence of all reality.[60]

All that is expressed here about the Andean way of living in the mark-
edly relational-communitarian *ayllu*, whose ultimate foundation is the
Pacha-Trinity, are traits that challenge and help shape a church community
that is more authentic and significant in its evangelical project of the fullness of life.

A Nomadic Style of Hospitality: "My Father Was a Refugee Aramean"

The Amerindian theologian, Eleazar López, pointed out that "nomadism is
the point of departure and the necessary reference point of all Indigenous
peoples of America."[61] We can say that nomadism and itinerancy are present
almost as a founding structure or profound archetype in the memory of
the Indigenous peoples, especially the Mesoamerican and Amazonian. It
is certainly an experience closely linked to the symbolic-religious concept
of life, where what is sacred represents the central motor or the axis for
articulating all that exists, because "in the religious and theological scheme
of nomadism, God is everything and everything has to do with God."[62] This
nomadic concept balances, in a certain way, what was expressed above about

59. Chalco, "El Zorro y la Ética Andina."

60. See Tomichá, *Trinidad y Relacionalidad*; Tomichá, "Teilhard de Chardin"; see
also Sarmiento Tupayupanqui, *Un Arco Iris*.

61. López Hernández, *Teología India*, 32.

62. López Hernández, *Teología India*, 33.

the meaning and the Indigenous communitarian cohesion. In any case, we are talking about a dynamic community—always on the move, itinerant, nomadic, in the full sense—that understands all the dimensions of the human being and human-cosmic relations. Such is the model of church that emerges from the Amerindian peoples.

In fact, according to the nomadic concept, human beings enter into a relationship with a dynamic Mystery, always "on the move," who listens, walks, takes initiatives, and comes close to the plural realities of the people, which are contrasting, ambiguous, and incomprehensible. Nomadism is communitarian, creaturely, and is founded in the same God who is nomadic, itinerant, wandering. Therefore, from an Indigenous point of view, we could postulate a nomadic existential principle which is the foundation of all that is created: the One-Triune God is dynamic and in permanent movement.

In this sense, the founding experience of the people of Israel's encounter with the divine Mystery is essentially nomadic. The patriarchs were nomads, migrants, and foreigners, and the people were called to recreate this as a memory in the present: "My father was a refugee Aramean who went down to Egypt with a small household and lived there as a resident alien. But there he became a nation great, strong and numerous" (Deut 26:5, NABRE). That is why we need to preserve the roots, not lose them, but recreate them, give them new meaning as an authentic lifestyle which is articulated and connected to hospitality. Nomadism and hospitality are two sides of the same coin that characterize the living out of the faith. It is a lifestyle that the Son of God himself proposes: he had "nowhere to rest his head" (Luke 9:58, NABRE); he sent his disciples out carrying "no food, no sack" (Mark 6:8, NABRE), no "second tunic, or sandals, or walking stick" (Matt 10:10; Luke 10:4, NABRE). On the contrary, the disciples simply had to live as "aliens and sojourners" (1 Pet 2:11, NABRE), in the midst of diverse peoples. To sum up, the Son lived the precariousness of traveling, together with the apostles, in an openness to all that exists. This had its maximum expression in the nudity on the cross, where he reached the inner nomadism of abandoning himself to the Father, the Ultimate Mystery.

This welcoming nomadism represents a central dimension of the Indigenous experience, especially in the South American lowlands, that preserves several historical memories. Here, we will limit ourselves to the memory of the Chiquito-Chiquitano peoples of the lowlands of Bolivia, focusing concretely on the term *poos*, which is central for the Chiquitana living with the cosmos. In fact, *poos* above all means home, dwelling, cell, cloister, colony, address, country, republic, residence;[63] it does not simply

---

63. Falkinger and Tomichá, *Gramática y Vocabulario*.

refer to a physical place, but is a space of encounter and interpersonal relations, of welcome and hospitality. For example, when one says, *oxima oitii iñemo au n'ipostii*—"he behaved well with me in his house"—it means "he gave me a good welcome."[64] In the same way, there is a close relationship between person and home: a woman who is married is *ipooca*; a man who is married, *izipocîca*;[65] an elderly person, *yarucĭrĭs poomaa*;[66] "coexist" and "coexistence" are *ipoôzaapaca* and *poozaapacas*;[67] a person from my same village, *poozaapas*;[68] "I am sick," *ipooruca*.[69] The meaning of home-dwelling is not limited to the extended family, but also relates to the community, to the "pueblo" or village to which one belongs:[70] *izecati auqui n'ipoostii Pedro*, "I come from Pedro's village";[71] *ichiicoca aucuza poôs*, "I come from near this village";[72] *iziuca au napoo*, "I was born in your village."[73] This home-family-village relationship is a social and cultural dimension that is very present in the Chiquitano people's process of formation and can still be appreciated today, not only as a patrimony of the past, but rather as a "living culture" in the concrete attitudes of its own inhabitants.

Concretely, *poozoca* means not only the guest or foreigner who deserves to be welcomed by the community, but also a person who, in some way, becomes part of the household, the family, or group. In fact, *poozoca* comes from the Chiquito root *poo-s*, or home, which means "the one who has a house";[74] the plural form *poozo-ca* means "those who have a home, those who live in their home." Therefore, for the Chiquitano people "of yesterday and today, the *poozo* is not a simple 'guest' or 'visitor' . . . but 'one of the household,' and as such, he or she should be made welcome with full honors. The *poozo*, on his or her part, must respond to that respect and hospitality by behaving well and assuming the duties and obligations of the members of the family that he or she is visiting."[75]

---

64. Falkinger and Tomichá, *Gramática y Vocabulario*, Vocabulario f. 13 and 355.

65. Falkinger and Tomichá, *Gramática y Vocabulario*, Vocabulario, f. 118.

66. Falkinger and Tomichá, *Gramática y Vocabulario*, Vocabulario, f. 46.

67. Falkinger and Tomichá, *Gramática y Vocabulario*, Vocabulario, f. 139.

68. Falkinger and Tomichá, *Gramática y Vocabulario*, Vocabulario, f. 505.

69. Falkinger and Tomichá, *Gramática y Vocabulario*, Gramática, f. 46.

70. Falkinger and Tomichá, *Gramática y Vocabulario*, Gramática, f. 35; Vocabulario, f. 31.

71. Falkinger and Tomichá, *Gramática y Vocabulario*, Vocabulario, f. 555.

72. Falkinger and Tomichá, *Gramática y Vocabulario*, Vocabulario, f. 77.

73. Falkinger and Tomichá, *Gramática y Vocabulario*, Vocabulario, f. 463.

74. Adam and Henry, *Arte y Vocabulario de la Lengua Chiquita*, 115.

75. Tomichá, *La Primera Evangelización*, 306.

This Indigenous concept of a home open to the public, without distinction or exclusion, is also an attitude that the whole ecclesial community should assume in some way. As Pope Francis reminded families, "Do not neglect to show hospitality to strangers, for thereby some have entertained angels unaware (Heb 13:2)."[76] He is, therefore, proposing this model for the church: "The Church must be a place of mercy freely given, where everyone can feel welcomed, loved, forgiven, and encouraged to live according to the good life of the Gospel."[77] Hospitality is possible when the Christian community allows itself to be inhabited and transformed by the Holy Spirit: "Whenever a community receives the message of salvation, the Holy Spirit enriches its culture with the transforming power of the Gospel."[78] For that, the community needs "approachability, readiness for dialogue, patience, a warmth and welcome which is nonjudgmental."[79]

76. Francis, *Amoris Laetitia*, 324.

77. Francis, *EG*, 114.

78. Francis, *EG*, 116.

79. Francis, *EG*, 165.

2

Beyond the Colonial Wound: The Emergence of the Indigenous Theological Movement in Latin America

STEPHEN P. JUDD, MM

The revival of a traditional Andean myth has surfaced in recent years at local and international gatherings organized to exchange stories among participants from diverse Indigenous groups around the Americas. Often referred to as the "Tale of Two Brothers," or *Iskay Hermanonimanta*, the myth has its origin in the highlands of Peru and Bolivia, but has come to symbolize narratives found in similar cultures that resonate with common archetypal experiences.

In the retelling of the myth, the younger brother of a family is forced by conditions of poverty to leave his ancestral home and go to a far-off place in search of a means of sustenance for his family. For the journey, all he takes is a handful of green vegetables. Along the way, he reaches a well-known crossroads identified by a pile of rocks called an *apacheta*. There, he meets up with a stranger who is obviously from a higher social and economic class. The ensuing conversation goes like this:

> "Friend, where are you headed?" asks the stranger.

> "Sir, I am very poor, so I am traveling to find work to help my family."

> "Don't go, my son, because in those places there is no work."

> "Then, sir, let's stop to rest awhile."

They both sit down to rest a bit, and the poor Indian lays out his poncho so that they can sit down. After resting for a while, the Indian takes out the only thing he has to eat, which is a bundle of greens. "Help yourself, sir," he says. The man serves himself and then says, "Don't go, my son, you will not find anything. It's better for you to return." "Yes, sir," says the Indian, "then I am going to return home." The man replies, "I am going to give you this flower." And so he gives him a bouquet of carnations with a single native flower. "Take it, bring it back home with you, and don't look back!"

After this encounter and dialogue, the young man returns home newly aware and more appreciative of the beauty of his ancestral homeland, having rediscovered the richness of his cultural heritage, which he was about to leave behind.[1]

Dialogues of this type at sacred *apacheta* sites are a frequent occurrence, with local variations on the same transformative narrative aimed at young people who are forced by push-pull factors to migrate to distant lands in search of an elusive lure of wealth or adverse conditions, only to experience the revelation of an epiphany experience. *Apachetas* of whatever kind are liminal spaces of encounter, dialogue, and transformation described by anthropologists like Victor Turner.[2] Liminality applied and lived out in a number of circumstances and situations provides a template for a deeper understanding of sociocultural phenomena among native peoples. Here, we apply it to the disruptions in the lives of Indigenous people and the myriad ways they affirm and celebrate their diversity in a world "turned upside down," a concept known since the times of Spanish conquest and colonization as a *Pachakuti*, or cosmic upheaval.[3]

The Maryknoll Experience of Encounter with the Indigenous World

Mythical transforming encounters like the one described have become intertwined with the narratives of the Maryknoll journey to missions among the Indigenous peoples of the Americas since 1942. The significance of the stories of our initial placements and insertion into the cultural, religious, and

1. Judd, "Indigenous Theological Movement," 210–30.

2. Social anthropologist Victor Turner is credited with introducing the concept of liminality into the social sciences and interdisciplinary scholarly research with his book, *Ritual Process*.

3. Most often, the Andean notion of *Pachakuti* joins the two Quechua words of *pacha*, which refers to time and space in the cosmos, and *kuti*, which signifies an upheaval, revolution, or historic reversal of relationships on many levels. One of the best summary statements can be found in Thomson, "*Pachakuti*."

social worldview and milieu of Indigenous peoples throughout the Americas have only recently begun to be told. They give witness to an awakening of Indigenous social actors, along with a bountiful harvest of new and original currents of theological thought to reflect the resurgence of Indigenous identity manifested in the emergence of vibrant social movements. What has just become increasingly apparent on a global scale was well-known to many in the missionary world and in the social networks we've inhabited for many years. A conference like this one, jointly organized by the Catholic Theological Union (CTU) and DePaul, widens the audience even more to share in significant developments in this life-transforming experience of peoples at these crossroads on the peripheries of the Americas.

Long ago, we in a community like Maryknoll recognized the many ways that Indigenous peoples have contributed to our greater self-understanding as a North American mission society. They have also contributed to the continuous process of renewal in the Spirit that has shaped our identity since that time in both large and small (but significant) ways. In a particular and lasting fashion, this kind of encounter has enabled and defined the mission of the women and men Maryknollers living and working among the Quechua, Aymara, Mapuche, and Mayan peoples in the peripheral areas of the countries of Bolivia, Peru, Chile, Mexico, and Guatemala. The Maryknollers have had a continuous, fruitful, and committed presence for over seventy years in these liminal spaces across the Americas, though it has not been without its share of mistakes, missed encounters, and squandered opportunities.[4]

Now that this decades-long missionary presence has diminished in a quantitative sense, appreciation by those who proudly lay claim to this legacy and have passed it on can be said to provide one of the foundations for building up Indigenous leadership in the service of creative initiatives in theology and in the promotion of vibrant social movements across the American continent and beyond. Originally, the assignment to accept a commitment to live and work in these frontier, peripheral, and remote areas—invited by the local church—was not so much an endeavor of planned design. Rather, it was a graced moment in the life and mission of the church, confirmed and validated by the Second Vatican Council and subsequent

---

4. From 1989 to 2002, there was a series of conferences convened by Maryknollers and their partners, Indigenous theologians, and organizations from throughout Latin America. The systematized results of these conferences have been collected in documented form by the organizers of the conferences held in Urubamba, Peru (1989); Cochabamba, Bolivia (1993); Arequipa, Peru (1993); Oaxaca, Mexico (1995); Antigua, Guatemala (1997); Chol Chol, Chile (1998); and again in 2002, in Arequipa, Peru. After 1990, a parallel development took place with the organization of several international conferences around the Americas in Peru, Ecuador, Paraguay, and Mexico.

developments. The face-to-face transforming encounter with people on the margins nurtured, motivated, and shaped our awareness of and commitment to the inculturation of the gospel with respect for the emergence of an Indigenous worldview and sociocultural imaginaries.

For the most part, the intentional operative missiology of the early years of evangelization was to plant the church and its structures in areas of Latin America where church institutions were weak or nonexistent, partly as a result of the long absence of missionary mendicant orders from the first evangelization of the early colonial period, followed by the utopian Jesuit model of the Reductions in the seventeenth century. A hiatus of two centuries followed this suppression of the Jesuits. Until Maryknoll arrived in the early 1940s, many of these places on the periphery of Latin America were abandoned, served only occasionally and sporadically by national diocesan clergy or circuit-riding priests, leaving the task of inculturation to lay *cofradías*, confraternities with popular devotions to local saints. The restoration of the mission churches and towns in eastern Bolivia stands as a living monument to that early period researched and studied so well by my Bolivian colleague Roberto Tomichá, who made a magisterial presentation at this conference.[5]

When the first Maryknollers arrived in the 1940s and 1950s, there was little semblance of a concentrated church evangelization effort among Indigenous peoples. However, in those remote areas of the continent, we discovered how the first seeds of a transformative encounter had begun to bear fruit, much like the parable of the seed that grows by itself (Mark 4:23–26). From the early years, an abiding awareness and conviction of the evangelizing potential and protagonist role of Indigenous people was implicitly recognized. Despite the deep wounds left from the colonial past of oppression and marginalization, the fruits of this mutually enriching encounter shaped the style and model of our evangelization among indigenous peoples.

Still, a residual persistence of the consequences of what Argentine sociologist Walter Mignolo describes as the "colonial wound" remains in the consciousness of many people still affected by the trauma of conquest and colonization.[6] However, recent processes of decolonization—for example, in countries like Bolivia—have begun to reverse the longstanding effects of the colonial order in order to enable new and creative expressions of these peoples' wisdom and worldview to emerge on a larger world

5. Two outstanding sources are Tomichá, *La Primera Evangelización*, and the magisterial study by Klaiber, *Jesuits in Latin America*.

6. Mignolo, *Idea of Latin America*. The author illustrates and documents the use of the term the "colonial wound" as the touchstone for a new generation of Indigenous leadership proposals for an alternative worldview.

stage. Yet, then and now, we see in the struggles of Indigenous peoples of the Americas inchoate resources of resilience and resistance for overcoming adversity and recovering the wisdom of ancestral worldviews to forge new and authentic relationships.

From centuries of the "colonial wound," they have emerged with a renewed sense of their unique role to create a historical project that engages all nations of the human family. In my view, Maryknollers by and large have observed this historical reversal of the role of Indigenous "witness people" who have suffered, endured, and survived the colonial experience with renewed consciousness of their role and purpose. Seventy years later, we can attest to signs of how these peoples have flourished in order to fashion and articulate an identity out of the pain and anguish of lamentation to construct local worldviews and narratives in particular narratives and ideologies of modernity and postmodernity. Now, we turn our attention to the ways Indigenous peoples have begun to articulate these alternative narratives at the service of all members of the human family.

Toward a More Systematic Understanding of the Encounters

The stage was set for these developments by the seismic shifts in mission methods that occurred in the 1970s and 1980s in these peripheral Indigenous regions of the continent, especially those inspired by the emerging liberation theology movement. The words of its acknowledged and acclaimed founder, Peruvian Dominican priest Gustavo Gutiérrez—a "physical and spiritual nearness to the poor"[7]—resonated with the encounter experiences of many Maryknollers from the outset in the context of a renewed appreciation for the emergent Indigenous worldview, the formation of new and highly creative sociocultural imaginaries, and potentially transformative narratives of survival, as well as the recreation of a compelling alternative worldview.

Two outstanding examples in particular demonstrate the depth of these face-to-face encounters. One is the exemplary life and witness of the late Indiana-born James Madden, whose eleven years living in an Indigenous community on the south side of Peru's Lake Titicaca is the testimony of a "spiritual and physical nearness" to the people. So, too, is the martyrdom of another Maryknoller, Texan Bill Woods, in Guatemala. Forty years ago, in 1976 in the midst of the country's civil war, he was assassinated by the Guatemalan army, which downed the plane he was piloting to bring supplies to Mayan Indians in the Ixcán region of that country.[8] During the

7. Gutiérrez, *Theology of Liberation.*

8. Diocese of Santa Cruz del Quiché, *Padre Guillermo Woods.* Fr. Woods was

subsequent years of the civil war, many Maryknoll missioners accompanied displaced Guatemalan indigenous refugees to camps in Mexico.

These diverse personal and collective experiences became the focus of a more systematic reflection process underway from the beginning in those aforementioned peripheral areas. They took on more explicit meaning through a series of seven periodic workshops and conferences that were held from 1989 through 2001 at different venues in Latin America: Urubamba, Peru (1989); Cochabamba, Bolivia (1991); Arequipa, Peru (1993 and 2001); Antigua, Guatemala (1994); Oaxaca, Mexico (1995); and Chol Chol, Chile (1998).[9] The choice of these sites reflects the diversity of the collective Maryknoll experience throughout the Americas and the present-day historical realities that have shaped our identity and mission—as well as our spirituality and mission methods—in both large and small (but significant) ways. The systematic accounts of these gatherings reflect the foundations for a profoundly unique mission spirituality lived out, often under adverse and conflictive conditions, in these remote, peripheral areas.

These workshops, initially convened for Maryknollers and close collaborators, opened up a space to reflect on the individual and collective experiences of encounter. Soon, they evolved to include the participation of invited Indigenous people, local theologians, and social scientists whose history was intertwined with ours; thus was forged the beginning of an Indigenous theology movement. This new theological current, and a younger generation headed by Nicanor Sarmiento, is articulated by local theologians of the stature of Jesuit Xavier Albó in Bolivia; the Aymara priest Domingo Llanque in Peru and Deacon Calixto Quispe in Bolivia; Chilean Diego Irarrázaval; and the Zapotec Mexican Eleazar López, along with the Aymara Methodist leader, Vicenta Mamani, and other pioneers of the movement.[10] As a result of their writings, they have woven an in-depth, systematic reflec-

---

killed on November 20, 1976, shot down in the plane he piloted transferring people and supplies to Indigenous colonizers in the Ixcán region of Guatemala. Initial reports attributed Fr. Woods's death to a mechanical failure. However, documentation obtained through the Freedom of Information Act confirmed that he was murdered by the Guatemalan army.

9. See the series of systematized documents from Maryknoll-sponsored conferences, 1989–2002.

10. Several articles and books published in different Latin American countries attest to the scope and quality of *teologia india* during the last thirty-five years. Among the significant titles is Marzal et al., *Indian Face of God*. Noted theologians like Domingo Llanque (Peru), Vicenta Mamani (Bolivia), and Eleazar López (Mexico) have published extensively. An example of a younger theologian who is writing and publishing in this vein is Peruvian Quechua Nicanor Sarmiento Tupayupanqui with his recent work, *Un Arco Iris*.

tion documenting the growing awareness and awakening of an Indigenous protagonist role in articulating an emerging theological movement that is in dialogue with other emergent currents of theological reflection with a feminist and ecological focus.

Relationship to the Latin American Church's Renewal Process, from Medellín to Aparecida

These theologians are influenced and inspired by the prophetic and collegial leadership style and witness of bishops formed in the spirit of Vatican II and the Latin American Church's renewal process—bishops like Samuel Ruiz, Leonidas Proaño, Bartolomé Carrasco, Sergio Méndez Arceo, Luis Dalle, and Luis Vallejos. They can also trace much of their inspiration back to the prophetic witness of the sixteenth-century "defender of the Indians," Dominican Fray Bartolomé de las Casas (1484–1566).[11] To a greater or lesser extent, by claiming the Las Casas spirit, they have fostered the growth and development of this movement throughout the continent. In the process, these women and men have become the scribes and chief proponents of this new ecumenical contribution which, in two distinct moments, I will attempt to describe.

Emblematic of the movement is the substantial corpus of articles and books over the past twenty-five years by Eleazar López and others. These writings stemmed from international conferences in the Andean countries of Peru and Bolivia, as well as in Mexico, Paraguay, Argentina, and Ecuador—conferences that were born of the kinds of face-to-face transforming encounters mentioned above. López and fellow theologians came out of ecclesial settings because of changed church structures and the creation of regional pastoral research and formation centers like CENAMI (Centro Nacional de Ayuda a las Misiones Indígenas) in southern Mexico, IPA (Instituto de Pastoral Andina) in Cusco, Peru, and centers in Bolivia promoted by the local church in dialogue with social scientists.[12]

---

11. Many Indigenous theologians find inspiration in the prophetic witness of life and extensive writings of the sixteenth-century Spanish Dominican friar, Bartolomé de las Casas (1484–1566), documented in the historical research of the late Helen Rand Parish of Bancroft Library at the University of California, Berkeley, and published in books such as *Las Casas en México: Historia y Obras Desconocidas* and *Bartolomé de las Casas: The Only Way*.

12. CENAMI's long pioneering work in Mexico's southern Pacific region gave birth to the original theological contributions of the Zapotec Indian theologian Eleazar López and many others in the post-conciliar era.

Immediately after the 1992 Santo Domingo conference, published articles and studies appeared which highlighted features of this emergent theological movement. Periodically, in different articles and publications, Indigenous participants and outside observers traced the contours of subsequent developments in and through local, national, and international conferences sponsored and organized by church-affiliated centers such as IPA; CENAMI; IDEA (Instituto de Estudios Aymaras), now known as IDECA (Instituto de Culura Andina) in Puno, Peru; and the Missiological Institute of the Catholic University of Bolivia and the Maryknoll Mission Center, both located in Cochabamba.[13]

Directly linked to the ecclesial and post-conciliar identity of the movement is the result of the Puebla, Santo Domingo, and Aparecida conferences of the Latin American bishops. In 1979, Puebla first opened the door in its "Conclusions" by noting the shift from the church as the "voice of voiceless" to recognizing the "evangelizing potential of the poor" as a central feature related to the emergent Indigenous presence. While stressing and highlighting the inculturation of the gospel, Puebla granted a privileged protagonist role to Indigenous actors in the larger scheme of the church's evangelization. It proclaimed another important shift, namely the need for Latin America to assume its own missionary call out of poverty and the originality of its ancestral traditions, expressions of popular religiosity, and faith witness experiences.

These were themes picked up and further developed in the Fourth Latin American Episcopal Conference at Santo Domingo, which took place in the symbolically charged year commemorating the anniversary of Christianity's arrival in the Americas in 1492. Neither observers nor participants at Santo Domingo missed the awarding of the Nobel Prize for Peace to the Guatemalan woman Rigoberta Menchú, announced during the conference to loud applause. The Santo Domingo Conference provided another platform on which to build and consolidate the movement that has grown from a largely clandestine lamentation to a full-fledged project.[14] No longer are Indigenous, Afro-American, and mestizo cultures considered peripheral to

13. Church-affiliated pastoral institutes have been one of the chief catalysts for promoting the development of *teologia india* throughout the Americas. In Peru, initiatives such as IPA—through its programs and publications like *Allpanchis*, with more than sixty issues published between 1969 and 2000—served as a forerunner and chronicler of this movement. The occasional bulletins of the Maryknoll-founded IDEA and its successor, IDECA, have carried on this tradition in Peru. Similarly, in Mexico, the bishops of the southern Pacific region—including the prophetic bishop of Chiapas, Samuel Ruíz—promoted a protagonist role for Indigenous theologians like Eleazar López through CENAMI.

14. Judd, "From Lamentation to Project."

the Western European cultural legacy. This leaves the door open for even greater intercultural dialogue that was central to sections of the Conclusions of the Aparecida Brazil Conference, convened in 2007 after a fifteen-year lapse, recognizing how the continent's Indigenous peoples are classified among those "missionary disciples" of a new evangelization.[15] Moreover, their self-identification as "peoples of memory, resistance, and hope"—first heard in the context of the five-hundred-year commemoration—becomes the matrix and template for which we continue to observe, accompany, and celebrate the movement.

Over and above these ecclesial developments, we return to the defining phenomenon of an initial, transforming face-to-face encounter that provides the motivation and mystique for the conversion to dialogue with the Indigenous worldview in Latin America. More importantly, in this historical process, we are constantly reminded of the authentic voice of Indigenous identity, of the voice of interlocutors who fully articulate the movement in its different stages like the Mexican Zapotec, Eleazar López. And now, we turn to the collective initiatives of these women and men who carry the movement into a new stage and context to shape the direction with ever-new thematic content.

Results and New Challenges: The Proposals and Prospects for a New Sociocultural Imaginary of Buen Vivir[16] for the Peoples of "Memory, Resistance, and Hope"

Validation of the movement out of the residue of the "colonial wound" arises from different but interrelated sources in the witness of Indigenous peoples in the thirty-year civil war and genocide of a country like Guatemala, as well as in the truth and reconciliation process that resulted in the Report. Church participation in the process was critical, and the martyrdom of Bishop Juan Girardi two days after its publication further underscores the power of the church's encounter.

Likewise, a church presence in southern Peru was a decisive factor in building a strong social network to offset the worst effects of the political

15. López, "*Aparecida*, Globalización y Cambio Cultural."

16. Within the past several years, the unique Indigenous concept of *Buen Vivir* has emerged as an alternative way of living in right relationships with the Creator God and with peoples all over the Earth, with respect for ancestral traditions reinterpreted in the contemporary context in several Latin American countries with large Indigenous populations. The language of *Buen Vivir* offers another worldview and invites dialogue with diverse cultures and civilizations.

violence during the 1980s. A commitment to accompany a theological movement among the Andean Quechua and Aymara peoples at that time contributed to the rejection of and resistance to the violence perpetrated by the Shining Path Maoist-inspired terrorists and the armed forces. In places where there was a weak church presence and little experience of intercultural dialogue, the violence reached catastrophic proportions, as documented in the Truth and Reconciliation process report.[17]

A direct result of this widely documented and courageous witness of this movement was the instrumental role it played in the 2007 passage of the United Nations Declaration on the Rights of Indigenous Peoples, complementary to the United Nations Declaration of Human Rights of 1947. Because of this cumulative experience of peoples of memory, resistance, and hope, the concept of human rights was expanded to incorporate the new understandings of sacred territories and the worldview of Indigenous peoples across the globe to live in harmony with the environment. Maryknoll-affiliated witnesses were invited to give testimony at the different hearings held at the United Nations and recounted by Peruvian Victor Maqque and Bolivian Jose Luis López.[18]

Another significant result is the development of a growing and vibrant movement and network of Indigenous theology with the uninterrupted series of international conferences and writings that first appeared in 1990. In a collection of articles in a book published in 2004, *Resurgent Voices in Latin America: Indigenous Peoples, Political Mobilization, and Religious Change*, I have attempted to present a survey of the key developments in thematic content and to profile the principal actors of the current of Indigenous theology, while building on earlier works by Eleazar López, Diego Irarrázaval, Xavier Albo, and Nicanor Sarmiento. A recent example of this literature can be found in the reflections of Eleazar López, Christine Perrier, and Simón Pedro Arnold, *Caminos de Herradura: Veinticinco Años de Teología Andina, Perspectivas* (2016). These reflections flowed out of one of the most recent international conferences in 2016 in Peru and marked the twenty-fifth anniversary of these kinds of Latin American events.[19] As the shift in reflections based on the liberation theology perspective turn toward the pneumatological,[20] proponents of the movement look toward retrieval of a Spirit-based focus in further developing this new and promising current.

17. Tovar, *Ser Iglesia*. See especially the selection by Lupe Jara, "El Sur Andino," 397–632.

18. López, *Derechos de los Pueblos Indígenas*.

19. López et al., *Caminos de Herradura*.

20. Cf. the Third Congress of *AMERIINDIA* held in Belo Horizonte, Brazil, 2015.

These so-called "barefoot theologians" have graduated to another category of dialogue partner, equal to their elder mentors and ideally positioned to articulate and expound an original theology to the academic world.

Intercultural dialogue has emerged as a compelling contribution from throughout the Indigenous world to enhance what Argentine sociologist Walter Mignolo calls "borderland co-existence," or consciousness-building on the momentum of international events like the World Social Forums that announce that "another world is possible." This is an epistemological revolution that offsets and counteracts Western cosmology and worldviews which pervade the discourse of academic debates provoked and exemplified by Samuel Huntington's polemical *The Clash of Civilizations and the Remaking of World Order*. Other possible worlds in this view can be constructed from newly revitalized civilizations of Indigenous peoples who claim inclusiveness and holistic approaches to such global problems as how humanity can learn to live together, sharing each other's witness. We need go no further than the emergent Indigenous theology movement to find an expression of the "decolonizing" trend.

A concrete result of the development of Indigenous consciousness offers strong claims for a proposal and not merely a lamentation or a protest. The "living well," or *Buen Vivir*[21] (*suma qamana* in Aymara), paradigm has taken on renewed relevance around the Americas and is expressed in local variants, explicitly in 2008 in the new Constitution of the Plurinational State of Bolivia. The prominent Indigenous theologian Eleazar López frames the question not merely as a return to an elusive romantic past, but as an application of the values embodied in ancestral worldviews and wisdom to the crisis of civilization and the mechanistic metaphor of modernity that looks on their cultures as commodities. Living well, according to this paradigm, is not living better or with more materialistic values and lifestyle choices.

---

21. Editor's note: For a helpful discussion of *buen vivir*, see Hicks, "Buen Vivir," esp. paras. 3–6: "*Buen vivir* has existed as a worldview for millennia and, at its core, is about communities living sustainably with mother nature . . . Maria Estela Barco Huerta of DESMI . . . eloquently described *buen vivir* as being based on a concept of deep, great respect, or *Ich'el Ta Muk* in the Mayan language, that each person has for the spirit, or *Ch'ulel*, of every other living being, which includes humans, animals, nature, and the spiritual realm . . . Professor Mauricio Phélan of the Central University of Venezuela . . . explained three distinct harmonies which exist within communities practicing *buen vivir*: (1) Harmony within yourself: physical, mental, and spiritual components; (2) Harmony between communities: between yourself and your family, your community, your neighbors, your colleagues, institutions, and markets; (3) Harmony with nature: mutual balance between human activities and environmental health. When harmony with and amongst individuals, communities, and the natural world are achieved, then *buen vivir* is achieved."

Together with and closely linked to these tangible results is the challenge from Pope Francis to live out the demands of "missionary discipleship." This call was first heard at the Aparecida Conference and is now spelled out more clearly in his 2013 apostolic exhortation, *Evangelii Gaudium,* along with his call in *Laudato Si'* to heed the message of Indigenous peoples. Chapter 4 of that groundbreaking document on "integral ecology" incorporates much Indigenous wisdom in calling for a new way of living with and in right relationships of solidarity with the cosmos. His much-acclaimed 2015 address to representatives of social movements from around the continent in Santa Cruz, Bolivia, captures well his acknowledgement of these developments I mention here.[22]

This perspective of Indigenous wisdom now articulated through the concept of *Buen Vivir* has been adopted by many Indigenous peoples throughout the Americas in a growing movement to express a notion of the importance of living in right relationships among peoples and the created world. It serves as a confirmation and a validation of the emergence of the Indigenous theology movement over the past thirty years of developments of a creative new vital synthesis. This new vital synthesis can also be seen as a variation of what is called a subversive "Pachakuti," the epistemological upheaval of turning the world order upside down by imagining new and deeper ways of relationship, such as those that have been forged for decades at the real and symbolic and transformative *apachetas.* The metaphor of the *apacheta* was the organizing theme in the memoir of my encounters throughout the Indigenous world of the Americas from 1975 onward, and it has served me as an interpretive key for this journey.[23]

22. Francis, *Evangelii Gaudium.* Pope Francis's use of the language of *peripheries* resonates with the missionary Maryknollers living and working among Indigenous peoples in remote areas of the American continent since 1942–43.

23. See also the book memoir by Judd, *De Apacheta en Apacheta.*

Regional Indigenous Theological Voices and Responses

B: Canada

3

My Experience Working as an Indigenous Person with Indigenous People

Eva Solomon, CSJ

Megizique n'dijnicas, waswaskesh/mkwa n'dodem. My Indigenous spirit name is "Eagle Woman," and my clans are deer and bear. My baptismal name is Eva Solomon. I wish to begin by acknowledging that we are standing on the traditional lands of the Potawatomi Indigenous people until the early nineteenth century. Then major portions of Potawatomi lands were seized by the US government. In the Treaty of Chicago in 1833, that tribe was forced to cede its lands in Illinois.[1] Most of the Potawatomi people were removed to Indian Territory west of the Mississippi River, but some returned to Manitoulin Island in Canada, also part of their original territory, where to this day we have "The Council of Three Fires—the Potawatomi, Odawa, and Ojibwa."

I grew up in the small, isolated fishing village of Killarney, Ontario, with a population of about three hundred people. We had no roads, with water access just to Manitoulin Island and other areas on the shores of Lake Huron's Georgian Bay. Although it was isolated, I was aware of a much larger world, because Killarney was on the Great Lakes water system, and we saw many American yachts come into our village from Florida and elsewhere. Even President Franklin D. Roosevelt used to go there. There is a commemorative plaque at McGregor Bay to remind us that he was fishing there when news came of the end of the World War II.

I knew at the age of four that I would be a religious sister when I grew up, and I never wavered from that conviction. Around that same time, I watched my dad build a log cabin with a stone fireplace in it to house an

1. Hornbeck Tanner, "Treaties."

archeological team from Flint, Michigan, that was digging up one of our traditional Indian burial grounds which was 3,000 to 4,500 years old. I remember thinking that meant "we had been here forever!" Killarney's original name was Shebanoning, which meant "Inland Passageway," because it provided an inland passageway protecting people traveling to the head of the lakes—Thunder Bay, Ontario—through Sault Ste. Marie. My mother was from Sagamok reserve (a reservation, in your language) on the Spanish River, and my father was from Henvey Inlet reserve on Georgian Bay. Our family was relatively large—five boys, five girls, and five adopted as well, because my parents lost three children at birth, or shortly before and after. I currently live in Winnipeg.

As Indigenous peoples, racism is everywhere for us, at both the personal and social levels; my first experience was at seven years old. I came home from school in tears at 11:30 AM. I found my mother sitting on the green wooden armchair by the table. I asked her why the other children were calling me "a dirty Indian." She put her arm on my shoulder and said, "They do that because they are ignorant, and ignorant means they have never learned anything different." She had comforted me without putting anything negative on those who had hurt me. That was my first experience of racism and prejudice, and I and many other Indigenous continue to experience it even today. I have been working most of my life in Indigenous ministry, currently covering more than two-thirds of our country of Canada. Indigenous ministry is one of the largest pastoral issues today.

Racism is systemic in our society, our education, our political system, our immigration system, our churches, our health care, our justice system, and more. What racism does to us as people is extremely violent. It puts us down; it continues to impose the colonial system imposed by the settlers and blames us for not conforming to societal demands regarding living in a settler's colonial idea of our land. Let me give you an example of social racism. For more than a century, Winnipeg has obtained its drinking water from Shoal Lake 40 First Nation, a reserve that straddles the Ontario-Manitoba border. In order to do that, about one hundred years ago, the settler community built an aqueduct that cut off the reserve from the mainland.[2] While our city gets good drinking water, the people of Shoal Lake 40 First Nation have to live on bottled water; they have been under a "boil water" advisory for almost two decades. They have no indoor plumbing, no winter road over the ice, a broken-down ferry in the summer, and several weeks in fall and spring with no access to the outside world at all. The health care workers and ambulances won't risk going to the reserve, so the sick have

2. CBC News, "Shoal Lake 40," paras. 1–2.

to find their own way out, and children have to leave the reserve after the eighth grade to go elsewhere to finish their education. Imagine waiting a century for potable water when others are taking yours daily! And we are told "that was in the past; get over it, and get on with living." At least one provincial government, the federal government, and the city of Winnipeg have promised money for a road, but very little has materialized. After a century of isolation, construction finally began in July 2017 on this road, which Shoal Lake 40 Chief Erwin Redsky says "sends a strong and important message about taking reconciliation seriously."[3]

Lack of employment is also a problem on reserves. Even the mainline churches have often abandoned Indigenous peoples because they cannot sustain their own churches. But how can they with little or no employment on the reserves? Like Shoal Lake, many reserves have no access to places where they can work because of distance and lack of roads.

Another great loss is the loss of life, by intent and by accidents such as tragic fires, drowning, and plane crashes, where perhaps three to six people lose their lives in a single event. There are over one thousand documented cases of murdered and missing women and girls. It is phenomenal! Talk about compounded grief! I recall one period of two years in my own life where we lost sixteen people to tragic deaths. That's a lot to deal with in two years. We are not finished grieving one or more deaths before another one is upon us.

All of the governments' empty promises lead to a loss of hope, continued addictions to alcohol, and even newer kinds of addictions to many kinds of prescription drugs and street drugs, gas and glue sniffing, and related gang memberships. Another issue that we are constantly dealing with is suicides. Pikangikum, another isolated village in northwestern Ontario, has the highest suicide rate per capita in the entire world.

Because of the many dysfunctions in the community—the desperate poverty, the lack of education, the struggle just to live, and what I call the compounded (some call it pathological) grief that communities are suffering due to the many deaths both in the past and in the present—there is a kind of numbness, or paralysis, in many villages. Much of this compounded grief comes from the communities' experience of the whole process of colonization and the intense and rapid speed of it. While most of Europe took centuries to move from the Stone Age to the Space Age, many of our people—especially in the isolated communities of the northern provinces— were only "discovered" when planes started flying over those territories to England during the Second World War. I have been in many communities

3. Malone, "It's Everything for Us," para. 13.

that still had the stakes in the ground noting the year the government "discovered" them and forced them to relocate—small extended families of twenty or so had to go to certain villages in order to adhere to the treaties. I can remember one old man telling my parents and me, "I remember when the first white man came to our village." Some villages started as small family bands that moved, at the encouragement of a Catholic missionary, and established a village of about three thousand people. They could not learn to adjust to an imposed government and establish the social structures to live together as one people in the short time it took them to arrive. European peoples took centuries to move from the Stone Age to the Space Age, even at the level of social structures, which they themselves probably developed rather than had imposed on them.

The adhesions to the treaties and Canada's Indian Residential Schools were part of an overall assimilation strategy to civilize and Christianize Indigenous peoples with the ultimate goal of making them into citizens, even though it was only in the 1960s that we got the right to vote and were deemed citizens. Children became the focus of the Indian Residential Schools because a consensus arose between government and church officials that "[a]boriginal . . . 'savagery' could be solved by taking children from their families at an early age and instilling the ways of the dominant society," popularly described as "killing the Indian in the child."[4] Adults were deemed to be incapable of this transformation from savagery and an impediment to it by continuing to transfer their own knowledge and culture on to their children.[5]

---

4. The phrase "killing the Indian in the child" is widely used in referring to the goal of Canada's Indian Residential Schools and is difficult to attribute to any particular source. It may have evolved from "Kill the Indian, Save the Man," a phrase used by Richard Pratt, the architect of the US Residential School System. For more information, see Churchill, *Kill the Indian*. See also Canadian Press, "Text of Stephen Harper's Apology":

> Two primary objectives of the residential schools system were to remove and isolate children from the influence of their homes, families, traditions, and cultures, and to assimilate them into the dominant culture. These objectives were based on the assumption aboriginal cultures and spiritual beliefs were inferior and unequal. Indeed, some sought, as it was infamously said, "to kill the Indian in the child." Today, we recognize that this policy of assimilation was wrong, has caused great harm, and has no place in our country. (paras. 3–4)

5. See the report of the Royal Commission on Aboriginal Peoples (RCAP), which comprised five volumes and four thousand pages, at https://www.bac-lac.gc.ca/eng/discover/aboriginal-heritage/royal-commission-aboriginal-peoples/Pages/final-report.aspx. The RCAP was established in 1992 to investigate the situation of the Aboriginal peoples of Canada.

I think that by now you have a broad picture of our reality. But the negative is only one part of our story. Just as the negative things have brought shame and destruction, so also have the good things brought honor and integrity. In our land, we have this saying: "The honor of one is the honor of all." So, let's look at some of the positives.

I would like to begin by sharing some thoughts on one of these, the Truth and Reconciliation Commission (TRC), which just finished its work in 2015. The TRC was established by the Supreme Court of Canada to respond to the concerns of Indigenous or Aboriginal people about the abuses that took place in or because of the boarding schools or residential schools. Those abuses could be summarized as cultural, spiritual, emotional, and various forms of physical abuse—in particular, sexual abuse—that took place. The effects of this system are intergenerational, and I am part of that system since both of my parents went to one of those boarding schools. For many years, the residential school system could be described as a function of colonization intended to "kill the Indian and save the child," even when it may not have been understood that way by the religious working in them. By giving that responsibility over to the various churches—predominantly the Catholic, Anglican, United, and Presbyterian—without sufficient funding, staffing, or professionalism, the government tried to absolve itself of its responsibility. Led by Indigenous Judge Murray Sinclair, the TRC spent much of its first year developing a community among the commissioners. They traveled to various parts of the country to hear the stories of the survivors of the residential schools which really epitomized the process of colonization of Canada's Indigenous peoples by the settlers who were supported by legal documents like the Indian Act, written by the settler people in government, with no Indigenous involvement.

The TRC commissioners recognized early on that they could not summarize their findings in "recommendations" but rather required "calls to action" which would imply concrete actions that would help everyone to change their mentalities, their attitudes, their behaviors, the education system, the health care system, the legal system, and governance patterns. Action Forty-Eight of the TRC's ninety-four Calls to Action required that the churches issue a statement no later than March 31, 2016, as to how they were going to implement the United Nations Declaration on the Rights of Indigenous Peoples and to repudiate the Doctrine of Discovery and *terra nullius*. They envisioned a Canada transformed from a colonized nation to a decolonized nation, based on living fully as treaty people, fully human with equal dignity. This demanded real change. It forced Canada to take another look at the concepts of the Doctrine of Discovery and *terra nullius* that had been used as foundational documents for our country.

The Catholic leadership in Canada repudiated the Doctrine of Discovery and *terra nullius* and committed to implementing the United Nations Declaration on the Rights of Indigenous Peoples as a framework for relationship. Here is a small quote from their letter:

> We acknowledge that many among the Catholic faithful ignored or did not speak out against the injustice, thereby enabling the violation of Indigenous dignity and rights. It is our hope and prayer that by naming and rejecting those erroneous ideas that lie behind what is commonly called the "Doctrine of Discovery" and terra nullius, we may better recognize the challenges we face today so that we may overcome them together.[6]

The text includes eight commitments by the bishops which are recommended as better ways of walking together with Indigenous peoples.

By making the United Nations Declaration on the Rights of Indigenous Peoples the framework for reconciliation, the TRC also shifted the foundation of the Indigenous/non-Indigenous relationship back to our friendship treaties. The Indigenous understood their participation in the treaties to be as sovereign nations. This is now beginning to be acknowledged by our governments. In his informative online essay, Mohawk leader and legal academic Stephen John Ford says this:

> The need to exert sovereignty by Indigenous Nations flows from the Colonizer's assertion that the Crown became sovereign over all the lands and peoples living upon Turtle Island at "Discovery." The Doctrine of Discovery and the concept of *terra nullius* . . . are the legal foundations upon which European Crowns made pompous claims of sovereignty over Indigenous lands and populations. The Courts have used these doctrines and principles and upheld them in favor of the Settler State.[7]

In January 2007, I began working for the Assembly of Western Catholic Bishops' Standing Committee on Indigenous Affairs (AWCB–SCIA) as the executive director of Building Bridges, an umbrella project that was started in the fall of 2006. Our main task is to seek to build bridges with the non-Indigenous peoples of our land. The work includes four major areas:

1. developing an annual conference on Directions in Indigenous Ministry with a team;

---

6. Canadian Conference of Catholic Bishops et al., "Doctrine of Discovery," 2.
7. Ford, "Sovereignty," para. 5.

2. developing a biennial Catholic Indigenous Elders Dialogue with a team;

3. organizing a one-day meeting for the SCIA and local Indigenous people prior to the annual AWCB meeting in the diocese hosting the meeting; and

4. conducting or assisting in diocesan workshops in whatever diocese requests my assistance.

We have been through some adaptations over the years, and now I am ready for another. We have changed from using "Aboriginal" to using "Indigenous" to reflect a more common and correct name, and now, I would like us to change the name of the committee from "Aboriginal Affairs" to "Indigenous Relations." Using the word "Affairs" seems to have a connotation that something is under the control of another. Using the word "Relations" in the title implies more mutuality. I have already begun this discussion with the committee.

In the 2016 "Directions in Indigenous Ministry" conference, we wanted to have as many Indigenous as non-Indigenous participants to meet for a number of days. If the church were to learn anything about us Indigenous peoples, it requires hearing us over a period of days, not just for an hour or so. Since the very first gathering, the bishops present and the Newman Theological College staff members on the team realized the value of our presence. Initially, the intention of the gathering was to teach non-Indigenous clergy and pastoral workers how to work in Indigenous communities. In order for that to be successful, they needed to know something about our Indigenous spirituality and some of our ceremonies, such as the smudge, the sweat lodge, the Sacred Pipe ceremony, the Sun Dance, and other rituals. Not only did they need to experience them, but they also needed to dialogue with us about the language and theology behind them.

Our other regular gathering is the Catholic Indigenous Elders' Dialogue, with Catholic theologians present to help the Indigenous theologians find a common language that speaks to our reality in such a way that is clear to both the church and us. We are blessed to have among us an Indigenous Peruvian theologian who has some common understanding of our spirituality and who can help us with this task.

Every February, we have a dialogue with Indigenous peoples in whichever diocese that is hosting the Assembly of Western Bishops' regional annual meeting. Local Indigenous people meet with the Standing Committee on Indigenous Relations for one day prior to their meeting. It is another way for the Indigenous people to be in dialogue with the bishops, and it is normally the Indigenous peoples who do the talking. The bishops are serious about listening and acting. Indigenous ministry is one of the largest pastoral issues today, at least in western and northern Canada. Because of those meetings, some dioceses have now started to establish Diocesan Indigenous Councils. At our 2013 "Directions in Indigenous Ministry" conferences, we had Kateri TV from Toronto present to film the conference. A series of twelve short videos were produced about the conference featuring Archbishop Emeritus Sylvain Lavoie and myself.[8] There are so many other good things that are happening that I cannot include them all, but will mention a few more below to give some more examples.

Idle No More is a grassroots peace movement begun in 2012 by four Indigenous and non-Indigenous women in response to Prime Minister Harper's Bill C-45, which threatened the sovereignty of Indigenous rights, particularly over land, water, forests, and the environment.[9] The movement has a strong educational component, too. It also works to rebuild our sense of nationhood and a nation-to-nation relationship with the government, which is how we originally made our treaties. With this peace-focused movement, Indigenous and non-Indigenous groups rise up everywhere in peaceful demonstrations of Round Dances on major street corners to bring awareness to Indigenous issues. Another positive thing that happened recently is the federal government's establishment of the independent National Inquiry into Missing and Murdered Indigenous Women and Girls.[10] Winnipeg is one of the hot spots for these missing and murdered women, and in 1992, a community safety patrol formed called the Bear Clan Patrol, a mixed group of Indigenous and non-Indigenous people.[11] The group was inactive for some time, but has recently started again to patrol the streets of the city of Winnipeg every weekend.

Reconciliation

An important and positive thing I learned during my Doctor of Ministry work at Catholic Theological Union—and which I have expanded to adapt to our Indigenous peoples' reality—is the steps for reconciliation. I learned that reconciliation is a lifelong journey; it means finding a healing/redeeming way of dealing with violence. It is a basic human act that

8. The series is available online at http://www.villagersmedia.com/kateritv.

9. "Idle No More is Founded," http://www.idlenomore.ca/idle_no_more_is_found ed_by_4_women.

10. Visit their website at http://www.mmiwg-ffada.ca/.

11. Bear Clan Patrol, "History," https://www.bearclanpatrolinc.com/.

demands effort and involvement, time and patience. My reflections are mostly based on Robert Schreiter's ideas about reconciliation.[12] But from my own life experience, I have also learned other steps and have added them, or perhaps focused more attention on them. The steps for reconciliation I describe below deal more with personal or individual reconciliation. Following those steps, I will then talk about the "Returning to Spirit" program, which addresses reconciliation on a broader social scale and is working very well for us in Canada.

1. *Awareness*: This is our recognition of oppression. Colonization and its effects are the most all-pervasive destructive force that must be dealt with if healing, peace, and reconciliation are to be achieved in Canada.

2. *Anger*: This is the feeling that arises once we know that we have been offended or lied to in word or action, etc. It is a just anger that needs to be expressed.

3. *Crying out*: There is a need to cry out both *loud* enough and *long* enough, until the oppressed feel that they've been heard. Someone needs to gives legitimacy to the crying out of the oppressed in a context in which they can feel that they have actually been heard and may now begin to move on in their healing process.

4. *Creating a new, redeeming narrative*: The offended must create/reconstruct a new and redeeming narrative. Only when the offended one is able to see the offender as a human being, with frailties just like him/herself, can healing take place. The victim reaffirms his or her own humanity, goodness, and dignity in the image of God, thus providing a redeeming meaning to suffering.

5. *Forgiveness of self*: This step is the one I have articulated more directly as its own distinct step. I have found that forgiveness of self is probably the most difficult. As Indigenous peoples, we need to forgive ourselves for having believed the lie given by the settler peoples. It is like our "original sin," if you will, when we realize that we, too, have offended others, and our merciful God has forgiven us. Forgiveness is opening oneself to love. Jesus himself has given us a model of redeeming suffering. Forgiveness restores right relationships with God, self, others, and all of creation.

6. *Forgiveness of the offender*: Self-forgiveness allows us to forgive our offender, and that opens a doorway. Forgiveness can be offered, because

12. See these two books by Schreiter: *Reconciliation: Mission and Ministry* and *The Ministry of Reconciliation*.

the offended themselves recognize that they have been offenders at other times (i.e., that they've sinned, and they've been forgiven by Jesus and by others). Jesus forgave his offenders—"Father, forgive them, for they don't know what they are doing" (Luke 23:34, NLT). It is worth noting that, within the Ojibway language, there is also an ancient verb structure called, in English, the "forgiveness tense." Perhaps other Indigenous languages are similar in this way. This verb tense means that "everything is resolved to the satisfaction of all." That means that everyone involved is able to move on to a new and positive future. Reconciliation means finding a healing/redeeming story and dealing with violence in a creative, forgiving way. It is what we are called to live in our daily lives. That is the message of Jesus through the Paschal Mystery. In reconciling us to the Father, Jesus healed our relationships, restoring right relationships for us with God, self, others, and all of creation. We know from the Scripture that this did not happen overnight. It took Jesus' whole thirty-three-year lifetime, including his suffering, passion, death, resurrection, and sending of his Spirit. Reconciliation demands effort and involvement, and takes time and patience.

7. *Opening for repentance*: This final stage of the reconciliation process happens when the offended one forgives the one who prompted the offense. The offended opens the possibility for the offender to ask forgiveness and to gain openness to love. In the Christian story, that is what happened at the crucifixion as well. One of the two men crucified with Jesus was able to recognize himself as an oppressor and was able to ask Jesus to remember him when he came into his kingdom. The other was stuck in his story.

For me, one important aspect in the healing process of Indigenous reconciliation is to identify and accept the reality that colonization happened. This is part of—and maybe the beginning of—the forgiveness stage. We cannot change or undo colonization. It happened! What we can change is how we relate to it. We can allow it to hold us in the past, or we can pass through it as a kind of death experience, and with others' help (the Creator's help, one's Higher Power's help, or Jesus' help), move on to create a new reality, a new identity for ourselves as peoples and as Canadians.

On the cross, Jesus asked his Father to forgive those who had condemned him to death. In that act of forgiveness, the door is opened for the offender to repent. It is the same with us. The offender recognizes and acknowledges the wrong he/she has done and changes his/her ways of behaving. This must be the reality of the broader Canadian society, too. Our society must acknowledge the wrong that has been done in colonization and change its way of behaving to find a more accepting and loving way to live together in harmony. After the resurrection, Jesus' wounds remained, but they had a new and redeeming power. They gave him a new identity. And like Mary Magdalene, we must not cling to the new identity, but rather, allow it to go before us into broader healing service in our world. In this way, we too can provide hope in the possibility of a new future for all of us. The process of reconciliation is not a one-time event; it is a lifelong process. It is this healing medicine of love that allows us to create a new future for ourselves, our community, our country, and our world.

Social Reconciliation

I completed the "Returning to Spirit" (RTS) program in 2007, and I am now the chair of its board. RTS is a nonprofit charitable organization born out of the vision and partnership of an Aboriginal Algonquin man, a religious sister, a chief, a bishop, and a talented design team; its goal is to address the divisive legacy of the Indian Residential Schools.[13] Its program follows three steps: 1) Indigenous people participate in a five-day program by themselves; 2) non-Indigenous people participate separately in the same five-day program; 3) Indigenous people come together for two days to prepare for reconciliation with non-Indigenous participants, and for the program's last two days, both groups come together for the actual reconciliation. Miracles happen. Indigenous and non-Indigenous trainers form the heart of the organization and are supported by the Keepers and the Board of Directors. They help individuals, families, organizations, and whole communities move forward through the principles of personal empowerment and community leadership. They welcome community partners to continue the process of transformation. The work of RTS goes beyond healing. It provides conditions for transformation and mindfulness in all relationships. All Canadians are invited to engage in this process and help the nation to move forward more powerfully toward hope for the next generation.

Thank you for the privilege of sharing our story with you. It has been an honor for me. *Meegwetch*! Thank you.

---

13. For more information about RTS, visit http://www.returningtospirit.org. There are several short videos available there which explain the program.

4

The Truth and Reconciliation Commission
of Canada

BRIAN MCDONOUGH[1]

Introduction: The Residential School System and Its Objectives

During the nineteenth century, the government of Canada established a network of residential schools for Indigenous children.[2] Most of these schools were administered by various Christian churches. This system emerged out of a deliberate policy seeking the cultural assimilation of Indigenous peoples. At a very young age, Indigenous children were removed from their families. Parents were prevented from visiting their children, and if they did manage to make their way to the school, their visit was strictly supervised. Signs of Indigenous identity were abolished. Speaking in one's native tongue was punished.

In certain residential schools, there was abuse—not only physical violence, but also sexual assault—which caused severe harm to these children, and which likely contributed later on in life to alcohol and drug addiction,

1. The author wishes to thank Mrs. Rose-Anne Gosselin, member of the Timiskaming Algonquin First Nation, and Mrs. Christine Zachary-Deom, elected chief of the Mohawk Council of Kahnawake, for having taken the time to read and comment on this article.

2. The first residential school opened its doors near Brantford, Ontario, in 1828. Following the adoption of the Indian Act in 1876, all Indigenous children fell under the responsibility of the government of Canada. In 1920, the Indian Act was amended to allow the government to compel any First Nations child to attend residential school. The government of Canada has estimated that at least one hundred and fifty thousand First Nations, Métis, and Inuit students spent time in one of the 139 residential schools. The last residential school was closed in 1996.

criminal activity, and serious behavioral problems. Overcrowding in dor-
mitories and in classrooms, the poor quality of the food, and inadequate
or nonexistent medical services contributed to the grave deterioration of
the children's health. In such conditions, it is not surprising that infectious
diseases caused a higher proportion of deaths among Indigenous youths
than among the general population.

As a result of repeated demands by former students, who had succeeded in their actions before the courts, a Truth and Reconciliation Commission (hereafter, the Commission) was established to study the consequences
of the residential school system upon Indigenous communities and upon
Canadian society as a whole.[3]

Impact over Multiple Generations—and Across Cultures

Imagine a little girl of six years old in an isolated Indigenous community.[4]
One day, she sees a police car arriving in her village, followed by a school
bus. Without her parents having had the opportunity to explain to her what
was about to happen, she finds herself in the bus, with not much more than
a bag containing a few clothes. She is being taken far away from the world
she had known. Perhaps she is asking herself what she must have done such
that her parents would allow her to be taken away. "Was I a bad girl?" She
observes the police officer, a huge man who speaks in a strange language and
gives out orders to the leaders of her village. From that moment on, she will
feel a certain wariness toward law enforcement officers she will meet. Upon
her arrival in the residential school, she will be told to change her clothes
and to put on a school uniform like the other little girls. Her hair will be cut
and the necklace which her grandmother had given her will be confiscated.
In the large dormitory, the girls in the bed to the right and to the left of hers
speak languages which she cannot make out. In the following weeks, she
will be punished every time she speaks the language she learned from her
family. She feels lonely, isolated, abandoned. She gradually withdraws more
and more into herself. She even shows signs of depression.

3. The Commission was launched on June 2, 2008, under the terms of the Indian
Residential Schools Settlement Agreement, which was signed in 2006 and came into
force in 2007. Following the coming into force of the Settlement Agreement, the Canadian Conference of Catholic Bishops expressed its support for the creation of the
Commission as a path toward healing and hope.

4. This account is fictional, but it does bring together elements from the lives of
persons who went through residential schools. To read authentic accounts, please see
Truth and Reconciliation Commission of Canada, *Survivors Speak*.

A few years later, she begins to rebel against the religious authorities who run the school. She refuses to do homework, and she is told that she is stupid, without talent, and will never amount to anything.[5] She has never gotten used to the food served in the school, and she complains more and more often of indigestion. Some of her classmates have died following mysterious illnesses. Now an adolescent, she dreams of leaving residential school. She escapes a few times, but is caught and is severely punished. One day, she manages to escape and hitches a ride to the big city. But there she discovers that she is all alone in an unfamiliar world. And she's getting hungry. A man, who promises to help her, offers her a place to stay—in exchange for "favors." She begins to drink and to take drugs. Once she falls pregnant, the father abandons her. To feed herself, she shoplifts and is soon arrested by the police. She refuses to cooperate and displays what might be characterized as antisocial behavior. When the day comes to give birth, she is told that it would be better if she gave her baby up for adoption, because she is not able to take proper care of it. She receives the message that she's incapable of being a mother and that, furthermore, she has become a burden to society. She's drinking more and more, and she's exploited by men. She learns that she must not trust men.

The years go by, and she now has several children. She depends on social welfare. Once again, the message she receives is that she's good for nothing. This negative image of herself is reinforced by racial profiling from people she meets and from the media. She does not have the means to return to her native village—in any case, who would remember her? For many years now, the bridges have been burned. She is becoming more and more dependent upon her children to meet her affective needs. As the children grow older, they need to take some distance from their mom. Once again, she feels abandoned, and she begins to slip into episodes of mental illness, cut off as she is from her family, her Indigenous culture, and her spiritual roots. She has become a "statistic." Her children will, in turn, be marked by the tragic story of their mother, and some of them, in spite of themselves and perhaps unconsciously, begin to repeat their mother's patterns of behavior which, in turn, will be transmitted to their own children. How to break out of this dynamic in which trauma and

5. This is what the former prime minister of the Northwest Territories, Stephen Kakfwi, declared at one of the Commission's hearings: "The nun used to say, 'You know, Steve, you don't listen. You're just like a devil.' And I often wondered about it. You know, you go through depression and all these things, and you think, maybe she was right, you know, maybe as a nine year-old, maybe I was a devil. Why else would I be punished by a nun? Why would she hit me? Why would she beat me? I must be so bad that God's people would do that [to me]" (Truth and Reconciliation Commission, *Canada's Residential Schools*, 97).

dysfunctions are passed on from one generation to the next?[6] Where to find the resources to reaffirm one's sense of belonging to a culture and to reconstitute one's identity in a positive way?

But we must also ask what impact, if any, this tragic story had on the police officer who came to take the little girl away from her family to bring her to residential school. Did he ever remember her face when he looked at his own daughters? And how about the nurse who said that the baby should be given up for adoption? Or the social worker for whom this Indigenous mother was yet another case for family services? Or whether the legislators who maintained this policy thereby poisoned the national soul by failing to respect the original inhabitants of this land?

Cultural Genocide, According to the Commission

On June 3, 2015, after six years of work during which the testimony of seven thousand former students of residential schools were heard in every region of Canada, the Commission submitted a summary of its final report—a summary of almost six hundred pages. The Commission came to the following conclusion:

> Cultural genocide is the destruction of those structures and practices that allow the group to continue as a group. States that engage in cultural genocide set out to destroy the political and social institutions of the targeted group. Land is seized, populations are forcibly transferred, and their movement is restricted. Languages are banned. Spiritual leaders are persecuted, spiritual practices are forbidden, and objects of spiritual value are confiscated and destroyed. And, most significantly to the issue at hand, families are disrupted to prevent the transmission of cultural values and identity from one generation to the next. In its dealing with Aboriginal people, Canada did all these things.[7]

---

6. See the 2015 report by Aguiar and Halseth, "Aboriginal Peoples and Historic Trauma."

7. Truth and Reconciliation Commission of Canada, *Honouring the Truth*, 1. In the 1948 Convention on the Prevention and Punishment of the Crime of Genocide, the definition of "genocide" includes "forcibly transferring children of one group" to another, but specifies that this removal must have been committed with the intention of destroying a national, ethnic, racial, or religious group. According to former Prime Minister Stephen Harper, the intention of the governments of the period, in removing children from their families and placing them in residential schools, was not to destroy them, but rather to assimilate them.

The term "cultural genocide" had already been used in 1997 by the commission that investigated the treatment of Indigenous children by governments in Australia. It was also used by such high-ranking Canadian officials as former Prime Minister Paul Martin, when he appeared before the Commission in 2013.

The Responsibilities of the State

According to the Commission, the government of Canada pursued a policy of cultural genocide because it wished to rid itself of its legal and financial obligations toward Indigenous peoples, resulting from various treaties, and to ultimately gain control over Indigenous lands and resources.[8] If Indigenous peoples were absorbed into Canadian society, there would be no more reserves, no more treaties, and no more Indigenous rights.

And so, the Canadian government separated Indigenous children from their parents by sending them to residential schools, not to offer them an education, but primarily to break their ties to their culture and identity. To justify the government's policy in favor of residential schools, the first prime minister of Canada, Sir John A. Macdonald, declared this in the House of Commons in 1883:

> When the school is on the reserve, the child lives with its parents, who are savages; he is surrounded by savages, and though he may learn to read and write, his habits, and training and mode of thought are Indian. He is simply a savage who can read and write. It has been strongly pressed on myself, as the head of the Department, that Indian children should be withdrawn as much as possible from the parental influence, and the only way to do that would be to put them in central training industrial schools where they will acquire the habits and modes of thought of white men.[9]

Residential schools were an integral part of a coherent policy to eliminate Indigenous peoples as distinct peoples and to assimilate them into mainstream Canadian society. "Our object," stated the deputy minister of Indian

---

8. In the numbered treaties which enabled colonization of the Northwest, the most significant clauses, from the Canadian government's perspective, were those where the First Nations agreed to "cede, release, surrender, and yield up" their traditional lands to the Crown. See Aboriginal Affairs and Northern Development Canada, "Treaty 1" and "Treaty 2."

9. Truth and Reconciliation Commission of Canada, *Honouring the Truth*, 2.

Affairs, Duncan Campbell Scott, "is to continue until there is not a single Indian in Canada that has not been absorbed into the body politic."[10]

As late as the 1950s and 1960s, the primary mission of residential schools was the cultural transformation of Indigenous children. A school principal wrote in 1953: "we must face realistically the fact that the only hope for the Canadian Indian is eventual assimilation into the white race."[11] Since Indigenous persons would have to work and to live with "whites," they should learn to think like "whites."

The coercive measures adopted by the Canadian government did not succeed in attaining their policy objective. Even though Indigenous peoples and their cultures suffered serious harm over the many decades, they have continued to exist. The Commission, throughout its report, insisted on the fact that Indigenous peoples have refused to give up their identity. In fact, it was former students—survivors of assimilationist policies—who succeeded in putting the residential schools issue on the public agenda. Their courage and perseverance led to the negotiation of the 2006 Indian Residential Schools Settlement Agreement, bringing together survivors, the federal government, and various church entities.

Thus, on June 11, 2008, the Prime Minister of Canada, Stephen Harper, made a Statement of Apology to former students of residential schools, on behalf of the government of Canada:

> We now recognize that it was wrong to separate children from rich and vibrant cultures and traditions, that it created a void in many lives and communities, and we apologize for having done this. We now recognize that, in separating children from their families, we undermined the ability of many to adequately parent their own children and sowed the seeds for generations to follow, and we apologize for having done this. We now recognize that, far too often, [residential schools] gave rise to abuse or neglect and were inadequately controlled, and we apologize for failing to protect you. Not only did you suffer these abuses as children, but as you became parents, you were powerless to protect your own children from suffering the same experience, and for this we are sorry.[12]

10. The Commission pointed out that this goal was reiterated in 1969 in the Federal Government's Statement on Indian Policy (more often referred to as the "White Paper"), which sought to end Indian status and terminate the treaties binding the federal government to First Nations.

11. J. E. Andrews, director of a Presbyterian school in Kenora, Ontario.

12. Harper, "Statement of Apology," para. 7.

The Indian Residential Schools Settlement Agreement established a $2 billion compensation package. Almost eighty thousand former students have received an average lump-sum payment of $28,000.

The Responsibilities of the Churches

The Canadian government had entrusted the running of the residential schools to Roman Catholic entities as well as to the Anglican, United, Methodist, and Presbyterian Churches. For the purposes of this article, I will be concentrating on Catholic entities, specifically those religious orders and those dioceses which were directly or indirectly involved in the residential school system.[13]

How did Roman Catholic entities become willing partners of the Canadian government in the setting up of a colonialist system, whose consequences are said to constitute nothing less than cultural genocide? How did they become complicit in what might be characterized as *structural sin*?[14]

In considering the responsibility of Catholic entities, it is essential to understand the historical context of the nineteenth century and the pressures that led to their involvement in the residential school system. It must be said from the outset that missionaries, both women and men, displayed immense courage and perseverance in learning the languages of the peoples who inhabited the territories to which they were sent and in trying to adapt as best they could to the very difficult living conditions in which they found themselves.

Imagine the following situation:[15] A team of missionaries establishes itself close to an established fur trading post. When local Indigenous people come to trade the furs harvested during the winter, they are met by missionaries who seek to initiate them into Christian beliefs. Over time, a relationship of friendship and trust develops. But fur-bearing animals are becoming increasingly rare because of extensive trapping and because of the arrival of white settlers. Furthermore, Indigenous traders are facing stiff competition, which brings down the price of fur pelts. Poverty and hunger become generalized. The situation of the Indigenous communities

13. We are referring here to the seventeen dioceses and thirty-seven religious institutions who are parties to the Indian Residential Schools Settlement Agreement of May 8, 2006.

14. John Paul II, *Sollicitudo Rei Socialis*, 36. Each generation has its blind spots. Each generation needs prophets and artists, not only to challenge their contemporaries' moral conscience, but also to reveal their blindness.

15. In constructing this scenario, I have drawn on elements presented in Huel's fascinating study, *Proclaiming the Gospel*.

becomes critical when their numbers are decimated by epidemics. Orphans are entrusted to the missionaries who call upon religious women for help. A rudimentary school is built with a dormitory where the orphans can be housed. The local Indigenous leaders are relieved that the orphans have been taken in by the missionaries, because food is increasingly scarce.[16] Through their interaction with these missionaries, these Indigenous youths, who are becoming numerous, begin to learn the ways of the "whites" and are prepared for the sacraments. The time comes when the school must be expanded, an orphanage built, and a crèche organized—all of which costs a great deal of money. The missionaries write to their religious superiors, describing not only their work, but also the perilous conditions facing the local Indigenous people. But the religious congregations are running out of financial resources. At this point, the government steps in with an offer of partnership, with substantial financial support.

It is also important to understand the religious mentality of the time.[17] Catholic authorities, locked in fierce competition with Protestant groups,[18] considered sound instruction in the church's doctrines and proper preparation for the sacraments to be essential for the eternal salvation of souls. The heads of the missionary orders reminded their benefactors what was at stake when they solicited them for financial assistance. But the donations received were insufficient to meet the need. The government's offer became very difficult to resist, especially when certain Indigenous groups refused to meet the missionaries' expectations and refused to adopt the customs of the "whites."

Let's consider the example of the Missionary Oblates of Marie Immaculate, who arrived in Red River in 1845 and became the dominant Catholic missionary order of men in the western and northern regions of Canada over the next hundred years. For the Oblates, residential schools had two objectives: to inculcate Catholic ideals and morality in their students and to enhance the material welfare of these students by providing them with the skills necessary to survive after they left the school. Students would thereby be able to contribute to the evangelization of their parents and

---

16. I recall being taken aback when an Indigenous woman from Alberta told me that, if her brothers and sisters had not been in residential school, they would probably not have survived the years of poverty and hunger in her community.

17. "The past is a foreign country: they do things differently there," as we are aptly reminded by L. P. Hartley (1895–1972) in the opening line of his novel, *The Go-Between.* Regarding the challenges involved in writing about the past, see Geertz, *After the Fact.*

18. See Miller, "Denominational Rivalry," 139–55.

communities—or at least encourage them to adopt a more regular practice of Christian precepts.[19]

By collaborating, the federal government and the oblates hoped to rid Indigenous people of their nomadic habits and impose upon them a sedentary lifestyle. Hayter Reed, who would later become deputy superintendent general of the Department of Indian Affairs, wrote about transforming Indigenous people into "a self-supporting peasant class" in which poverty would be banished by hard work.[20]

The residential school system was founded on the belief that the Christian religion and European civilization were superior to Indigenous cultures, which were held to be savage and brutal. The missionaries saw the residential schools as the best way to eliminate traditional Indigenous practices.[21] This hostility toward Indigenous cultures and spiritualities continued well into the twentieth century. An oblate missionary, Omer Plourde, declared before a parliamentary committee in 1947 that, because Canada was a Christian nation committed to having "all its citizens belonging to one or other of the Christian churches," he could see no reason why the residential schools "should foster aboriginal beliefs."[22]

This kind of mentality led to *spiritual violence*, which the Commission held as occurring when

a. a person is not permitted to follow her or his preferred spiritual or religious tradition;

b. a different spiritual or religious path or practice is forced on a person;

c. a person's spiritual or religious tradition, beliefs, or practices are demeaned or belittled; or

d. a person is made to feel shame for practicing his or her traditional or family beliefs.[23]

Regarding the spiritual violence perpetrated against Indigenous youth in residential schools, the Commission was especially severe in its judgment of the churches:[24]

19. Huel, *Proclaiming the Gospel,* 147.

20. Titley, "Hayter Reed and Indian Administration," 139.

21. See Truth and Reconciliation Commission of Canada, *Canada's Residential Schools,* 96.

22. Truth and Reconciliation Commission of Canada, *Canada's Residential Schools,* 5.

23. Truth and Reconciliation Commission of Canada, *Canada's Residential Schools,* 96.

24. Truth and Reconciliation Commission of Canada, *Canada's Residential Schools,* 98.

That Christians in Canada, in the name of their religion, inflicted serious harms on Aboriginal children, their families,
and their communities was in fundamental contradiction to
what they purported their core beliefs to be. For the Churches
to avoid repeating their failures of the past, understanding how
and why they perverted Christian doctrine to justify their actions is critical knowledge to be gained from the residential
school experience.

Happily, there are signs that the mentality that acquiesced to such
spiritual violence is no longer acceptable in Catholic circles. Thus, on the
occasion of the 2009 National Day of Reconciliation, marking the first anniversary of the apology addressed to Indigenous peoples by Prime Minister
Stephen Harper, Archbishop Paul-André Durocher, as delegate of the Canadian Conference of Catholic Bishops, participated in the traditional sunrise
ceremony and exchanged gifts with Indigenous elders and leaders.

In a collective response to the Commission's Calls to Action (which
will be discussed below), the Catholic signatories—including the president
of the Canadian Conference of Catholic Bishops and the president of the
Canadian Religious Conference, representing Catholic religious congregations—were unequivocal in calling for the respect of Indigenous spiritual
practices:

Although many priests, brothers, sisters, and laypeople served
in the residential schools with generosity, faithfulness, care, and
respect for their students, this was not always the case. The TRC
Final Report rightly observes that when Christians, through the
residential schools, belittled Indigenous students as "pagans"
or "demonized, punished, and terrorized them into accepting
Christian beliefs," this was in fundamental contradiction to the
core beliefs of Christianity. While Christians have at times failed
to live up to the standard to which they are called by God, the
glaring failures to respect the identity and freedom of Indigenous children outlined in the TRC Final Report are particularly
saddening and must never be repeated.[25]

25. Canadian Conference of Catholic Bishops et al., "Catholic Response," 2. This
response also referred specifically to the Second Vatican Council's *Dignitatis Humanae*,
4, which urged that "in spreading religious faith and in introducing religious practices,
everyone ought at all times to refrain from any manner of action which might seem
to carry a hint of coercion or of a kind of persuasion that would be dishonorable or
unworthy."

Apologies from the Catholic Entities during Commission Hearings

Even before the Commission had begun its work, expressions of regret and formal apologies had been offered by the spokespersons of the different churches—not only for the physical and sexual abuse that had been committed, but also for the systematic repression of Indigenous languages, cultures, and spiritualities.[26] In 1991, Catholic bishops and the leaders of religious orders had declared publicly that they were "sorry and deeply regret the pain, suffering, and alienation that so many experienced" in residential schools.[27] And, in its 1991 Apology to the First Nations of Canada, the Oblate Conference of Canada acknowledged that oblate missionaries had in the past dismissed the riches of Indigenous religious traditions:

> We broke some of your peace pipes, and we considered some of your sacred practices as pagan and superstitious. This had its origins in the colonial mentality, our European superiority complex which was ground in a particular view of history. We apologize for this blindness and disrespect.[28]

The Commission's Calls to Action and the Responses by the Churches

In its report, the Commission formulated ninety-four calls to action in order to redress the legacy of residential schools and to advance the process of Canadian reconciliation. In respect of the *legacy*, the Commission called for action in the areas of education, language and culture, justice and health. It is beyond the scope of this paper to address each one of the areas. Special attention, however, must be drawn to the area of child welfare. The Commission called upon the government to commit itself to reducing the number of Indigenous children in its care and to redress the imbalance in resource allocation between Indigenous and non-Indigenous children. This call is of particular importance in light of the January 2016 decision by the Canadian Human Rights Tribunal, which held that welfare funding for Indigenous

---

26. See the apologies by the Anglican Church in "Apology—English," https://www.anglican.ca/tr/apology/english/; the Presbyterian Church in "Confession of the Presbyterian Church," http://caid.ca/PresChuApo1994.pdf; and the United Church in "Apologies," http://www.united-church.ca/social-action/justice-initiatives/apologies.

27. "Statement by the National Meeting," 1. But as Agathon declared some twenty-five centuries ago, "Even God cannot change the past."

28. Crosby, "Apology to the First Nations," 2.

children on reserves was 38 percent less than that for non-Indigenous children living off reserves and which ordered that the government of Canada put an immediate end to such discrimination.[29] Today, there are more Indigenous children in out-of-home care than there were at the height of the residential school system. Indigenous children make up nearly half of the children in foster care, while making up only seven percent of children in Canada. Why are so many Indigenous children in foster care? Among the contributing factors are dilapidated housing, extreme poverty, and drug abuse—the long-term consequences of the residential school system. With so many children in out-of-home care, are we collectively in the process of repeating the residential school tragedy?

In respect of reconciliation, the Commission insisted a great deal upon Canada's adoption and implementation of the United Nations Declaration of the Rights of Indigenous People.[30] The Commission stressed the importance of putting in place educational programs regarding Indigenous peoples, their historical contributions, and the impact of residential schools.

Among the calls to action to promote reconciliation, the Commission considered apologies by the churches. It specifically asked the pope to come to Canada to offer, on behalf of the Roman Catholic Church, an apology to the survivors, to their families, and also to the communities which were affected by the spiritual, cultural, emotional, physical, and sexual mistreatment which Indigenous children endured in the residential schools run by Catholic entities. One month after the issuing of this report, Pope Francis, in an address at the world meeting of popular movements in Bolivia, did ask for forgiveness, "not only for the offenses of the Church herself, but also for crimes committed against the native peoples during the so-called conquest of America."[31] The pope added that it was important to remember the thousands of Catholic leaders who had defended the rights of Indigenous peoples.[32] It is impossible to state at this time whether, during an official visit to Canada, the pope will offer an apology to Indigenous persons who were harmed by the residential school system.

---

29. Fontaine, "Canada Discriminates Against Children."

30. See *United Nations Declaration on the Rights of Indigenous Peoples.*

31. Francis, "Participation at the Second World Meeting," 3.2. Pope John Paul II, during his 1992 visit to the Dominican Republic, had issued an apology for the pain and suffering caused by the church over the previous five hundred years.

32. The pope also asked believers and nonbelievers alike to think of those many bishops, priests, religious sisters, and laity who have preached the gospel and who have stood alongside Indigenous peoples, accompanying their popular movements even to the point of martyrdom.

In another call to action, the Commission invited church parties to the Settlement Agreement to collaborate with residential school survivors and representatives of Indigenous organizations to establish permanent funding for community-controlled healing and reconciliation projects, as well as for cultural revitalization projects. Certain Catholic dioceses have invested in organizing healing and reconciliation workshops, such as "Returning to Spirit," a program originally developed by an Indigenous man in collaboration with Indigenous and non-Indigenous partners.[33]

Challenges Facing the Churches on the Path Toward Reconciliation

Church representatives have repeated their apologies and requests for forgiveness, in the hope that these will be accepted by Indigenous peoples and, particularly, by the survivors of the residential schools and their descendants who are suffering the consequences of the residential school system. They have expressed their desire to work with Indigenous peoples to build a future based on mutual respect, peaceful coexistence, and sharing.

Thus, on March 19, 2016, the Canadian Conference of Catholic Bishops, the Canadian Religious Conference and the Canadian Catholic Organization for Development and Peace called upon all Catholics to take on eight commitments "in the hope and desire to continue to walk together with Indigenous Peoples in building a more just society where their gifts and those of all people are nurtured and honored."[34] These commitments are:

1. To work with Catholic educational institutions and programs of formation to tell the history of Canada in a way that is truthful and to ensure proper treatment of the history and experience of Indigenous peoples;[35]

---

33. For more information, see www.returningtospirit.org. The Commission noted that this program brings Indigenous and non-Indigenous "participants together to gain new insights into the residential school experience and develop new communication and relationship-building skills" (Truth and Reconciliation Commission of Canada, *Honouring the Truth*, 233).

34. Canadian Conference of Catholic Bishops et al., "Catholic Response," 7.

35. One of the best tools for increasing public awareness regarding relations between settlers and Indigenous peoples is the "Blanket Exercise," originally developed by Kairos Canada and now existing in different versions. See http://justicepaix.org/wp-content/uploads/2016/02/Blanket-Exercise.-B.McD_.pdf.

2. To work with centers of pastoral and clergy formation to promote a culture of encounter by including the study of the history of Canadian missions, with both their weaknesses and strengths;

3. To call upon theological centers to support Indigenous reflection within the Catholic community;

4. To encourage partnerships between Indigenous groups and existing health care facilities;

5. To strengthen restorative justice practices within the criminal justice system;[36]

6. To support the current national inquiry into missing and murdered Indigenous women and girls;[37]

7. To deepen and broaden relationships, dialogue, and collaboration with Indigenous peoples;

8. To encourage parishes and Catholic organizations to become familiar with the United Nations Declaration on the Rights of Indigenous Peoples.

To these eight commitments, I would add another: "To honor and create better awareness regarding Indigenous spiritualties." Many survivors continue to live in spiritual fear of the traditions of their ancestors, because of religious beliefs imposed on them by those who ran the residential schools. This spiritual fear can be internalized over several generations and becomes difficult to shed. The Commission stressed the importance of this task and declared that

> the Churches, as religious institutions, must affirm Indigenous spirituality in its own right. Without such formal recognition, a full and robust reconciliation will be impossible. Healing and reconciliation have a spiritual dimension that must continue to be addressed by the churches in partnership with Indigenous spiritual leaders, Survivors, their families, and communities.[38]

This task has become urgent as more and more Indigenous Catholics draw from the deep well of Indigenous spiritualties and are seeking within

36. Such initiatives include sentencing, healing circles, and other traditional Indigenous ways of dealing with offenders. Incarceration rates among Indigenous people are many times higher than among the general population, and prisons are not sufficient places of reconciliation and rehabilitation.

37. See the National Inquiry into Missing and Murdered Indigenous Women and Girls website, http://www.mmiwg-ffada.ca/.

38. Truth and Reconciliation Commission of Canada, *Honouring the Truth*, 227.

the church itself a place where Christianity and Indigenous religious traditions might coexist. The words of Presbyterian minister Margaret Mullin
should offer inspiration to all the churches:

> Can the Rev. Margaret Mullin/Thundering Eagle Woman from
> the Bear Clan be a strong Anishinaabe woman and a Christian
> simultaneously? Yes, I can, because I do not have my feet in two
> different worlds, two different religions, or two different under-
> standings of God. The two halves of me are one in the same
> Spirit. I can learn from my grandparents, European and Indig-
> enous Canadian, who have all walked on the same path ahead
> of me. I can learn from Jesus and I can learn from my Elders.[39]

Perhaps Indigenous and non-Indigenous persons who are blessed
with religious faith and who honor those who have passed on may ask for
insight and guidance on these matters through the intercession of saints like
Kateri Tekakwitha and Rose Prince.[40]

Impact of the Residential School System on Images of God

Many survivors have indicated that the Christian faith, which they may
have received from their parents or grandparents, was shattered by their
residential school experience, particularly in cases where there was physical
or sexual abuse. Some survivors may have lost any faith in the existence of a
god. Others may have been drawn to traditionalist Indigenous spiritualties.

---

39. Truth and Reconciliation Commission of Canada, *Canada's Residential Schools*,
106. Consider also the heartfelt hope expressed on the same page by Alf Dumont.
See also the groundbreaking research over many decades accomplished by Professor
Achiel Peelman, OMI, of the University of Saint Paul. Achiel Peelman, in a recent work,
has shown how the Christian notion of the communion of saints may be enriched by
drawing upon the Ojibway concept of *Bimaadiziwin*. See Peelman, *La Communion des
Saints*.

40. Born in 1915 into a Dakelh (i.e., Carrier) family, Rose Prince was sent like other
children to Lejac Residential School. As she grew up, she developed a severe curvature
of the spine, which caused her great difficulty, though she was never heard to complain
about the pain. When she was sixteen and still attending school at Lejac, her mother
and two sisters died from influenza. Rose opted not to return home for the summers,
but to stay on at the school instead. Classmates as well as the sisters who ran the school
remarked that Rose had a deep spiritual life and a special devotion to the Eucharist.
Rose contracted tuberculosis, and by the age of thirty-four she was confined to bed. On
August 19, 1949, she was admitted to the hospital and died that same day. Several years
later, when the residential school was closed down and the graves were to be moved to
a new location, it was discovered that Rose's body was incorrupt. Pilgrimages to her
gravesite have been growing in number.

Still others have sought to blend Christian beliefs about God with traditionalist Indigenous beliefs.

It may be asked whether some survivors and their descendants have been led to a new image of God—a suffering God—who understands their experience, who was mysteriously present to them in their darkest moments, and who continues to summon them.[41] Duane Gastant Aucoin, a Wolf Clan member of the Tlingit Nation in the Yukon and also a Carmelite brother, writes this:

> Just as God brought good out of the evil done to His Son after they crucified Him, by raising Him up from the dead, so too must we work with God and with each other to bring good out of the evil done to our people. So that we as a whole may be given new life and rise up from the tomb in which we have been placed, stronger and more alive than before.[42]

For Christians, both Indigenous and non-Indigenous, the church is born of the mystery of redemption in the cross of Jesus Christ and, as such, Christians have to try to meet people on their path of suffering.[43] Meeting face to face with Indigenous persons who are suffering from the consequences of the residential school system must, therefore, remain an important way of being the church in a Canadian context. But church representatives have to prepare themselves for encounters where their well-intentioned efforts will be rebuffed as violations of interior sacred space. The church herself must ask for mercy.

In due course, Indigenous persons may choose to share their spiritual experience and to help non-Indigenous believers to deepen their understanding of the mystery of human suffering[44] and of the gift of mercy.

---

41. In *Christ is a Native American*, 109–10, Achiel Peelman refers to an Indigenous woman named Mary who worked with Indigenous persons learning to survive in an urban environment, and who regularly met young persons scarred by the residential school system. Mary indicated that, for her, Christ was a very concrete person who had suffered from different forms of abuse, was in prison, or had traveled with homeless persons. She said, "We must resurrect Christ in the life of our people . . . because the history of Christ's suffering goes on, in a very real way, in the human suffering I see every day."

42. Gastant Aucoin, "Residential Schools," 1. On this point, see also Gerhart, "Bernard Lonergan's Law of the Cross."

43. See John Paul II, *Salvifici Doloris*, 3.

44. "Suffering seems to be particularly *essential to the nature of man*. It is as deep as man himself, precisely because it manifests in its own way that depth which is proper to man, and in its own way surpasses it. Suffering seems to belong to man's transcendence: it is one of those points in which man is in a certain sense 'destined' to go beyond himself, and he is called to this in a mysterious way" (John Paul II, *Salvifici Doloris*, 2).

Reconciliation: A Problematic Quest?

Some Indigenous commentators have criticized the notion of reconciliation. They have gone so far as to claim that the Commission itself was compromised by including the term "Reconciliation" in its name.[45] For them, reconciliation smacks too much of a Christian agenda, rooted as it is in the New Testament (e.g., Matt 5:24; Rom 5:10; 2 Cor 5:18; Eph 2:16) and, as such, ultimately serves the interests of the churches and of the state.

Gerald Taiaiake Alfred, professor of Indigenous governance at the University of Victoria, claims that reconciliation must be intellectually and politically deconstructed as the goal of Indigenous peoples' political and social struggles:

> I see reconciliation as an emasculating concept, weak-kneed and easily accepting of half-hearted measures of a notion of justice that does nothing to help Indigenous peoples regain their dignity and strength. One of my concerns in any discussion of reconciliation is finding ways to break its hold upon our consciousness so that we can move towards a true and lasting foundation for justice that will result in meaningful changes in the lives of Indigenous peoples and in the return of their lands.
>
> Without massive restitution made to Indigenous peoples, collectively and as individuals, including land, transfers of federal and provincial funds, and other forms of compensation for past harms and continuing injustices committed against the land and Indigenous peoples, reconciliation will permanently absolve colonial injustices and is itself a further injustice . . .
>
> Something was stolen, lies were told, and they have never been made right. That is the crux of the problem. If we do not shift away from the pacifying discourse of reconciliation and begin to reframe people's perceptions of the problem so that it is not a question of how to reconcile with colonialism that faces us but instead how to use restitution as the first step towards

---

45. The Commission defined reconciliation as "an ongoing process of establishing and maintaining respectful relationships. A critical part of this process involves repairing damaged trust by making apologies, providing individual and collective reparations and following through with concrete actions that demonstrate real societal change" (Truth and Reconciliation Commission of Canada, *Canada's Residential Schools*, 11). Note that the Commission drew upon the United Nations Declaration on the Rights of Indigenous Peoples to list ten guiding principles of truth and reconciliation which it believed would help Canadians to move forward (Truth and Reconciliation Commission of Canada, *Canada's Residential Schools*, 16).

creating justice and a moral society, we will be advancing colonialism, not decolonization.[46]

According to Alfred, restitution—not reconciliation—is what would be needed to transform relationships based on centuries of injustice into a relationship where there is justice for Indigenous peoples. Alfred's insistence upon restitution is compelling when one considers how Indigenous peoples in Canada and elsewhere in the Americas have repeatedly been dispossessed of their lands—either by military force, outright theft, or shady backroom deals.[47] It is hard to disagree with the principle that restitution is the first step toward justice. However, when concrete measures to implement such restitution are—in the name of justice—actually adopted, objections will be raised by those who would be directly affected. Suddenly, many different interpretations of justice will be advanced and defended, leading to endless court battles and bitter conflict. Whose interpretation of justice must prevail? And why?

Perhaps a larger framework is required, one that takes into account not only the legitimate (and long ignored) demands for justice expressed by Indigenous peoples, but also the reasonable concerns advanced by settler communities.[48] Such a framework can only exist if there are clear signs of *willingness* on all sides to seek reconciliation.[49] Only then will the different

46. Alfred, "Restitution is the Real Pathway," 165–66.

47. Direct access to the Saint Lawrence River by the Mohawk residents of Alfred's natal village of Kahnawake was lost when a huge trench was dug for the purpose of establishing a seaway for merchant vessel traffic to and from the Great Lakes. The trench could have been dug elsewhere. How often have major infrastructure projects have been carried out on Indigenous land instead of on settler land? The recent construction of the Dakota Access Pipeline is a case in point: instead of the pipeline crossing the Missouri River upstream from the state capital of North Dakota, the government agency, bending to pressure from the local settler population fearing for its water supply, decided it would be built on lands considered sacred by the Lakota, a small distance upstream from the Lakota Standing Rock Reservation, ignoring Indigenous concerns regarding the safety of *their* only water supply.

48. Survivor and former United Church moderator Stan Mackay pointed out before the Commission that not only Indigenous victims require healing, but also settlers. A conversation can only take place if all involved adopt an attitude of humility and respect (Truth and Reconciliation Commission of Canada, *Canada's Residential Schools*, 6).

49. See Volf, *Exclusion and Embrace*, 220: "There can be no justice without the will to embrace . . . To agree on justice, you need to make space in yourself for the perspective of the other, and in order to make space, you need to want to embrace the other. If you insist that others do not belong to you and you to them, that their perspective should not muddle yours, you will have your justice and they will have theirs; your justices will clash and there will be no justice *between* you. The knowledge of justice depends on the will to embrace. The relationship between justice and embrace goes deeper, however. Embrace is part and parcel of the very *definition* of justice."

parties commit themselves to the hard work of finding just solutions—and these will certainly entail reparations and the transformation of colonial institutions so that Indigenous and settlers can coexist peacefully and fruitfully.[50] Restitution and reconciliation are interlocked.

Clearly, Indigenous peoples have, over the centuries, been the ones who have most often shown a willingness to work toward reconciliation, and they have much to offer to the process.[51] The Commission, its work, and its calls to action certainly provide evidence of such willingness. But will the governments of Canada and the settler populations—notably those who identify with the churches—go beyond words to signify a genuine willingness to work toward finding just solutions?

Possible Signs of Settler Willingness to Work Toward Reconciliation

Some people have asked whether the churches should not undertake further action in the spirit of restorative justice. One of the concerns repeatedly expressed at Commission hearings was the disappearance of Indigenous languages. Indeed, in its Call to Action 14, the Commission asks the Government of Canada to provide funding for the preservation and revitalization of Indigenous languages. In not a few Indigenous communities today, those who know their language well enough to speak it on a daily basis are in their sixties or older. Distinctive worldviews are in danger of disappearing.

Would it be possible for dioceses and religious congregations to establish a fund to sponsor centers for the teaching of Indigenous languages?[52] Such centers would ensure the transmission not only of languages, but also of systems of meaning and values to future generations of Indigenous (and even non-Indigenous) persons.[53]

---

50. As the Commission itself stated, "Reconciliation must inspire Aboriginal and non-Aboriginal peoples to transform Canadian society so that our children and grandchildren can live together in dignity, peace, and prosperity on these lands we now share" (Truth and Reconciliation Commission of Canada, *Canada's Residential Schools*, 4).

51. The Commission specifically mentioned Indigenous knowledge systems, oral histories, laws, and connections to the land, as well as the wisdom of survivors, elders, and traditional knowledge keepers. See Truth and Reconciliation Commission of Canada, *Canada's Residential Schools*, 5 and 12.

52. As proposed by the Commission in its Call to Actions 61(ii).

53. The Shrine of Saint Kateri Tekakwitha in Kahnawake, in the Catholic Diocese of Saint-Jean-Longueuil, has contributed to the revitalization of the Mohawk language by using that language in its liturgies, which are attended by Indigenous and non-Indigenous persons.

A concern shared by both Indigenous and settler organizations is the impact of oil and mining industries on the environment and of irresponsible exploitation of natural resources on Indigenous communities, some of which still do not have access to drinking water.[54] Alliances are being forged to protect the Earth, regarded as a sacred gift entrusted to humans by the Creator.[55]

Conclusion: Looking Back Upon a Complex Past in Order to Create a Hope-Filled Future

During the Commission's hearings and following the publication of its report—with its highly critical assessment of the missionary project as a whole and of the role played by Catholic entities in the residential school system—it was difficult for Catholics, and especially for members of religious congregations, to find adequate words. It was particularly difficult to speak after repeatedly hearing the testimony of survivors who had experienced physical or sexual abuse.[56] I recall, during the Vancouver hearings,

54. Before the Commission, Elder Reg Crowshoe explained that reconciliation between Indigenous and non-Indigenous Canadians, from an Indigenous perspective, also requires reconciliation with the natural world. "If human beings resolve problems between themselves but continue to destroy the natural world, then reconciliation remains incomplete." This was a perspective that the Commission repeatedly heard: "Reconciliation will never occur unless we are also reconciled with the Earth" (Truth and Reconciliation Commission of Canada, *Canada's Residential Schools*, 13).

55. See the 2015 encyclical by Pope Francis, *Laudato Si'*, 146: "It is essential to show special care for Indigenous communities and their cultural traditions. They are not merely one minority among others, but should be the principal dialogue partners, especially when large projects affecting their land are proposed. For them, land is not a commodity but rather a gift from God and from their ancestors who rest there, a sacred space with which they need to interact if they are to maintain their identity and values. When they remain on their land, they themselves care for it best. Nevertheless, in various parts of the world, pressure is being put on them to abandon their homelands to make room for agricultural or mining projects which are undertaken without regard for the degradation of nature and culture."

56. During the Commission's time in Montreal, I spent many hours in the listening areas, where survivors and their families could consult photo albums, provided by the religious congregations who ran the schools. An Indigenous man who was about seventy years old sat beside me to examine the collection of photos taken in schools run by the Oblates. After having examined in silence a large number of these photos, he began to speak with me and tell me about the difficulties he had experienced following his years in residential school: problems with alcohol and with violence, etc. He shared with me how he had had to apologize to his children for his attitudes and behaviors, which resulted from having been cut off from his own parents and finding himself in an anonymous institutional context without much human warmth. I do not know why this elder shared his story with me. Perhaps he needed to speak and to share. Certainly,

how a Catholic deacon, who was himself Indigenous, facilitated with great dignity and respect a sharing circle with survivors who needed to express their intense hostility toward the church. During the hearings, it was important that church representatives be present—to listen and to acknowledge the deep wounds—especially those of survivors and their families, but also those of members of religious congregations who ran the schools (some of whom are themselves Indigenous or Métis).

Clearly, the Commission's hearings did not lend themselves easily to positive testimony regarding the religious congregations who ran the residential schools.[57] And yet, there is evidence from the Commission report itself that a significant number of religious men and women were held in high esteem by Indigenous students.[58] The hearings did not offer an opportunity to learn about the occasions when the religious took up their Indigenous students' cause by lodging protests with government officials regarding the poor quality of food and the inadequate level of health care. Nor did we often hear words of appreciation regarding the colossal task accomplished by missionaries in preserving Indigenous languages and cultures,[59] in spite

---

I needed to listen and to learn.

57. See Truth and Reconciliation Commission of Canada, *Canada's Residential Schools*, 10–11, where the Commission noted the difficulty of reconciling the testimony of an oblate who had been supervisor of a residential school with the testimony of a former student: "These two seemingly irreconcilable truths are a stark reminder that there are no easy shortcuts to reconciliation. That there were few direct exchanges at Commission events between survivors and former school staff indicates that for many the time for reconciliation had not yet arrived."

58. Truth and Reconciliation Commission of Canada, *They Came for the Children*, 45–49. The interim report by the Commission says this on page 49: "The Roman Catholic Grandin College in Fort Smith, Northwest Territories, had one of the best reputations of any school. Established in 1960 as a preparatory school for Aboriginal priests and nuns, Grandin College's first director decided to turn it into a leadership training centre. The use of Aboriginal languages was common throughout the school, and students were encouraged to excel. Ethel Blondin-Andrew, the first Aboriginal woman to serve as a federal cabinet minister, said she was 'saved' by Grandin College, where she 'learned that discipline, including physical fitness, was essential.' She was just one of a number of Grandin graduates who went on to play leading roles in public life in the North. Others include former Northwest Territories premiers, ministers, Dene Nation presidents, and official language commissioners."

59. For example, efforts are currently being undertaken to teach Huron-Wendat children their ancestral language. Dictionaries and grammars prepared by Jesuit missionaries over several centuries are being relied upon by Indigenous scholars today to reconstruct the Huron-Wendat language, which no one has spoken fluently since the nineteenth century. See the December 15, 2015 Radio-Canada.ca article by Blais-Morin, "Comment Faire Revivire," available at http://ici.radio-canada.ca/nouvelles/societe/2015/12/15/001-enseignement-langue-huron-wendat-wendake-quebec-cpe.shtml.

of opposition from government officials.[60] These actions reveal how some members of religious congregations actively struggled against cultural genocide, albeit while participating in a colonialist system which would lead, over time, to such a result.

A fair appraisal of the legacy of religious men and women in their relations over several decades with Indigenous peoples in Canada has yet to be done—one that would bring out not only the negative aspects, but also the positive ones. Already the Missionary Oblates of Mary Immaculate have begun this important work, notably at the first symposium focusing on the history of oblate missions among Indigenous peoples.[61] Who will take over this colossal task from the missionaries? Might greater access to stories from members of the various religious communities contribute something vital to the healing process and to advancing reconciliation?

60. According to Roberto, "Les Relations des Autochtones," 252, "[t]he Oblates made efforts to maintain two principles: *first*, to teach in Indigenous languages anything that had to do with religion and have missionaries study these languages; and *secondly*, to teach Indigenous children not to be ashamed of their race or language. The notion that the students in residential schools should be proud of their culture appears frequently in Oblate documents" (translation mine).

61. Held at the University of Saint Paul, in Ottawa, in 2015. The proceedings of this symposium are published under the title "A Past to be Visited or Revisited," edited by Pierre Hurtubise, OMI.

5

Walking a New Path: A Harvest of Reconciliation—Forging a Renewed Relationship between the Church and the Indigenous Peoples

SYLVAIN LAVOIE, OMI

Background

It seems appropriate to place this article on the relationship of the church with the Indigenous peoples within the context of growing up as a French Canadian Catholic youth in my home province of Saskatchewan, Canada. This experience, I believe, serves as the underlying basis of both my life of ministry among the Indigenous peoples and also my interest in forging a renewed relationship with the Indigenous peoples.

My home was near Highgate Siding, on land that my father home-steaded and broke with a McCormick steel-wheeled, hand-cranked trac-tor. I still have vivid memories of helping him pick roots on that virgin prairie soil. I attended a one-room elementary school named after a Chief Whitecap that we neither knew nor were taught anything about. During recess, we innocently played in a cemetery adjacent to the school grounds from which the bodies had all been exhumed. We vaguely knew that it had been an "Indian cemetery." I rarely saw Indigenous people in town the Saturdays we went in for our music lessons and shopping. What I didn't know was that the pass and permit system had limited their movement to the reserves and made it almost impossible for once successful farming Indigenous communities to survive.

Two striking childhood memories were of an alcoholic couple (non-Indigenous and Métis) as neighbors and meeting an Indigenous boy my

age when I was twelve at a nearby resort. The late Archbishop Daniel Bohan commented, after being installed in the Archdiocese of Regina, that
the Indigenous peoples in his archdiocese were "the most invisible people
he had ever seen!"[1]

Only later did I learn that the fertile land between the two rivers (North
Saskatchewan and Battle Rivers) was the focus of a land grab decades before
my birth, a sad story that Jack Funk wrote about in his book *Outside, the
Women Cried: The Story of the Surrender by Chief Thunderchild's Band of
their Reserve near Delmas, Saskatchewan.*

The First Nations communities of Moosomin and Thunderchild were
pressured into surrendering their lands and relocated onto hilly, less fertile
land further north. It seems that even one of my brother oblates, Fr. Delmas,
was involved in this process. His hope was to establish a French Catholic
community on that land, which became my home parish and was named
after him. Ironically, much later we would read in the parish records that he
was being asked to negotiate land that was better suited for the needs and
desires of the Indigenous peoples!

This reality came home to me even more deeply when I was language
learning on Onion Lake First Nation (*wîhcekaskosîwi-sâkahikan*). One
of my language helpers, Maryann Carter, told me that her mother, Susan
Whitecap, used to live in Highgate. From her perspective, I had grown up
on land that was stolen from her people.

A shameful and striking incident happened to me as a university student at a conference in Cleveland, Ohio. Someone asked me what we were
doing about the Indian problem in Canada, and I was almost duped into
thinking we had one, not realizing that it was the Indigenous people who
had endless problems with us and our unconscious "white privilege."

I think it was that incident that woke me up to the historical injustice I
was so deeply steeped in that I could not even recognize it. The words of the
late Bishop Samuel Ruiz in Chaipas, Mexico, resonate with me: "I was like a
fish asleep in the water with my eyes open."[2]

The Road to Greater Awareness

Within this context, forming a lifelong friendship with Harry Lafond (who
later became chief of his Cree community of Muskeg Lake, Saskatchewan)
helped instill in me a desire to do what I could to make things right and

1. Statement made during the meeting of the Assembly of Western Catholic Bishops, in which I participated, to set up its Standing Committee on Aboriginal Affairs.

2. Andraos, "Bishop Samuel Ruiz's Early Theological Insights," 11.

to make a difference. So, when given the opportunity as a young oblate, I accepted to minister among the First Nations and Métis peoples, a decision I will never regret.

Harry went on to become an educator, chief of his community of Muskeg Lake, and now works in the office of the Treaty Commissioner out of Saskatoon. Our relationship provided us with the opportunity to conduct workshops together, along with elders, on Indigenous ministry, issues, and spirituality. Through his commitment to the church and involvement on numerous committees and boards, Harry has dedicated himself to this process of educating Canadian society on Indigenous issues and furthering the rights of Indigenous peoples.

One early incident stands out in my memory as a young oblate. Before ordination, I was part of a team running an Indian and Métis youth club. Even though we had elections, they were largely a sham because the team was really running the club, until a decision was made to move the scholasticate to Edmonton. We met with the youth, explained the situation, and told them they would have to take over the club or we would shut it down.

Sensing that we were serious, the meeting went silent. For over ten minutes, no one moved or said a word. Finally, one person asked what that would mean. We explained they would have to choose a leader. More silence, as they realized this would really be their choice and their responsibility, not ours, and finally one young lady said, "OK—I'll do it," and they were off and running. They really took over the club and even threw a farewell party for us in the spring.

Reflecting on this incident, I realized that a psychological transfer of power took place during that silence, and the club finally became theirs. Perhaps, after over a century of colonization, that same transfer of power has to happen on a much larger scale.

My first mission as an ordained priest was to the northern Métis community of Beauval. Although the people there did not appear that different than in the south, what I eventually realized was that I had entered into an *internalized culture*. What was different was the way of thinking and acting, the sense of humor, and attitudes toward time, money, work, and relationships, and it was up to me to adjust.

That was a struggle until my father's death in 1980 during harvest. After the reception following the funeral, my brother stated that he was going combining out in the fields. Shocked, I asked how he could do that—we had just buried our father. He replied, simply, that it was what Dad would have wanted. The next morning, I went out to the field to see how things were going, and ended up helping with the harvest all day. Deep within, however, I was profoundly conflicted—in the north, everything stopped for a wake or funeral. But when it rained a few days later, I realized we had done the right thing, and I was able to accept two different economies: both were okay and I should not judge one better than the other—they were just different. In the north, the fish and animals are always there; in the south, the crop had to be harvested to avoid great loss.

Once, at a conference, the speaker talked about an original wound or core grief that most people have, sometimes without realizing it. It did not take long before I was face to face with the woundedness of the First Nations and Métis people, especially prevalent through rampant alcoholism, a welfare mentality, a sense of inferiority, painful shyness, sexual abuse, suicide, and family breakdown.

The loss of the traditional livelihood of hunting, fishing, and trapping was especially devastating for the men, leading to a loss of dignity that is so destructive. Premature deaths from so much dysfunction have affected everyone, leading to what late Elder Joe Couture called a "collective grief"[3] in which so many were stuck. Added to the pain was a subtle racism on the part of many non-Indigenous people, who, without even realizing it, formed a kind of upper class in the communities.

My first visits and liturgies at the Beauval Indian Residential High School (BIRHS), as it was known at the time, were a systemic shock. Even though it had long ago become a high school, and some of the students were eighteen years old, the staff were still called "childcare workers," and the students were still being treated like children, especially when they were herded into the chapel for Mass at 9:00 AM, just as breakfast was finishing. It did not take long before we changed that to 5:00 PM for those who wanted to attend.

As the last chaplain at the school, I was shocked to discover much later on that sexual abuse by some of the staff had been happening at the school. So, the legacy of the school was very mixed—a good education was offered, lifelong friendships were formed, and leaders were trained, but the negative effects of the system and a prejudiced society seriously negated much that was good.

One elder in the south, when he realized at a culture camp that I was a priest, pointed his finger at me and told me point blank, "You are the one! You destroyed our language! You destroyed our culture!" When he passed away, even though I knew his family well and they wanted me to attend the funeral, his sister and niece were adamant: his will stated that he did

---

3. Joe Couture (respected elder, cultural advisor, educator, academic, and psychologist) at a men's wellness conference in which I participated in Saskatoon in the mid-1990s.

not want the church to be present at the ceremony, so I was not invited or allowed to come.

I realized that this all added up to the original wound or core grief that the conference speaker had addressed. The challenge was how to address it, how to make a difference, and how to bring reconciliation and healing to this painful situation.

Early Attempts at Reconciliation

As a pastor, I chose to visit homes as often as possible, and to empower the Indigenous parishioners by forming church councils they would chair. We started up movements such as the Christopher Leadership course with Indigenous instructors, which taught leadership skills and instilled self-confidence; a marriage encounter movement with Indigenous teams; search weekends for youth with talks given by the youth themselves; and a lot of addictions awareness ministries that eventually led to my authoring of the book, *Walk a New Path: From Hurt to Healing*, which integrates Indigenous, Twelve Step, and Judeo-Christian spiritualities.

In 1983, and again in 1999, I took time off to learn the Cree language. That, I think, is one of the best ways to bring about reconciliation with the Indigenous peoples. Language learning involves a shift of power, similar to the youth group incident. It involves becoming a learner and a receiver, depending on an Indigenous language helper and an Indigenous community for immersion. It also demonstrates great respect for the language, builds strong bonds with the people, and inspires them to revive and learn their own language.

Jean Vanier, son of the former governor general of Canada, teaches that the poor are always being given things. What they need most, and the best thing we can give them, he claims, is dignity. To offer the Indigenous people the opportunity to give us the gift of their language is to humble ourselves and give them that dignity.

Language learning, for me, also included involvement in the culture and spirituality. I attended every social and cultural event I could—round dances, sweat lodges, chicken dances, powwows, spirit lodges, pipe ceremonies, cowboy dances, and especially dancing in a Sun Dance with the support of the family with whom I was staying. This experience led to an article entitled "Worship Without Walls."[4]

---

4. I wrote this in 1990 for the Lebret Task Force, described in the following paragraphs.

Although on the surface, language learning does not seem like ministry, I experienced it as a privileged experience of ministry. This led to a whole new approach to my ministry as an oblate missionary: when beginning in a new community, I would go door to door, introduce myself, practice my Cree, get to know the people in their homes, and build relationships before starting any kind of programs or even doing any sacramental ministry other than the Eucharist. Now I cannot imagine doing ministry any other way. *Tâpwe miyasin!*[5]

The Missionary Oblates, from 1978 to 1983, began hosting "Summer Amerindian Leadership" sessions for Indigenous laity and missionaries. These sessions were very effective and led to the formation of regional gatherings for quite a few years, such as the "Lighting the Sacred Fire" events in Manitoba, the Faith Family Festival in Saskatchewan, and gatherings in British Columbia as well.

In 1988, the Missionary Oblates held a national conference in Lebret, Saskatchewan, of all the oblate missionaries to the Indigenous peoples in Canada with our superior general at the time, Fr. Marcello Zago. The vision we came up with for our ministry among the Indigenous, while creative and well-crafted, was flawed, because we did it without the Indigenous peoples themselves. Looking back, I am amazed at how naïve and blind we were, to make such a mistake without even realizing it.

The Lebret Task Force (LTF) that was created as a follow-up to the conference, however, went on to organize an annual Indigenous Awareness Experience led by the late elder Mike Steinhauer of Saddle Lake, Alberta. This became a five-year series of four-day fasts attended by up to thirty participants. Previous to that development, some oblates were involved in similar experiences in the Little Red River area of northern Alberta.

The LTF also began a series of summer sessions in Alberta to provide orientation for Indigenous ministry for pastoral agents who would be replacing the oblates as we diminished, and the Canadian Church took on greater responsibility for ministry among the Indigenous peoples. This initiative was actually a forerunner of the present Directions for Indigenous Ministry of the western bishops, headed up by Sr. Eva Solomon, CSJ.[6]

We also produced a booklet entitled *Who Leads the Leaders?* that gathered up all the experience and wisdom from years of assemblies and

5. I would translate this as "Yes, very good!" or "Truly good!"

6. Directions for Indigenous Ministry is a program of Building Bridges Project that functions under the Standing Committee on Aboriginal Affairs of the Assembly of Western Catholic Bishops of Canada. For more information on this program, see chapter 3 in this volume by Sr. Eva Solomon, director of the project.

sharing. Some of the key learning that emerged from this shared experience is as follows:

- The importance of relationships, extended family, and clan systems for the Indigenous peoples. Ministry is all about developing relationships. This was exemplified by the question one young family asked me during a visit: "Father, are you going to grow old with us?";

- The importance of personal development, including regaining dignity, self-worth, and self-confidence;

- Dealing with grief and loss, as there are so many premature and tragic deaths directly connected to the legacy of colonization and the residential schools;

- Recognizing the role and importance of emotions, as the Indigenous are a very sensitive and feeling people;

- The need for a ministry that provides a lot of affirmation and teaches the importance of self-awareness;

- Respect for and appreciation of Indigenous spirituality, including the worldview of the sacred, the ethic of noninterference, and the importance and power of rituals and ceremony;

- A varied approach to learning using especially right-brained methods. For example, the training that the Nechi Institute in St. Albert, Alberta offers is 20 percent lecture and 80 percent experiential;

- Learning the history of the Indigenous peoples and seeing Canadian history from an Indigenous perspective.

A Historical Perspective

Regarding history, it is said that those who do not learn from their mistakes are bound to repeat them. The following is my own personal, broad assessment of the history of the relationship of Canadian society with the Indigenous peoples:

1. Precontact

   Indigenous communities were autonomous and self-sufficient, with highly developed social, economic, political, spiritual, and family systems in place.

2. Fur Trade Partnership

First Nations were valued partners as trappers and for military alliances. This was a time of mutual cooperation.[7]

3. Métis Interim Stage

As the Métis became more numerous through intermarriage, their involvement also increased. Île-à-la-Crosse, a Cree Métis community, dates its history back to the Fort Black trading post in 1776, as old as the United States.

4. Creation of a Caste System

The 1821 union of fur companies led to a retrenchment of the fur trade and some denial of employment for full-blooded First Nations people. The racist attitudes of then governor George Simpson (who denied upward mobility to any non-Indigenous person married to a First Nations person) marked the beginning of cultural denial and an attitude of second-class inferiority toward First Nations peoples.

5. Treaties

In the 1763 Royal Proclamation, the queen recognized the nationhood of the First Nations peoples. A land base for settlements was to be negotiated, and the surrounding traditional territories protected under the treaties. Land would be shared with the settlers to the depth of a furrow of a plow. Education and healthcare benefits were promised. The treaties were to be seen as "mutual cooperation" between two equal parties (the First Nations and the European colonists) and their descendants.

6. Colonial Policies and Residential Schools

The next century and a half witnessed efforts to "civilize" and assimilate the First Nations people. Treaties were broken, residential schools created, spiritual and cultural practices prohibited, and political systems undermined. The buffalo were killed off, and disease took the lives of many. This social upheaval hit so hard and so swiftly that this stage was marked with little resistance—it was like being hit by a fast-moving train.

An example of this is a woman I once met named Marie, originally from northern Manitoba. As a child, she was placed

7. For more information on this topic, see the works of Robert J. Miller and Bruce G. Trigger.

in a residential school in the south. Shortly after she was taken away to the school, her father died, and her mother, reasoning that the children needed a father and having met the right man, remarried within the year. As there was no means of communication at that time, Marie was not aware of this development in her family. When she returned home the following summer, she was shocked to find out that she had a different father. She rebelled, ended up in a reform school, and led a dysfunctional life of addiction and abuse. It was only as an adult during a parish renewal session held in her community that she was reconciled with her mother and stepfather, an emotional moment for the whole community.

My appreciation of the deep scar caused by the schools deepened when I heard the story of one woman who asked us to imagine a small community of five hundred members and its experience losing all of its children the first week of September—no more children playing and laughing, no parents parenting, and no grandparents and great-grandparents grandparenting. On the other end of the spectrum, former students lacking parenting skills and their children were robbed of the parenting they needed.

The same woman, who for some reason did not go to the school, shared that she now understood that her mother took her to a different home after church every Sunday so that the family would have a child in their home for one afternoon at least.

7. Attempts at Resistance

Saskatchewan saw some attempts at resistance. The most noteworthy was the Riel rebellion of 1885 in which the Métis, supported by some Indian bands, fought government troops for their rights and land. The Frog Lake Massacre in Alberta was another isolated attempt at resistance. There was also some resistance that involved some military action around Loon Lake (*Mâkwa Sâkihigan*) in Saskatchewan.

8. Hitting Bottom and Survival

By the late 1960s, the Canadian government's policy was deemed a failure. Instead of civilizing the First Nations, the government's policy, over the course of over a century, had created severely broken First Nation communities. In the 1950s and 1960s, many communities hit bottom. There was no place to go but up. Alcoholism ravaged the people and families, causing the breakdown of family systems. Miraculously, though not without much pain, hardship and loss of life, the people and the culture survived.

9. Gradual Recovery

Attempting to totally assimilate the First Nations, the 1969 White Paper—formally known as the "Statement of the Government of Canada on Indian Policy, 1969"—actually served to mobilize them.[8] Leaders emerged, and the National Indian Brotherhood (which became the Assembly of First Nations) was formed. A more educated and politically astute Indigenous population lobbied for real change, although differing internal views and fear on the part of civil leaders led to a stalemate in 1987.

10. Healing and Wellness (Cultural and Spiritual Renewal)

In 1999, a clear connection was made clear between the movement for self-government and First Nations' need for communal healing. Treatment centers and elders involved in correctional institutions made a difference. Wellness movements and a variety of healing programs started to have an impact.

Canadian Initiatives: RCAP,[9] IRSSA,[10] and the TRC[11]

There were also developments happening within Canadian society, such as the Royal Commission on the Aboriginal Peoples (RCAP, 1992–95) doing a full inquiry on the situation of the Indigenous peoples in Canada. Unfortunately, the environment in the country at the time was not conducive

---

8. This federal policy paper attempted to eliminate "Indian status"; incorporate First Nations under provincial government responsibilities; and impose land decisions, notions of private property, and economic agendas on Aboriginal communities. The backlash to the 1969 White Paper was monumental, leading not only to its withdrawal in 1970, but to a wave of activism, academic work, and court decisions over the next five decades. For more information, see the University of British Columbia's First Nations and Indigenous Studies article, "White Paper 1969," at http://indigenousfoundations. arts.ubc.ca/the_white_paper_1969.

9. Royal Commission on the Aboriginal Peoples. For more information, visit https://www.aadnc-aandc.gc.ca/eng/1100100014597/1100100014637.

10. Indian Residential School Settlement Agreement. For more information, visit http://www.residentialschoolsettlement.ca/english.html.

11. Truth and Reconciliation Commission of Canada. For more information, visit http://www.trc.ca.

to receiving this monumental work, and it primarily sat on the shelves of government, educational, and ecclesial institutions.

It wasn't until the question of the Indian Residential School system's negative impact was brought to the attention of the media—especially by Phil Fontaine, former Grand Chief of the Assembly of First Nations—that the Canadian public and churches woke up. This activism, which coincided with litigation in other areas of the country, led to a class action suit against the government, who third-partied the churches. That, in turn, led to the whole process of the Indian Residential School Settlement Agreement (IRSSA), signed in 2007, as well as the Truth and Reconciliation Commission (TRC). It is unfortunate that it took the threat of litigation (what everyone was afraid of and trying to avoid) to bring about concrete change and action.

One of the actions that the churches took at that time was to issue public apologies, first by the United Church and then by the oblates in 1991 at the Lac St. Anne pilgrimage in Alberta. Although controversial among the oblates at the time because it was issued quickly with little consultation, it has proven to be providential and prophetic, and was renewed at the last national TRC event in Edmonton in 2015 by the provincial, Ken Forster. Interestingly, one former Indigenous student told me that she left the church for ten years after witnessing that apology at Lac St. Anne, because no one took the time to hear her story.

That is a reminder of how important it is for these stories to be shared and for the individuals to feel that they have been listened to and heard. The apologies that were issued need to be completed with action, through making amends and ongoing education. Expressing regret and sorrow is commendable, but it is spiritually and psychologically inadequate. For an apology to be sincere and complete, these steps are essential:

1. Taking the time to hear the story and soaking up the pain of the victim;

2. A humble request for forgiveness without expectation;

3. Making a declaration to change and to try never to act in that hurtful way again;

4. A sincere effort to make amends and make things right.

Although the legacy of the residential schools was only one segment of the RCAP, that issue dominated the narrative in Canada for the ensuing years. Under the terms of the Indian Residential School Settlement agreement, the government would provide a Common Experience Payment (CEP) to all who attended a residential school and put into place an

Independent Assessment Process (IAP) for additional compensation to those who claimed they were also abused in the schools in some way.

Unfortunately, this last process was very open to abuse itself and made it politically incorrect to say anything positive about the residential schools. Although our archdiocese received donations of over eighteen thousand dollars out of the CEP of former students who had positive experiences at their schools, we were advised by our lawyers not to publicize this during the process, as it would be seen as being defensive.

What was more fruitful was the setting up of the Truth and Reconciliation Commission, composed of three commissioners that would run for five years, hear the stories of residential school survivors and former students, attempt to write the missing chapter of Canadian history regarding the schools, and leave behind a research and information center for future generations.

This process managed to garner much greater attention from the Canadian public, with an opening session in Ottawa involving the governor general, seven major conferences across the country, and a closing event in Ottawa. Thousands attended these gatherings, which included ceremonies, public testimonies, private testimonials, healing circles, archival materials (always popular with everyone), one-on-one reconciliations, and the arts.

Survivors or former students of the schools were encouraged to tell their stories of being taken away from their families (some at the tender age of five) and placed in the very forbidding and cold environment of the schools, sometimes not seeing their families for ten months of the year.

Part of the healing that happened at these events occurred as children and grandchildren heard their elders speak of their trauma and experience at the schools for the first time, and they began to understand their elders and why they behaved the way they did. This understanding led to greater forgiveness and personal freedom, a true healing.

As the TRC process was about to unfold across the country, the United Nations General Assembly adopted the *Declaration on the Rights of Indigenous Peoples* (UNDRIP) on September 13, 2007, after more than twenty years of discussions and negotiations that included representatives of Indigenous peoples and civic political groups. Although the *Declaration* is a symbol of triumph and hope to the Indigenous peoples, the then government of Canada initially voted against it and tried to undermine it, until finally endorsing it with ideological qualifications in 2010, a position that was widely criticized by international and domestic experts.

Colonization

The residential school reality, which has been the focus of national attention since 1990, has overshadowed the more basic and pervasive destructive reality of colonization mentioned earlier, which spawned the schools. It is this reality that calls for much more attention. One definition of colonization is the policy or practice of acquiring full or partial political control over another country, occupying it with settlers, and exploiting it economically. That is truly what happened in Canada.

The late Indigenous activist, Arthur Manuel, had this to say about colonization:

> Colonization is a complex relationship but simple to understand if you know that dispossession, dependency, and oppression are the consequences that it is designed to produce between the colonizer and the colonized . . . That is what the first Canadian Constitution rendered under the British North America Act, 1867. Our lands were put under Crown title, and we were left with 0.2 percent of the land on our Indian Reserves . . .
>
> I believe that, under the existing colonial system in Canada, Indigenous Peoples are not Canadian because of the systemic impoverishment we are forced to live in and because we are alienated from our traditional territories. If we accept colonization as a foundation of our relationship to Canada, we are endorsing our own impoverishment.
>
> You cannot have reconciliation under the colonial 0.2 percent Indian Reserve System. It is impossible. Nothing can justify that kind of human degradation. The land issue must be addressed before reconciliation can begin.[12]

One factor that enters into the picture is the reality of the Doctrine of Discovery and its adjunct, the notion of *terra nullius*. The Doctrine of Discovery is a complex legal tradition that arose in Western Europe during the medieval period, and in which the church played a central role. A series of papal bulls—particularly, *Romanus Pontifex* and *Inter Caetera*—both reflected the thinking of dominant European powers and reinforced the trajectory of justifying conquest by Christian powers.[13] This gave Christopher Columbus and other European explorers the mandate they needed to conquer and exploit the territory they "discovered." Even when they knew the land was

---

12. Manuel, "Until Canada Gives Indigenous People," paras. 3, 8, 21–22.

13. For example, see the text of the 1455 papal bull *Romanus Pontifex* by Pope Nicholas V in Davenport and Paullin, *European Treaties*, 23, and the text of the bull *Inter Caetera* issued in 1493 by Pope Alexander VI in *European Treaties*, 77–78.

occupied, the notion of *terra nullius* was applied under the pretext that the land was not being cultivated and utilized as it was in Europe.

What many are not aware of is that, in 1823, the US Supreme Court quietly adopted the Doctrine of Discovery into law in the celebrated case of *Johnson v. McIntosh*. As Steven Newcomb, who has done extensive research on this topic, explains, the reasoning was "that Christian European nations had assumed 'ultimate dominion' over the lands of America during the Age of Discovery and that, upon 'discovery,' the [Indigenous] had lost 'their rights to complete sovereignty as independent nations' and only retained a right of 'occupancy' in their lands." As Newcomb goes on to say, "[a]ccording to the U.S. government, Indian nations were 'domestic dependent nations' subject to the federal government's absolute legislative authority—known in the law as 'plenary power.' Thus, the ancient doctrine of Christian discovery and its subjugation of 'heathen' Indians were extended by the federal government into a mythical doctrine that the U.S. Constitution allows for governmental authority over Indian nations and their lands."[14]

This situation is rather confusing at present. There are calls for Pope Francis to repeal the Doctrine of Discovery, but the response from the Vatican is that subsequent bills negating the doctrine mean it has already been repealed, so what can be done is unclear.

One of the main points of interest at the moment is the Indian Act. Inspired by Prime Minister John A. MacDonald, many consider it the most well-used, racist colonizing tool the government has ever instituted. The Indian Act reversed the stance of the 1763 Royal Proclamation which recognized the Indigenous in Canada as nations within the understanding of *wahkohtowin*, or relationship-building. Reconciliation cannot occur under the umbrella of the Indian Act. There can be no compromise—it has to go, and Canada has to work its way back to the original relationship of the treaties.

My lifelong Cree friend Harry Lafond[15] believes, as he has told me in numerous conversations, that all government policies relating to

---

14. Newcomb, "Five Hundred Years of Injustice," paras. 8 and 13. A more comprehensive treatment of the ongoing impact of the Doctrine of Discovery can be found in a preliminary study put out by the Economic and Social Council of the United Nations at the Ninth Session of the Permanent Forum on Indigenous Issues in New York in April 2010; the document is entitled "Impact on Indigenous Peoples of the International Legal Construct known as the Doctrine of Discovery," and is available at https://www.un.org/esa/socdev/unpfii/documents/E.C.19.2010.13%20EN.pdf.

15. Harry Lafond was chief of Muskeg Lake Indian band in Saskatchewan, Canada, and was a special representative at the Synod for America held in Rome from November 16 to December 12, 1997. See Chief Lafond's important address to the synod in *Origins: CNS Documentary Service* 27.27 (December 18, 1997).

Indigenous peoples are based on that legislation. He sees nothing good about it, and believes that it was designed to destroy the Indigenous social fabric and control the Indigenous peoples. And that continues to this day, because it is still in effect. That claim can be verified, Harry says, simply by reading the Act itself.

There is a cultural shift happening in Canada at the moment and a greater openness to having a conversation and taking positive action about Indigenous rights, partly due to the Truth and Reconciliation process. This could lead to genuine healing and reconciliation, if we take advantage of this *kairos* moment.

Decolonization and Ongoing Colonization

Given this history and reality, decolonization must take place within both society and the church. Decolonization is a call to be humble and enter into a new relationship with the Indigenous peoples. It involves letting go of white privilege—and the power that goes with it—as well as our Eurocentric way of behaving. Decolonizing is happening among the Indigenous peoples as they recover their traditions and the elders participate once again in the fabric of their communities.

Despite a focus on decolonization, however, colonization continues. One example is the clear-cutting of thousands of acres of traditional territory in northern Canada. There is no consultation with the people who have used these lands for thousands of years, and trapping cabins are being burned. The lumber is essentially being stolen, thus allowing Canadian companies to sell on the international market for less. This is a microcosm of what is happening all across the country: mining, damming, fracking, pipeline construction, lumbering, and drilling for oil are often carried out without the consensus of or consultation with the Indigenous peoples involved.

The Calls to Action

The TRC final document issued ninety-four Calls to Action that are proving to be opportunities for governments, churches, and Canadian society in general to "move forward together" in ways that will bring about greater justice, healing, and reconciliation with the Indigenous peoples.

There are many ways this can be and is being done. One is by implementing *Laudato Si'*. This encyclical by Pope Francis provides a blueprint for renewing our relationship with the Indigenous peoples. It speaks of "showing special care for Indigenous communities, involving them as principal dialogue partners, and supporting their view of the land as a sacred space."[16] We must allow this document to keep guiding our steps as we move forward together.

Learning about the treaties, and living them out, is another direction we can take. Many Canadians do not realize that we are all treaty people. We are all party to the treaties that our ancestors made with the Indigenous people.

Choosing to get involved in cross-cultural experiences is to be encouraged. Any such experience offers an opportunity for growth, learning, and understanding. The Indigenous have no choice here—they are facing a cross-cultural experience every day, always having to deal with non-Indigenous teachers, politicians, social workers, police, etc. That is a source of their richness, but it also takes a lot of energy and can often be a source of great stress and frustration. Choosing to participate in cultural events can place us in a position of great vulnerability, but that is a price worth paying for the sake of greater understanding and reconciliation.

Becoming more aware of and changing our colonial mindset—the way we think and speak—is another challenge. I remember casually inviting the participants at one workshop to come and "circle the wagons" and immediately had to face the indignation of the Indigenous participants in the group.

We can also educate ourselves by reading authors such as Steven Newcomb, Sylvia McAdam, Thomas King, and Sheelas McLean, to name a few, and magazines like *Geez*, out of Winnipeg, which put out issues on colonization and decolonization. We can take part in educational events that are happening in our area and watch movies like *Rabbit-Proof Fence*.

Appreciation of Indigenous culture and spirituality, and even learning a few words of an Indigenous language, are all positive steps that can be taken as follow-up to the TRC.

Initiatives Toward Reconciliation

One of the main initiatives that has taken place in Canada is that, for the first time, the major Catholic parties (bishops, religious, the Aboriginal Council, Knights of Columbus, Catholic Women's League, Development and Peace, and St. Vincent de Paul) as well as the laity in general, including Indigenous laity, and priests and deacons have come together to form an Our Lady of Guadalupe Circle. The Circle serves as a national Catholic voice, provides a forum for discernment on various initiatives with Indigenous people, and engages in action in response to the TRC.

16. Francis, *Laudato Si'*, 146.

A think tank leading up to this Circle put out a statement on the Doctrine of Discovery, admitting its errors and falsehoods, and published seven commitments to walk with the Indigenous peoples. It also put out a statement in support of the *United Nations Declaration on the Rights of Indigenous Peoples*.[17]

Harry Lafond stresses the importance of this United Nations document as a framework for the church to use to review its relationship with the Indigenous peoples. It needs to be adopted, not just supported. Viewing this document as a good idea while standing by on the sidelines is actually ongoing colonization.

Elder Maggie Hodgson of Edmonton was instrumental in establishing a National Aboriginal Day in Canada. It is held annually on June 21st to celebrate the unique heritage, diverse cultures, and outstanding achievements of the First Nations, Inuit, and Métis peoples. A National Day of Prayer in Solidarity with Indigenous Peoples is celebrated every year on December 12, the feast day of Our Lady of Guadalupe, patroness of the Americas, who appeared in 1531 to a humble native peasant, Juan Diego, in Mexico. The Canadian Catholic Aboriginal Council celebrates this day for prayer, solidarity, and reconciliation by issuing an annual message honoring Indigenous people who were inspired by their Catholic faith.

Many dioceses are doing their best to implement follow-up to the TRC Calls to Action and move forward together. The following is merely a sampling of what some dioceses and parishes are doing:

- Researching the deaths of children at Indian Residential Schools and composing, for All Soul's Day, a prayer for them as well as for murdered and missing Indigenous women (MMIW);

- Exploring Indigenous traditions that could be incorporated into the liturgy;

- Disseminating the national statement on support for UNDRIP, the seven commitments to walk with the Indigenous peoples, and the statement on the Doctrine of Discovery;

- Organizing a diocesan synod to empower healing and Indigenous leadership;

- Hosting healing programs such as Returning to Spirit, Twelve-Step Pilgrimages, and Grief to Grace, along with committing to host further healing, addictions awareness, and family support programs. A visitor to one diocese from the Middle East marveled at what was happening,

17. The full text of this United Nations document is available online at http://www.un.org/esa/socdev/unpfii/documents/DRIPS_en.pdf.

leading us to an awareness that the eyes of the world are on Canada more than we realize;

- Establishing diocesan structures such as an Office for Indigenous Affairs, an Office for Truth and Reconciliation, and an Urban Aboriginal Peoples Advisory Committee;

- Organizing a diocesan study and workshops on MMIW and issuing a pastoral letter on this issue;

- Hosting an annual diocesan day of healing and reconciliation with Indigenous Peoples on April 17, the Feast of St. Kateri Tekakwitha, and other celebrations in her honor;

- Establishing Indigenous parishes such as Kateri in Winnipeg, Guadalupe in Saskatoon, and Sacred Heart Church of the First Peoples in Edmonton;

- Hosting a Cree language initiative and evening sessions on Indigenous spirituality taught by elders;

- Offering ongoing education on Treaty Six, including an explanatory plaque in the diocese's cathedral and churches;

- Rewriting the diocesan history through a film project guided by Indigenous scholars and supporting the creation of a diocesan Indigenous film festival;

- Giving financial support for Indigenous ministry in an adjacent diocese;

- Creating a variety of programs for Indigenous students, including nutrition, health, language, culture, and Indigenous spirituality through a partnership between a Catholic School district and First Nations governance;

- Offering outreach to Indigenous students at St. Thomas More College at the University of Saskatchewan, where, in 2016, a chair for Indigenous Studies was also established;

- Conducting healing and family support workshops;

- Forming a First Nations, Inuit, and Métis (FNIM) committee within the St. Albert Catholic School district, which meets monthly with elders in order to educate committee members and initiate positive action toward reconciliation;

- Participating in ecumenical initiatives such as the KAIROS Blanket Exercise;

- Offering special inculturated eucharistic celebrations for the feast of Our Lady of Guadalupe and St. Kateri Tekakwitha;

- Establishing an Aboriginal and non-Aboriginal Relations Community (ANARC) to build relationships;

- Participating in Indigenous ceremonies and spirituality;

- Hosting monthly potlucks and sharing circles to share stories;

- Developing a strategic plan to follow up to the TRC.

One unique inter-diocesan initiative is a three-stream, two-year, live-in lay formation program (a diocesan stream, an eparchial stream for Ukrainian Catholics, and an Aboriginal stream) that takes place in Saskatoon, Saskatchewan. This is the collaborative initiative of three dioceses in which candidates have both separate and joint sessions, learning from each other.

Our own Oblate Star of the North Retreat Centre has adopted the umbrella of a Culture of Encounter for our ministry. As a follow-up to the TRC, we have initiated "Breaking New Ground Together," a series of sessions on Indigenous issues such as colonization. The last powerful session, "Decolonizing Our Hearts and Minds," involved a young Slavey mother, an elder, and a settler as resource persons. Participants were challenged to step forward and to open their hearts.

We also hosted a "Long Ago Parenting" course taught by elder Elsie Paul, who is recovering the traditions of the ancestors. A young Indigenous presenter will also be conducting a program called "Becoming a Warrior" on mature male adulthood.

One of the most effective educational tools is the Blanket Exercise, developed by the ecumenical group KAIROS.[18] It is a hands-on, experiential walk through the history of colonization and the residential schools using quilts, scripts, and role-playing. This exercise and the debriefing that takes place afterwards have brought many of the participants to tears.

Some participants in the "Directions for Indigenous Ministry" sessions were invited on a social justice tour of the Diocese of San Cristobal in Chiapas, Mexico. There we were inspired by the work of the late Bishop Samuel Ruiz, who transformed the situation of the Indigenous of his diocese. When he arrived, the Indigenous were not permitted to walk on the sidewalks or to actually live within the city of San Cristobal. By promoting their rights, holding Indigenous congresses, forming Indigenous leaders, and translating the Scriptures into their own languages, they are now subjects of their own history. In turn, in the summer of 2016, local leaders traveled to Canada

18. For more information on KAIROS, visit its website at http://www.kairoscanada.org.

from Chiapas to serve as resource persons for our "Directions in Aboriginal Ministry" and "Elder's Dialogue" sessions in Canada.

On a civic level, the city of Vancouver had declared itself a "City of Reconciliation" during the TRC process. Having done so, members of the city council were hesitant to celebrate the one hundred and fiftieth anniversary of Canada because of our colonial history. A consultation of the local First Nations led to the decision not to cancel the celebration, but to celebrate the Indigenous history of the area. With some fear of pushback, they are forging ahead with this idea and planning a festival honoring the art, history, and culture of the Musqueam, Squamish, and Tsleil-Waututh First Nations.

Conclusion

An elder once swore at me and threatened me with a hockey stick when he realized that I was a priest. When I learned that he was dying of cancer in the hospital, I went to visit him with some trepidation. His first comment to me was that being sick had given him time to think. I wondered if he remembered the incident that had happened between us. Then, suddenly, he said that he was sorry for what he did to me that day. Relieved, I asked if it was his experience at the IRS that had made him so angry. He said that it was not his experience, but rather the fact that he had lost so many of his friends to suicide or violent deaths because of the schools that had angered him so. I apologized for that, and we shook hands warmly.

I was filled with joy at this reconciliation and left for Kenya to conduct workshops for the oblates at the pre-novitiate. They invited me to stay in Kenya because of the harvest of vocations there. I shared this story with them and told them I would stay in Canada, hoping for a harvest of reconciliation here, in which there is genuine healing of our history and of our spirits.

In 1993, at a North-South Dialogue of oblates and Indigenous from South, Central, and North America in Uspantan, Guatemala, the participants urged the oblates not to abandon them now and not to walk before them or behind them, but to walk with them. That, I think, is our challenge today: to journey together into a renewed relationship.

Regional Indigenous Theological Voices and Responses

C: Chile

6

My Experience as a Mapuche Christian

ROSA ISOLDE REUQUE PAILLALEF

*Marri marri kom pu che/Buenas Tardes/*Good afternoon!

Indigenous spirituality and interculturality are the main themes that bring us together in this place in the North. The Indigenous peoples are calling on the Catholic Church to recognize them in a real way, to accept their culture, spirituality, protocols, and distinct rights. I would like to make a contribution to this call by presenting to you my experience as a Mapuche woman and leading social activist.

In the first place, I must say that I am neither a journalist nor a sociologist; however, I have always lived in the space between observing and communicating. When I accepted the challenge of this invitation to speak to you, I thought I would share my experience as a Mapuche Catholic. What came to mind are a *lonko*,[1] a community, and a *werken*.[2] I am thankful to *Nguenechen*[3] for being here with us today.

It is often difficult to remember the path that I have followed and recall what I have learned during the journey. For me, it is quite a challenge to talk about myself and be in front of you all. I look and I see that you are interested in my life experience as a woman belonging to the Mapuche people, a Catholic Christian woman, a Chilean woman, and a worker.

I was born in a Mapuche community (*lof*) in the traditional way. In the delivery, my mother was assisted by an herbal medicinal woman

1. *Lonko* is the head or chief of the community.

2. *Werken* means messenger. It is the person who carries the message of the *Lonko*.

3. *Nguenechen* is the name of the superior being and creator of all things.

(*lahuentuchefe*) and a matron (*gutamchefe*). I do not have clear memories of my childhood; the memories are like a passage or photographs that represent important facts. I am the oldest female of seven siblings. My mother gave birth nine times. From her, I learned a sense of responsibility in the care of my younger siblings. I learned to work in the fields and take care of the animals. I was a happy child and enjoyed contact with nature, learned about the importance of plants, and assumed my responsibility as the oldest daughter.

I remember that my father always repeated that I should observe well how to work the land and take care of the animals. My mother also said, and still says, that I must observe well what others do in order to do the same, especially referring to learning the art of weaving and growing medicinal herbs. It is a process of learning without asking too many question but by observing a lot, and attentively. It is what social sciences refer to as "learning by doing."

Even though during my childhood and youth I did not understand much of what my parents were doing, my father was the *lonko* of the *lof* (head of the community), and my mother the daughter of a *lonko*. After I left home, I began to better understand what my father did every morning at dawn; he did his *llellipun* (personal prayer)[4] by the well. I saw the water falling as a cascade through his fingers, and I saw him giving the gift of a branch of *hualle* (what we know as oak) to my mother in the spring. I witnessed his prayers in the fields after planting the seeds, the prayers for rain, and the conversations he held with the trees and animals as if they were other people.

The memory of these experiences is still alive with me and in my practices. My participation in the *guillatún*[5] became increasingly important for me and made my father happy. I used to help my mother in the *guillatún* with the chores such as making *muzay* (traditional drink) or *sopaipillas* (fried bread)—the meal for the participating families and guests—taking care of the fire, and disposing of the leftovers, both in the house and in the *ngillatuwe* (the open area where the *guillatún* is celebrated). I learned that food leftovers should not be profaned. I also learned *purrun* (dance) by participating, becoming my father's partner for the dance, and then being my father's helper with the *kultrun tailfe* (drum instrumentalist).[6]

---

4. *Llellipun* is a time of personal or communal prayer done anytime of the day and before starting different Mapuche rituals.

5. *Guillatún* is a family or community religious ceremony that includes moments of celebration, prayer, sharing food, and communicating the message of God through the *Machi*, the medicine man or woman.

6. *Kultrum* is a repercussion instrument made from wood and covered with

All these things I continue to practice in my daily living, and they are part of my identity and reality.

My Identity as a Mapuche, Christian, Catholic Woman

I am an extrovert, and it would not be difficult for me to demonstrate who I am in the complex Mapuche-Christian reality. I am often asked who I am. Depending on the context, my answer could be Mapuche, Christian, Catholic woman, or Mapuche social and cultural activist woman leader.

One does not notice cultural difference when living in the family, but when we go to school to receive a formal education, one lives the differences. The experience in the city today is very different from the countryside fifty years ago. We experience life differently, from the simplest things to the most complex things of daily living. Everything changes at school: we have to be quiet; we have to learn how to write; and we see that the sentences are put together the opposite way, because we think in Mapuche and write in Spanish. The teachers would always highlight what was badly constructed or expressed and criticized our bad pronunciation, but never did teachers put themselves in our place, and never did they realize the fact that they were dealing with a different culture.

My cultural Mapuche identity blossomed after passing from elementary to middle school because I faced the unknown differences in my work in higher education, where I felt discriminated against as a person; it felt like I had to learn everything again from scratch. I discovered that, in the Mapuche teachings, what is learned is learned with conviction from the deep roots of the soul and culture. It is a question of faith and knowledge. In this sense, as a Mapuche woman, I integrated the different and cannot deny that this was important learning for what I have become today.

In relation to my encounter with Christianity, I also learned to first know the religion, the sacred Judeo-Christian Scriptures, where there is no room for dialogue with the Mapuche worldview. The acknowledgement and valuing of the Mapuche culture in the Catholic Church has been a slow process and has included resistance from priests and religious of the Mapuche culture itself.

In this regard, even though the magisterium of the church, on various occasions, recognized the good and true in the religious experience of Indigenous peoples, Catholic communities are not prepared, or lack the sensibility, to receive this wisdom and this diversity among us. They question our

---

leather; it symbolizes the Mapuche worldview in its different stages.

ways of praying and calling *Nguenechen* God, as if the Christian God were the only way of talking about God.

In my opinion, in the experience of prayer and liturgy, the differences and similarities between being Mapuche and being Christian become more evident. When it comes to prayer, where the Christian must learn to give meaning to the simplest of prayers, repeat established formulas, and spend a lot of time in life trying to feel the Holy Spirit as an outside sensation and witness to the faith, prayer for the Mapuche is spontaneous. Prayer comes from the heart, from what the heart feels, from the strength of nature that moves, and from what it sees and feels. It involves the whole person, which is not only the rational, but also the physical and affective; in the Christian experience, I relate this to the Holy Spirit that integrates all that is human. The *newen*[7] (force, energy) that moves our lives makes us aware that there is a supreme being that exists. The forces of nature teach us to respect all the beings of the earth, but there is only one supreme being that exists, *Nguenechen*—God, for the Christian. We learn that each of us is part of the earth and must live with all that is created. Therefore, when a person is born, it is a moment of happiness; it is the manifestation of the *Nguenechen*, the prolongation of the history of the creation of human beings on earth.

Some may wonder if it's possible to analyze the different points of view that give strength to being Mapuche and the values that reinforce our personality. An individual's way of daily living is a continuous, permanent process. We continue learning every day, creating knowledge and spreading what we've learned. There is not a moment to stop and reflect philosophically (in the Greek sense) when faced with situations; it is a continuous and permanent *kimün* (learning or wisdom), an invitation to be always attentive with all our senses, including the interpretation of what we dream and what nature tells us on any particular day.

How Have I Lived That?

With the passing of time, and in the different roles that I have had to perform, I have been an instrument for spreading Mapuche spirituality as well as the practice of the rituals that are part of our ancestral culture. First, by self-identifying with them, and then, by participating in the different activities that the family performs in the community, and in the tasks of daily life I face at work.

---

7. *Newen* is understood as the spiritual force that certain spaces have such as a mountain, water, waterfalls, and volcano, which communicate this force to human beings.

Secondly, I have had to direct and adapt the Mapuche protocol to a reality outside the community, to groups of people with different creeds and political visions with the goal of showing the non-Mapuche world the value of Mapuche spirituality and the pertinence of the respect Mapuche have for their ancestral authorities and for the elders in their communities.

From the Mapuche point of view, we face discrimination and mis-understanding about our life and Christian faith. In my experience, the two realities—the Mapuche way of life and the Christian faith—are not mutually exclusive but rather complementary. That is to say, I have to live keeping clear what it means to be Mapuche from the perspective of my values, identity, and culture, and see how to deepen that through my Catholic Christian experience, in which we believe that we are all children of the same God. This is primarily a spiritual experience and reality that is difficult to explain outside this spiritual context. In fact, in diverse rela-tionships, we see a confrontation of the viewpoints that question living or identifying as Mapuche and Catholic Christian. We experience criticism and discrediting of our way of living by those who say that our religion is mere syncretism, which implies that Mapuche spirituality, because it is not an "official religion," is not valid.

In recent years, the Catholic Church has recognized the Mapuche peo-ple as being different from the dominant Chilean society in their worldview, language, religion, particular ways of cultivating land, and close relationship to nature. For example, the bishops of the Ecclesial Province of the south of Chile issued a pastoral letter in May 1979 in support of the Mapuche people, promoting Mapuche culture through workshop leaders, skill building, de-fense of Mapuche rights, and leadership formation.[8] This strengthened the traditional organizations as well as the organizations that function out of clear Mapuche identity and supported their demands. In 1987, Pope John Paul II gave a speech in Temuco valuing and defending the culture and expressions of the Mapuche people.[9] In 2003, another ecclesial document was issued: "In Support of a New Treaty with the Mapuche People."[10] This document was studied in different social institutions and organizations and has served to help people learn about the Mapuche and their history.[11]

8. See the unpublished letter by Obispos de Concepción, Los Ángeles, Temuco, La Araucanía, Valdivia y Osorno, entitled "Carta Pastoral: Evangelización del Pueblo Ma-puche," written in Temuco, Chile on May 4, 1979.

9. See John Paul II, "Celebración de la Palabra."

10. Obispos Católicos del Sur de Chile, "Al Servicio de un Nuevo Trato," http://docu-mentos.iglesia.cl/documento.php?id=44.

11. Editor's note: To further explore this topic, see the following two documents in Spanish: (1) *Informe de la Comisión Verdad Histórica y Nuevo Trato con los Pueblos*

What Are the Challenges in the Face of This Reality?

The encounter between these cultures (or realities) presents us with the challenge of interculturality. Knowledge of the Mapuche people and valuing their spiritual practices leads us to a dialogue of mutual learning, which will have an effect on the identity of both cultures.

In the pastoral context of the Mapuche people, we need to think about the practice of the sacraments and how to give meaning to them from within their culture so that it is not merely a ritualistic practice or a formal administrative requirement. In other words, the sacramental practice would need to be thought through from within the cultural practices.

In the realization of celebrations—both of the Mapuche and the Christian—it would be necessary to maintain the integrity of both and avoid falling into liturgical syncretism. This would depend on the recognition and value given to the diversity of cultural expressions.

In relation to ecclesial statements, studies, and documents, the church needs to embody this wisdom in practices on the ground. This requires formation, especially of the clergy, pastoral parish leaders, and the whole Christian community.

And finally, I would like to say that it is a great challenge to all to acknowledge our Indigenous peoples and be consistent in doing so in an active, nonviolent way. It is important to search for the truth about who we are and what our demands are as Mapuche people and to support our integral cultural, political, economic, and social development.

I thank the organizers for this opportunity, which invites us all to reflect on the life and existence of Indigenous peoples. Faith in a superior being is the force that has convened us and has us ponder a God who unites all peoples.

Mañunkuley ta mu alkutumafiel kom pu che. Thank you for listening to me. *Fey müten*! I said all I want to say!

Indígenas [*Report of the Commission for Historical Truth and New Treatment of Indigenous Peoples*], issued in October 2003 to Chilean President Ricardo Lago Escobar and available online at http://www.memoriachilena.cl/602/articles-122901_recurso_2. pdf, and (2) "Construyamos 'el Buen Vivir' en la Araucanía: Carta Pastoral sobre la Iglesia y Pueblos Originarios" ["Building the 'Buen Vivir' in Araucanía: Pastoral Letter on the Church and Native Peoples"], issued in November 2016 by the Diocese of San José de Temuco and available online at http://institutoindigena.cl/web/wp-content/uploads/2017/10/Carta-Pastoral-sobre-la-Iglesia-y-Pueblos-Originarios.pdf.

7

Christian and Mapuche Dialogue: A Theological Reflection Toward Mutual Understanding

JAIME C. BASCUÑÁN

I am a Chilean-American who was born in Chile and have lived and worked in the United States for many years.[1] Since 2011, I have been teaching in Chile at the Catholic University of Temuco, where I got involved in developing an intercultural dialogue between our Institute of Theological Studies and the Mapuche people. I have to say from the outset that this is just one experience in Chile in relation to the church and Indigenous people. The experience described in this chapter represents the dialogue and work done by a small community of Christian Mapuches and non-Mapuche. My cross-cultural experience in the United States as a Latino has certainly given me a particular perspective that informs the dialogue I discuss below.

In particular, this chapter is a theological reflection on an experience of intercultural dialogue between Christian spirituality and Mapuche spirituality in the context of *mesas de diálogo,* or dialogue encounters, that have been taking place over the past few years at the Catholic University of Temuco, organized by the Institute of Theological Studies.

The Catholic University of Temuco is located in the Araucanía region, in the southern part of Chile. This is the region where the Mapuche people have lived since before the *conquista.* Mapuche communities are located in several other areas which are called *reducciones indígenas,* designated territories given to the communities after a vast portion of the land was given to *colonos,* the settlers who came to Chile around the end of the nineteenth century and the beginning of the twentieth. The *reducciones*

1. I lived and worked in the Chicago area for twenty-two years, and my three children still live there.

indígenas are, in many ways, similar to the Native American reservations in the United States and Canada.

A key dimension of the mission of the Catholic University of Temuco is to serve within this regional context and be attentive to its intercultural reality. Consequently, the university supports many projects toward this end, and in doing so, it tries to make a specific and unique contribution to the region and the country.

Two disclaimers before I continue: First, this chapter does not intend to cover in detail the culture, history, or reality of the Mapuche. And second, it does not represent necessarily the position of the Chilean Catholic Church as a whole in relation to the Mapuche. I would say that what I describe here is an experience of dialogue that prepares the ground for rethinking our theology of church and mission in this context. In this sense, the pastoral work would be understood as a mutual dialogue, and mission as intercultural dialogue.

The Experience

Starting in 2015, a dialogue roundtable was formed of Mapuche people, academics from the university and the larger community, and pastoral agents, meeting monthly to find ways to dialogue about spirituality. We began by sharing our experiences of being Christian Catholic, Mapuche Christian Catholic, and Mapuche. Eventually, we planned a meeting for a wider and more diverse group in the form of a symposium. We invited representatives from the Catholic Mapuche communities, people in Mapuche pastoral ministry, academic faculty and staff, and others interested in intercultural dialogue. Twenty-six people gathered for three days.

Some of the objectives for the symposium were

- To reflect on possible dynamics of intercultural-interreligious dialogue in Araucanía;

- To bring to light issues that can be obstacles to this dialogue;

- To look for themes from culture and spirituality that might facilitate this dialogue; and,

- To systematize our reflections and publish them, in order to help others to dialogue within their own context.

The format for this gathering was a circle of sharing not only stories and reflections, but also dance, food, silence, and prayer. We wanted to create and share in an environment where our whole being could be expressed.

That is, we wanted to share and dialogue, not just by focusing on spoken language, but also by using gestures, symbols, prayer, and dance, all incorporated into the dialogue. We wanted to reflect by engaging the whole person in an integral way.

The following are some of the elements that facilitated the dialogue:

- Creating an unconditional and open disposition to welcome the other in a circle, a symbol of mutuality and equality. Coming together in a circle and actually looking at each other. Finding the window to each person through the eyes, each participant made a real effort to come out and encounter the other as person.

- Inviting participants to relativize their prejudices: to be flexible and free from the dogmatism of possessing the truth, allowing oneself to become vulnerable and let the other reach out to us in our deepest convictions.

- Acknowledging our past differences but without dwelling on them, and in such a way that would enable us to move forward toward healing and finding a new path for a shared journey, becoming aware that the weight of history could become an obstacle for dialogue.[2]

- Sharing experiences of what was vital and meaningful in the cultural relationships between Mapuche and *Winka*,[3] revealing in each other the sense of the sacred that is inclusive of all aspects of life.

- Dancing together in a circle, an important dynamic, enabling us to see our bodies in a common place with music, trying to freely find the rhythm together. Our bodies are the first place where we experience differences, wrong steps, and clumsiness. The support of the group helped each person visualize the possibility of not only tolerating but also integrating the differences.

- Engaging in a dynamic of dialogue the symbols and gestures, which were valued and seen as key for communicating with each other in a meaningful way. In other words, these symbols and gestures provide

---

2. For instance, the Mapuche people were forced to assimilate to the dominant culture by attending schools in the official national educational system, learning Spanish and disregarding their own language and culture. This served them to become educated in Western ways of being and become assimilated into the country, which was part of a process of nationalization at the end of nineteenth century. See Díaz Fernández, *Misión y Pueblo Mapuche*, 30.

3. *Winka* is the name used among the Mapuche for people who are not Mapuche, such as white people or other Chileans.

an open door to connect with the experiences and meanings that each participant brings.

At the end, this experience became a genuine exercise of dialogue involving people with diverse identities as we identified several key attitudes in regard to the other as interlocutor.

Interior Disposition

As we began the roundtable dialogue, we all agreed that we needed to create conditions to enable us to listen to each other. We began presenting our basic rules for listening to each other and suspending judgment from previous experiences of dialogue that were not positive.[4] We agreed to be open and express our thoughts to each other in freedom and honesty about our expectations of being together for three days.

As each person was introducing him or herself, there was a clear realization that, at the moment of sharing with people from another culture, we might feel inadequate, clumsy, or even fearful to talk about ourselves. Sharing was done through personal stories and what we experienced together during the dance.

At the moment of exploring our identity and life experience in order to present ourselves to others, there is a realization of our own transcendence. This is a humbling experience that requires being vulnerable to exposing ourselves and going beyond our own fears and prejudices. It requires authenticity and genuine concern for being able to encounter the other as different, yet the same in many ways. The group came to a common understanding that the place and meeting space was sacred as we share our lives and God's Spirit and wisdom within and among us. It was required that we listen with respect and reverence to each other, encountering the best of each person and culture.

Safe Environment

As each participant shared their experiences, they felt heard and appreciated. This favored a greater understanding of each other's histories and of

---

4. Many of those present at this gathering, especially the Mapuche, have had similar previous experiences with the intention of improving dialogue and valuing diversity. However, there was no follow-up. The lack of effectiveness of such past gatherings made people apprehensive about participating again in other initiatives that might lead to similar results.

the processes that were oppressive and demeaning to our cultures and to us as human beings. The first and the most important barriers that appeared in the stories were those of discrimination and misunderstanding of the other. The Mapuche have been discriminated against as being uneducated, poor, too relaxed, lazy, and not taking initiative.[5] They are different, because they are "not like us." "Racism" was the word that summarized this experience: it is a reality that nobody wants to name, but it is the real experience in many encounters and structures where Mapuche live and work.

Thus, we have found ourselves in front of the other with respect and appreciation; we have recognized and put a name to the different situations we have experienced in relationship with those from another culture. The participants agreed that an experience like this—coming together and listening to each other with mutual respect and appreciation—was not something they were used to. Many participants noted that something happened when we shared in this way. We discovered that we entered into a dynamic of internal movement, even when that moving caused insecurity. This implied moving to new images of self, God, nature, spirit, knowledge (*saberes*), and reflecting on our own assumptions, learning to be reflexive in our practice of encountering the other. To make this a more intentional process, we asked the following question: what happened to us in this encounter?

We Are Apprentices

As we embarked on this experience of dialogue, several images began to flow, expressing this encounter. Each person encountered the "other" as an apprentice. We learned that it is important to be aware that, in dialogue, we are always apprentices. The image of the apprentice gave us a sense of being constant learners in practice. We acknowledged that we learn by listening to the stories and memories both of others and ourselves. Our individual selves are involved when we listen to the other's stories. Listening with empathy means putting ourselves in the other's place, even when our own history has to be reviewed.

A Dialogue Drawing from Gospel Insights: Mission as Encounter and Dialogue

We know that the gospel is not without culture and cannot happen without dialogue with a particular culture. It is expressed and takes form in

---

5. See Curivil, *La Fuerza de la Religión*, 99.

dialogue with the culture in all of its dimensions. In this way, it is necessary to understand the gospel, the good news, as the process of God's self being in dialogue with humanity, with the very gifts that God has given each person. These gifts are found in the life and cultural expression and memories of the people. Theology, then, in this respect, is the process of finding and reflecting God in the life of the people as pure gift. From this perspective, we need to rethink the theology of the church from its very nature: mission. Theology of mission should reflect not only on the purpose of the church, but also ought to envision ways and models to be nourished by encountering the other as God's gift, namely, understanding mission as encounter and dialogue.

Mission as theology and practice becomes a space of mutual conversation that provides us an opportunity to see the historical wounds of discrimination and lack of appreciation, even in the womb of the church. As a community that preaches love, we have not been able to live out what we preach, namely, being the other's neighbor and caring for the well-being of the other. This echoes what the US bishops said decades ago in their pastoral letter on racism: "Catholics must acknowledge a share in the mistake and sins of the past. Many of us have been prisoners of fear and prejudice. We have preached the Gospel while closing our eyes to the racism it condemns."[6] This calls us to rethink how reconciliation can be possible after the experience of cultural and religious colonization. Religion, the church as human body and structure, has been the cause of violence and imposition, not only by failing to provide a positive image of God, but also by failing to recognize other people's own experiences of life and spirituality. Basically, we have fallen short when it comes to recognizing the ways in which God can be manifested in the dynamic of the diversity of cultures and in every human being; we have failed to realize that God cannot be reduced to one image or formula.

This historical experience has marked the identity of each group: the church on the one side and the Mapuches on the other. From the time of the conquest until today, these identities have been formed in a context of oppression, forcing the Mapuche people to adapt to models and structures of church and civilization. For Christianity's part, this has always been an asymmetrical relationship, and one effect of this is that Mapuche religious or spiritual practices have not been recognized or accepted until very recently. Even now, the church views some of their practices with suspicion.

Mission as encounter and dialogue inspires at its core a deep commitment for encountering what is meaningful and life-giving to each people

6. "Brothers and Sisters to Us," 8.

and culture. It calls for the realization of how a true religious experience that is culturally meaningful can be an expression of the good news to all. As mentioned above, we need to do a critical reading, as the church, of our Catholic experience in relationship with the *pueblos originarios*, not only in terms of our social approach, but also in terms of our spiritual and theological approach.

We need to be strongly aware that the gospel and the church, in many cases, have contributed to manipulating and disregarding culture, and to imposing the Christian message in a cultural package, rather than as good news that unfolds God's presence and grace, therefore preventing us from encountering the other in his or her uniqueness. This implies the awareness that God also speaks in and through the other culture, and that God's Spirit is in all of creation, not just in the church. We can learn from the experiences of Jesus, who takes on the reality and the life of the one he encounters, and from that reality speaks in a way that gives new meaning. In his encounters with Zacchaeus (Luke 19:1–10, NAB), the woman at the well (John 4:1–30, NAB), and the centurion (Matt 8:5–13, NAB), all of them were invited to see in a different way by being encountered in their own reality and worldview.

The key challenge for us, beyond the doctrinal and catechetical realm, is this: how we can recognize God, or the experience of God, especially in the culture and life of Indigenous peoples? The experience of the Mapuche in reasserting their identity has been to become more radical about their culture as a way of enchanting themselves with their ancestry. They have been going back to the sources to find the *Kimün* (wisdom/knowledge) and also to protect their culture from what they say are damaging elements that disregard its meaning and power. Mapuche people find it difficult to practice dialogue with others, because this has not been the experience they have had with Western culture. The relationship with Western culture and the church has been one of power and domination, subordination and superiority—not of equals. The Mapuche understanding of diversity implies complementarity, new possibility of life. All is related: the power of nature, people, and the divine. Reality is already diverse and plural for them. Their consciousness about their culture is that of an intercultural and dynamic reality.

As Christians, we also need to answer this question. Today, we ask ourselves what it means to be a Christian in the midst of this diversity. We have been socialized to exclude the other. This blocks us from seeing plurality within the Christian experience. Is that not a rigid way to conceive of being a Christian? As a Catholic, what does "being universal" mean? This might give us a clue to be attentive to Christ and committed to the gospel, where God is manifest in what is diverse and unique as a sign of God's own creative self. But what is our image of God? Do we conceive of God as a creative relationship, rather than a confessional formula? What is the Christ we believe in? How do we interpret Jesus' message? Our praxis will come from what we believe in and the images we have of God.

Interreligious Dialogue

In our context, the interreligious/intercultural dialogue appears as if it is being done for academic interest because, in practice, it has not developed many new relations or structures. For theologians and many people in ministry, this activity is seen as suspicious and almost dangerous. The desire for this dialogue seems to be coming from a position of superiority and power with the intention of communicating a truth from within certain cultural paradigms where it was formed.

This experience tells us something different. Dialogue requires cultural reciprocity and symmetry. The history of seeing the other has been marked by words like idolatry and paganism. The church sees the process of evangelization so far as incomplete and calls for the need for a "new evangelization," with a paradigm of inculturation. However, this term still poses a problem. It tells us that, although we respect your culture, the message to be transmitted is superior to it and others from outside the culture, such as theologians and church officials, speak for the Mapuche. Notwithstanding the good intentions of this inculturation perspective, the Mapuche voice has not been heard and will not be heard officially in the church. The Mapuche people have not been able to communicate their vital and profound experiences in the dialogue, which raises questions about the dialogue. What experiences are being heard, and how do we interpret those experiences?

Back to the experience of the symposium, we listened to each other from the heart, trying to understand the profound meaning the other was trying to communicate. In the end, all experiences are different. But in this process, we are able to value and appreciate them.

The theme of power came up several times. Acknowledging this is key to a productive dialogue that is different from domination and imposition. The power is in the community, and it is given by the people. The power comes from the community and its identity. Fear also comes from power, as if something can be taken away if I share it with someone who is different.

As we spoke about diversity, we considered it necessary to go from an anthropology of diversity, which is an always present reality, to an anthropology of complementarity. As in the forest, diversity generates life; the new comes from diversity. The *pueblos originarios* keep something that is vital to conserve the equilibrium and the harmony of all. With this practice of dialogue, it seems that we are starting to value what is diverse as complementarity. The idea is not to homogenize and see the wisdom found in the other. As Paul Knitter stated,

> It is not the objective of the interreligious dialogue to impose uniformity of rites, symbols, beliefs, and worldviews, either to reduce each religion's identity into one religious universe or even to agree on religious or philosophical differences or doctrinal issues . . . The differences will remain even after the dialogue, but the easy disqualifications and unfounded mistrust will disappear.[7]

This implies that the interreligious dialogue is not an imposition but the ability and the willingness even to disagree and come to consensus. This has not been a historic reality in our context. The *pueblos originarios* have lived in subordination, which has put them in a place of inferiority. And when this takes places in a dialogue encounter, real dialogue is not then possible. Considering the subordination experience, we need to facilitate an intracultural process together with a process of decolonization. The church in this respect, I humbly offer, ought to be able to accompany this process to ensure a truly intercultural dialogue and, in turn, participate in its own process of conversion, as individuals, as a church, and as a people.

The gospel experience has life-giving power and requires to be good stewards, taking care of and being responsible for our neighbor. When we say that God has power, God is giving life to all: "I came so that they [you] may have life and have it more abundantly" (John 10:10, NAB).

Questions and Challenges that Have Emerged from this Experience of Dialogue

The following are some theological and anthropological questions that need to be addressed in order to advance in a more life-giving dialogue. I am sure that these questions have already been raised in other contexts, which would make them even more relevant and urgent today.

- Diversity is the most natural experience to human beings. We need to constantly ask ourselves what blinds us from seeing that plurality belongs to our nature as humans.

---

7. Knitter, "El Diálogo Interreligioso." The translation from Spanish is mine.

- We accept that, in the postmodern era, there are no certainties. Plurality and incertitude are the rule, and we are in constant tension, experiencing a lack of balance and instability. What are the insecurities that keep us from encountering the diverse other?

- We are sojourners. It is in the journey with others that we find identity: I am son, brother, father . . . How am I accompanied by, and how do I accompany, others on the journey?

- Even when we build individuality and community, there is a consciousness that we are with others. The relational or relatedness aspect of life and identity is paramount to individuality. The individual identity is a collective identity. With whom am I? How am I formed by others?

- We have experienced that vulnerability is what allows us to relate to others: it is the image of emptying oneself, an experience of kenosis. What are the prejudices and fears I need to let go of?

- The experience of Jesus is not an experience of religion per se, but a spiritual experience within the life of humanity, where love and empathy, as kenosis, were transversal in all aspects of human life: *Dios que se abaja* (God who came down to us). This is so important at the level of intercultural dialogue, in *lo cotidiano de la vida* (the day-to-day of life), as well as in the structure of societies, cultures, and religion itself.

- We are more aware of the fact that culture is dynamic. It develops by interacting with the other. If that encounter is in a genuine dialogue, it can be transformative and creative for a new identity. You continue being Mapuche or Christian, but with new horizons. You can be Christian and Mapuche at the same time. What does intercultural dialogue mean to you? Am I open to learn?

- As the church, we need to recover the image of the people of God, which we have not been able to wholly experience as the inclusivity of God, which includes all of life and creation. Are we as God's people as welcoming?

- The challenge of interculturality is also for the church as structure and as theology. How are the church and theology able to integrate in their reflections what is holy and true from the *pueblos originarios*?

- The intercultural dialogue is a spiritual process which will lead to transformation, producing small steps to encounter the other. It is a gradual process of growth toward transformation. Are we willing to be transformed in the process of dialogue?

- Intercultural dialogue is a sign of the times; it is the spirit that irrupts through the diversity in the world and in cultures. Do we believe in the Spirit that creates and makes everything new?

This process of dialogue we have developed must continue if we want to deepen reflection on these questions. The idea is not to obtain new formulas or final answers, but to understand ourselves in relationship to God, nature, and our neighbor. By doing so, structures and thought patterns might change to become more conscious of the needs of the other to be complete. The path of our personal journey must also be the path of the Christian community. The church must learn the path of kenosis by being more gospel and less religion, namely by paying more attention to Jesus' mission and words in context than to the cultural expressions of the faith as absolute structures.

I would like to end with the following text from the Book of Wisdom that challenges us to see the graciousness of an inclusive and caring God who loves all creation:

> But you have disposed all things by measure and number and weight . . .
>
> Indeed, before you the whole universe is like a grain from a balance,
>
> or a drop of morning dew come down upon the earth . . .
>
> For you love all things that are
>
> and loathe nothing that you have made;
>
> for you would not fashion what you hate. (Wis. 11:22–24)

Regional Indigenous Theological Voices and Responses

D: Mexico

8

Mayan Indian Theology: A Journey of Decolonizing the Heart[1]

PEDRO GUTIÉRREZ JIMÉNEZ

Greetings

I give my heartfelt thanks to all the people who were so kind to invite me to participate in this exchange of pastoral and theological decolonizing experiences. Accepting this invitation was difficult because the written word has never flowed easily for me. So, here I am before you to share what my eyes have seen, what my ears have heard, what I have learned on the path with my people, what my dreams have made me, what my great teachers have awakened in me, and what God continues to spark in my spirit. I'm grateful to our grandfathers and grandmothers for this opportunity they have given us. I'm grateful to life for allowing all of us to meet here at this event. I'm grateful to the universe and to those who came before us on the journey.

I. My Life Was Marked by Dreams

One night I dreamed that:

> I was at the foot of a great mountain, and there was a cave that one could enter.

> Someone told me to enter the cave.

> Once inside, I was handed two precious stones.

1. Translated by Karen M. Kraft and Michel Andraos.

I took them, and once in my hands, they changed into traditional musical instruments of my people.

Playing the strings brought forth songs of the great prophets . . .

Then I left the cave, went behind the great mountain, and sat down beneath the trees.

It was an unfamiliar place to me.

Then, people of different ages began arriving; they sat down next to me in a circle.

They asked me to speak, to tell them who I am, where I come from, and where I am going.

I spoke. I don't remember what I told them, but I watched their joy as they listened to my words.

When I was seventeen years old, I began to read the Bible in search of something that could give meaning to my life, something that could guide my way, or something that could inspire my heart in the face of the marginalization and poverty that we in my community were living in.

A strong desire to serve my people was born in me. "Shall I do that by becoming a lawyer or a priest?" I asked myself. I was not sure of the answer, and the question kept spinning in my head. Talking to my parents about my dream of becoming a priest was something unthinkable for them. Meanwhile, I used the little shack where we would store corn as a prayer space at night. It was a space to listen to and lighten my heart, a place to speak alone with God. After several nights, I began to have repetitive dreams. They provided me with a lot of clarity about God's invitation for my life, and I felt it was an invitation to serve through the priesthood. With great difficulty, I left my home and my community to enter the diocesan seminary in San Cristóbal. At the same time, I felt the desire and great necessity to learn about my ancestors, to better understand my own culture, and to accept my Tzeltal blood, name, and family name.

In my home and my community, I was always jPetul.[2] When I started high school, I wanted to reject my Tzeltal self in order to be accepted among the *mestizo* student population. But when I entered the seminary, I felt accepted as I am—with my identity, my history—and at the same time, I felt accompanied on the journey to encounter the spirituality of my ancestors. I would like to take this opportunity to thank all of the people who welcomed

---

2. Editor's note: "Petul" is "Peter" in the Tzeltal language, and "j" is the prefix used for men's names.

me into the diocese: the pastoral ministers (the missionaries, both men and women), the elders and people of my community, the seminary rectors, my advisors, and especially jTatic Samuel.[3]

II. The Emergence of Indigenous Theology in the Diocese

The seminary opened its doors to me and allowed me to connect with the diocesan pastoral programs. It made it possible for my heart and spirit to reconnect with the communities that preserve the spiritual practices of my ancestors and, at the same time, get to know some pastoral ministers who highly value the Mayan culture.

My heart opened to drink from the two fountains of spirituality. The seminary gave me what I needed to understand the Christian faith, and the Indigenous communities—along with their elders—began to fill my heart with ancestral wisdom. From the beginning, I felt deeply that both spiritualities fulfilled my expectations, and that the two paths made possible what I longed for in the depths of my heart.

I proposed to the rector that he allow me the opportunity to speak with the team of the National Center for Assistance to Indigenous Missions (CENAMI), so that, together with jTatic Samuel, they could help me pave the way for the formation that I desired from the depths of my heart.

My trip to Mexico City to speak with the priests at CENAMI and jTatic Samuel coincided with the First Latin American Meeting of *Teología India* (Indigenous theology) that was held in Mexico City in September 1990. Among those invited to that meeting were four priests from the diocese of San Cristóbal who had a long history working in Indigenous ministry. At the meeting, I also encountered Alberto Velásquez, a Jesuit seminarian who at that time was just becoming familiar with the San Cristóbal diocese. We both had a strong desire to participate in the meeting, but we weren't invited. When we spoke with the CENAMI team, they told us that there wasn't any space left for us. But then we made our case to jTatic Samuel, who told us that we could stay, and that he personally would talk with the event coordinators. He also told us not to worry about meals and lodging, because that could be resolved through some of his

---

3. Editor's note: "Tatic" is an affectionate term for "Father" in the Tzeltal Mayan language. The people used this term to address Samuel Ruiz, bishop of the Diocese of San Cristóbal de las Casas from 1960–2000. He died in 2011 at the age of eighty-six. He embraced the preferential option for the poor and Indigenous people since the mid-1970s. Ruiz's great legacy is the promotion of the Indigenous church in the diocese of San Cristóbal. See the article by Jorge Santiago Santiago in this volume to learn more about the work and legacy of Bishop Ruiz.

acquaintances. And that's what he did. We stayed at CENAMI and participated in the meeting. It was a blessing for both of us. Doors opened, and
my formation began just as I wanted.

When the meeting concluded, jTatic Samuel and the diocesan priests
commissioned us to become part of the regional Mayan coordination of the
teología india group, in which Mayan people from Honduras, El Salvador,
Guatemala, and Mexico would eventually participate. The first task assigned
to us was to prepare and hold the first meeting of Mayan Indian theology in
Mexico, and then the first regional meeting, which we held in October 1991,
in San Cristóbal de las Casas, Chiapas.[4]

The start of the journey was far from easy. Many of the pastoral agents
in the Diocese of San Cristóbal had doubts and suspicions with regard to the
words *teología india*. The most persistent questions were these: What is Indigenous theology? Why do we need Indigenous theology if we already have
liberation theology? Why talk about an Indigenous church if we're already
building the church of the poor? Wouldn't an Indigenous theology immobi-
lize the people in their search for liberation? Wouldn't Indigenous theology
serve just to send us back to the past and the practice of witchcraft? What
would happen with the word of God in the Bible that has been accepted in
the peoples' hearts? And so forth. These concerns were not only in the hearts
of the pastoral agents, but were also shared by most of those among the first
group of catechists. The first catechists were certainly trained to teach the
word of God as written in the Bible, to create community awareness about
social reality, to teach new practices that would improve community life, to
combat practices that weren't life-giving to the community, such as alcoholism and witchcraft (the misuse of gifts given by God), murder, etc. But they
were also encouraged to do away with our own way of seeing, feeling, and
living life, our proper ways of relating to and communicating with God, the
universe, and Mother Earth. And so, our traditional ways were getting lost.
We were losing our heart as a people, and the spirit of our ancestors was
drifting farther away from us.

As a result, when we began to develop a *teología india* program, the
wise women and men elders found it difficult to embrace what had been
earlier rejected, mocked, and demonized. They felt as if they were trying to
eat something they had vomited. And the first catechists resisted accepting
Indigenous theology, because doing so implied recognizing the mistakes
they themselves and the missionaries had committed.

---

4. For a record of the Teología India Mayense meetings since they first started in
1991, see Coordinación Ecuménica de Teología India Mayense, *El Aroma de las Flores*.

To begin the profound awakening of our heart and spirit, we had to hold a ceremony to reconcile with our traditions and with the spirit of our ancestors. The main focus was to ask forgiveness for having allowed, or having contributed to, the destruction of our spiritual way. Representing the first catechists, the church officials present at the ceremony asked for forgiveness, while the other pastoral agents did the same on behalf of the first missionaries who came to these lands. With tears in their eyes, the representatives of our ancestral spirituality granted us forgiveness in the name of our grandmothers and grandfathers. We all felt a very heavy weight lifted off our hearts, and this event brought us much clarity and strength to continue our journey in Indigenous theology.

III. Some Concepts of Indigenous Theology

1. What is Indigenous Theology?

   After several meetings, we came to the conclusion that Indigenous theology is a phrase that communicates, shows, and accounts for the deep sense of the experience of God we have as Aboriginal peoples. This theology—or spirituality, as others call it—is not something that was born in recent years, but rather something that has been present at every stage of our history as peoples. It has been—and is—the ferment and strength of our journey.

   Indigenous theology or spirituality is present in the practices and reflections of the Christian churches that believe in the possibility of developing a synthesis between the two spiritualities. It is equally present in the traditional religions that preserve a large part of the Aboriginal spirituality, as well as in the Indigenous social movements of resistance.

2. Who Does Indigenous Theology?

   We recognize that the subject of Indigenous theology is the community. The community experiences God in every moment of its life and, therefore, gives birth to its own theology. Those of us who have been the initiators, promoters, or partners in the process undertake the work as if we were midwives who help the community to open its heart and speak of its own experience of God. The pastoral agents, professional theologians, and bishops who participate in our ecumenical meetings accompany us on this journey.

The original impetus for Indigenous theology came from some Indigenous and non-Indigenous pastoral agents from the entire continent. This was also the case in the Diocese of San Cristóbal and in the Mayan region, but very quickly the coordination changed hands to community and parish leaders.

The current leadership is rich and vibrant with the participation of young people; men and women representing the Chol, Tzeltal, Tzotzil, Tojolabal, the peninsular Maya of the Yucatan; and mestizo peoples. The majority of the pastoral agents on the current leadership team are Indigenous who have been trained or formed through workshops and certificate programs.

3. The Main Purpose of Indigenous Theology

The theology that we do isn't meant to be published in books or discussed within academic contexts. Instead, it's intended first and foremost to inspire, encourage, animate, and guide the life of our communities, and to nurture and strengthen the hearts of those working to care for and defend life, and for those who walk in solidarity with other Indigenous peoples who dream and build "Another Possible World," or the "New Home for All."[5] Indigenous theology is also a voice of protest against any system of death, as well as a voice of resistance in the churches against continuing a colonizing evangelization. It is an alternative voice calling for the construction of "Another Possible World" and "Another Way of Being Church."

That's why, on several occasions, our leaders who have been able to participate in meetings convened by the bishops' conferences have insisted on saying that "we as Indigenous peoples are not the world's problem; we are rather part of the solution." We seek to be active within the churches without giving up being Indigenous. In our journey of Indigenous-Christian theology, we are not seeking to leave the churches, but rather to remain within, with the full right of living out our faith with our own face and heart as Indigenous people.

4. Sources of Indigenous Theology

Indigenous-Christian theology draws from two spiritual paths. First of all, we acknowledge as our own source the hundreds

5. Editor's note: In Spanish, these two slogans are "Otro Mundo Posible" and "Nueva Casa para Todos"; both are well-known in social movement contexts, especially in Latin America.

or thousands of myths held in the heart of the elders; the Maya Codices;[6] the Popol Vuh;[7] the Books of Chilam Balam;[8] the Mayan Calendars;[9] the traditional rituals, ceremonies, music, and songs; the content of the prayers; the dances, dreams, symbols, etc. And second, from the path of Christian spirituality, we acknowledge the greatness and sacredness of the Bible, the liturgy, rituals, traditions, etc.

Because the Christian faith was imposed on us and the Bible considered the only source of revelation, it has not been easy for us to accept that the books and stories that come from our Indigenous spirituality are also the word of God.

6. Editor's note: For a helpful explanation, see Zorich, "Maya Sense of Time," 29: "The Maya Codices are bark-paper books, estimated to have been "written no earlier than the twelfth century AD . . . and used to set dates for rituals, often by linking them to astronomical events. The pages of the codices usually depict a deity and include a series of glyphs describing what the deity is doing. Many pages of these books also contain lists of numbers that allowed the Maya to predict lunar and solar eclipses, the phases of the moon, and movements of Mars and Venus." Nearly all of the Maya's written records were burned by Franciscan missionaries in the mid-sixteenth century, and today, only three authenticated codices remain, all housed in Europe; there is a fourth, in Mexico City, whose authenticity is disputed.

7. Editor's note: For a helpful explanation, see Newberry, "Popol Vuh": Popol Vuh, which means "Book of the Community" in the K'iche' Mayan language, narrates the Maya creation account, weaving together "stories concerning cosmologies, origins, traditions, and spiritual histories. It is considered by Mayans as their equivalent to the Christian Bible and is held in deep reverence by them."

8. Editor's note: For a helpful explanation, see "Books of Chilam Balam": The Books of Chilam Balam are "a group of documents written in Yucatec Maya [the language of the Maya of the Yucatan Peninsula] with Spanish characters during the seventeenth and eighteenth centuries. A principal source of knowledge of ancient Mayan custom, they contain myth, prophecy, medical lore, calendrical information, and historical chronicles. Although originally there were probably many documents, only a few remain. Those of Chumayel, Tizimín, and Maní (towns where they were written) are particularly important for Mayan history. *Chilam balam* means 'secrets of the soothsayers.'"

9. Editor's note: For a helpful explanation, see Smithsonian National Museum of the American Indian, "Calendar System": "the ancient Maya developed one of the most accurate calendar systems in human history . . . [they] had a fascination with cycles of time. The most commonly known Maya cyclical calendars are the Haab [a 365-day cycle that approximates the solar year and is divided into nineteen months], the Tzolk'in [a 260-day cycle that matches the cycles of the moon], and the Calendar Round [made from interweaving the Haab and Tzolk'in]. Aside from these, the Maya also developed the Long Count calendar to chronologically date mythical and historical events . . . This is very similar to the Gregorian calendar system that counts days, months, years, centuries, and millennia" (Smithsonian National Museum, "Calendar System," para. 1).

5. Language and Indigenous Theology

Our theology is not about discourses or books. Above all, it is about myths, symbols, and rituals. Thus far, it has been more a lived experience than a reflection or a discourse, and in this lies its strength and newness. The theological lived experience is what nurtures the heart and strengthens hope. Trying to put our experience of God into words is very limiting. Speaking, dancing, and being together in community with God is what fills our whole being. There are no words that can fully express all that is lived and felt. We have discovered that we cannot talk about the Creator and Maker if we have not first discovered or felt him in life, in Mother Earth, in the universe, in our work, and in carrying out the tasks that He himself has entrusted to us.

IV. The Road Traveled Thus Far

The beginnings of Indigenous theology in the San Cristóbal diocese were the result of several courses and workshops with some diocesan pastoral agents and ecclesial ministers from various parishes. There was a need to discuss the urgency of a dialogue on the topic of the gospel and our culture, as well as the necessity for a true work of inculturation or incarnation of the gospel message. It was important at that starting point to acknowledge that God was already present with our peoples long before the conquest and colonization and that, as Indigenous peoples, we also have a salvation history, sacred books, spiritual guides, wisdom, our own spirituality, and great prophets.

The courses and workshops mentioned above helped us to see in a different way our own history and the spirituality in traditional religion. Before beginning the process of Indigenous theology, the catechists had an attitude of rejection toward Aboriginal spirituality. They had been taught to say that, before the Bible and the Catholic Church arrived to our lands, our grandfathers and grandmothers were lost.

As we began to discover the importance of Indigenous theology for the emergence of the autochthonous church and feel its effect and force in constructing the project of "Another Possible World" and a "New Home for All," interest began to grow in the communities, parishes, and the diocese in general. As initiators of the process, we began to accompany parishes that weren't getting support from the diocese's pastoral agents. We also saw the need for strengthening the coordinating teams by inviting more participation of brothers and sisters from the grassroots, while at the same time we initiated a process for training new leaders.

At the moment, the coordination is well established. We assume responsibility together for reclaiming and strengthening our historical memory, our symbols, our myths, our spiritual guides—wise men and women—our sacred places, our ceremonies, our cultural values, our traditional music and dance, our sacred books, and our dream of a "New Home for All," or the *Buen Vivir*.

Indigenous theology has been growing in the heart of every person and in the hearts of communities and parishes at the regional as well as the continental levels. As Mexican Mayan peoples, we have held twenty-five encounters so far. In addition, at the level of Mesoamerica, we have held eight regional and eight general encounters.

The encounters of the Mexican Mayan Indigenous theology movement are normally supported by the participants and the parishes that host them. We have learned from the beginning that this process can only be sustainable if the local communities take on the responsibility of hosting.

On our journey, we have so far reflected on the following themes:

- Indigenous theology as the leaven that ferments and strengthens our efforts to construct a good world;

- Indigenous theology and spirituality and our Mayan altars;

- Indigenous theology and the youth, our offspring;

- Our spirituality of water, the wellspring of life;

- The spirituality of corn (*maize*) and our task to serve as its guardians;

- The spirituality of Mother Earth and our task to defend her;

- Our experience of God in migration;

- The *Buen Vivir* as our heart's dream and desire;

- The Mayan calendar as a path of spiritual growth.

V. The Methodology or Way of Indigenous Theology

Our Indigenous theology workshops and encounters normally attend to the following five steps:

1. Experience and Feel What Is Going on in the Life of the People.

   This theology is born out of the life of our communities, out of our experience of God, and in the life we are living. It's a life mixed with flowers and thorns, joys and sorrows. To do theology, we must live and feel life deeply as it is.

2. Share Life.

A second step is to share life's problems and pleasures, to join and bring together—in community—our sadness and joy. As theologians of the people, we search for, or create, the spaces where we can talk about what makes us brothers and sisters in our life experience.

3. Touch the Heart of God.

This is when, together, we decide to live a deep experience of God in a sacred place, which could be a cave, a hill, a lagoon, or a church. In the ceremony, we open our hearts and our spirits to listen to God's heart, to hear what God feels and says in response to the reality we are living, and to hear the desire or dream of God's heart for humanity.

The ceremony is a special space where we enter into the life of God in order to look at things through him as we separate ourselves from normal life and enter into God's life. The celebration helps us to open our hearts and our minds to find God's response to our needs. In the ceremony, we reflect on the sacred texts from our ancestors and from the Bible; we give offerings to God; we say prayers; we dance; and we pray for dreams.

4. Explain God's Response.

During or after the ceremony, there are those who hear, feel, see, or dream God's response. After finishing the ceremony and experiencing God's presence, some men or women elders of the community explain or interpret for us the response that God is giving to us. The service of reading or interpreting God's response is undertaken by those who possess considerable wisdom and hearts that are in harmony with the heart of God. At our encounters—with the help of the Spirit—we seek together to understand God's response or invitation. In this way, we relearn how to collectively look for God's response to our lives. Often, the message we receive is an invitation for us to take on a commitment or a task in order to change our lives and change our reality.

5. Build a New Reality.

Coming down from the hill or out of the cave, or leaving the celebration, we return to reality to live out what we experienced together with God. In this step, we bring back with us all the strength to work for changing our reality. We build a Mayan altar to celebrate being in harmony with ourselves, with Mother Earth, with all of creation, and with God. Afterwards, we strive to live out this harmony at home and in the community. In this step, we prepare to give witness in our daily lives to what we believe, what we celebrate, and what we say.

VI. The Current Situation of Indigenous Theology

Our awakening as Indigenous peoples continues to advance. We have quickly moved from a passive to a very active resistance, making our voice heard—in protest and proposals—in the churches and in society. In the churches, those of us who are promoting Christian Indigenous theology have affirmed that we want to be Christians without giving up being Indigenous. For the good of humanity and Mother Earth, we must sit down to dialogue respectfully with openness of heart and spirit.

For many, our awakening as Indigenous peoples is a reason for joy, but it also causes worry and fear for others. In the institutional church, there are those who support and accompany us on our theological journey, and there are those who see our awakening, and speak of it, with fear and suspicion. And there are also those who openly speak out against Indigenous theology and search for ways to stop it. However, it is clear to us that there is no turning back on this journey.

The Catholic Church and some Protestant churches have been gradually transformed, especially in terms of statements, from being aggressors against Indigenous spiritualities and theologies to becoming our main allies in restoring and strengthening them. The Diocese of San Cristóbal, in particular, has gone a long way in this area. The Third Diocesan Synod (1995–99) and the diocesan pastoral plans of the last ten years acknowledge the contribution of Indigenous theology and make clear commitments to strengthen it. In practice, however, instead of carrying out the commitments of the pastoral plan, many pastoral agents ignore or obstruct the development of Indigenous theology. In the Protestant churches, the situation is more difficult, and there is still much work to be done.

In the reality in which we live as Indigenous people, we keep finding again and again that our spirit is rejected, and our sacred spaces, our history as seen by our grandfathers and grandmothers, our elders, our myths and symbols, our ceremonies, our gifts and charisms, our sacred books and texts, our spirituality, and our dreams are forgotten.

On our journey, we have realized how important it is to ensure that we have an ongoing support system for all the processes we have started. In particular, we invite and impassion the hearts of the new generation to be nourished by the wisdom and spirituality of our ancestors. Currently, many young men and women are drinking from the wells of ancestral wisdom. They are awakening and finding their own path and their own task and mission. There are five to six hundred representatives of the Indigenous theology program who come to the annual encounters. More than thirty percent of them are young people.

We continue to work toward reconciling the two spiritualities—the Mayan and Christian—that dwell in our heart. We continue to break the hold of what makes us deny who we are, where we come from, and where we are going. It has also been important and necessary to initiate a journey of reconciliation with the men and women elders of (non-Christian) traditional religious practice. They are spiritual guides for us, and together we can strengthen our spirituality, protect life, and defend Mother Earth.

VII. The Fruits of Indigenous Theology

The following is a summary of some concrete contributions Indigenous theology has made at the local community level. As Indigenous theology groups,

- We joyfully undertake and celebrate our work in the evangelization of our communities, and we collaborate resolutely in the building of an autochthonous church.

- We contribute to strengthening the prophetic voice of our communities, parishes, and diocese.

- We reclaim and integrate into our Christian celebrations our traditional symbols, signs, ritual drink, music and dance, and our myths and sacred books.

- We reclaim and strengthen our ceremonies for traditional healing, Mother Earth, water, crops, sowing, protection of life, occasions of taking on communal responsibilities, etc.

- We reclaim the importance of dreams in our personal, family, and community life. We interpret dreams together in community as we seek clarity and strength for our journey.

- We are restoring the sacredness of our myths and holy books such as the Popol Vuh and Chilam Balam and are reflecting on these books as God's word in our workshops and encounters.

- We reclaim our Mayan calendars as a path to human and spiritual growth, and as a guide to living in harmony with ourselves, with the community, with Mother Earth, and with all of creation.

- We seek that our hearts be one, even though we walk two different spiritual paths, so that we can cultivate life and defend Mother Earth.

- We recognize that the strength of our resilience to defend life lies in prayer, and for that reason, we make pilgrimages to our sacred places to nurture and strengthen our hearts to live out our mission.

- We recognize and celebrate the contribution of Indigenous theology to the journey of our communities in the different pastoral regions of the diocese. Indigenous theology contributed to the Third Diocesan Synod and to the pastoral plans of the diocese and parishes.

- We recognize our dignity and appreciate the seeds God has sown in our hearts and use that in service of a better life for our communities.

- We feel empowered to continue to strengthen the autochthonous church and to add our efforts to the building of "Another Possible World."

- We see more young people, men and women, participating in our encounters. They value the wisdom of our grandfathers and grandmothers, and their word is heard at these encounters.

- We see more involvement among parish Indigenous theology representatives in coordinating encounters and in the accompaniment of community programs.

- We have awakened as a community to protect and defend our Mother Earth, our territories, our native seeds, and our rivers, lakes, and springs from the threats of megaprojects such as mining, hydroelectric power, genetically modified corn, superhighways, etc.

- We recognize the importance of continuing to bolster our cultural values and our spirituality, because they are our strength and leaven in building the *Buen Vivir*, our collective dream as a people.

VIII. Challenges Ahead and Final Thoughts

We have learned many lessons in the twenty-five-year journey of Indigenous theology. There have been suffering and fatigue, setbacks and advances, disappointments and hopes. There have been many rewards in the personal, family, community, and parish lives of those of us who have been developing and mentoring these programs. Nevertheless, we realize that the road ahead is still long. Several of the men and women pioneers on this journey are no longer with us, but we know that they are watching over us from another place and they are walking with us. The following are some of the important challenges we are facing, as we think about the future. We need to:

1. Ensure that our Indigenous theology doesn't lose its vitality and mission and that it continues to awaken hearts and consciences, generate a spirituality that protects life and defends Mother Earth, serve as a leaven that strengthens the development of alternative ways of life, and bolster the autochthonous church in the diocese.

2. Inspire more participation by women and the younger generation—children and young adults—in the community and parish programs of Indigenous theology, and seek creative ways to pass on to them the ancestral wisdom and spirituality and to train them to live and carry out the mission they are discovering.

3. Continue to create spaces for the Indigenous spirituality and theology present in traditional religion, Christian churches, and Indigenous movements to be encountered, nourished, and strengthened.

4. Keep working to decolonize our minds, hearts, and spirits and, at the same time, help churches to overcome their colonizing attitude and ways of thinking.

5. Take on the task of systematizing our Indigenous spirituality and theology in order to continue to strengthen our communities, share our experience with other sister theologies, and prepare for genuine dialogue with Christian churches and theologies.

We realize that, when our hearts and spirit have fully awakened as Indigenous Mayan people, we will take the paths that make us feel the freest to sing our own songs, dance our own dances, think our own thoughts, speak our own words, live out our mission on this earth, and strengthen the *buen vivir* that we will leave to future generations.

May God grant that our hearts unite, that our colonized minds and hearts are healed, and that the colonizing minds and hearts of others are transformed in order to unite our spiritual efforts and energies to make possible the creation of a more human and divine world for everyone and everything.

9

Accompaniment in the Process of Dialogue-Encounter with the Indigenous Peoples from the Diocese of San Cristóbal de las Casas, Chiapas, Mexico: 1969–2019[1]

J. JORGE SANTIAGO SANTIAGO

The signs of the times are, in the first place, a call to a commitment to a historical situation. And only because I commit myself to that historical situation, I am able to interpret it. An outside interpretation is not an authentic interpretation of a sign of the times.

—GUSTAVO GUTIÉRREZ[2]

To evoke the faithful Holy People of God is to evoke the horizon to which we are called to look and reflect. It is the faithful Holy People of God to whom as pastors we are continually called to look, protect, accompany, support, and serve.[3]

—POPE FRANCIS

1. Translated by Michel Andraos. The original text that was presented at the November 2016 conference was translated by Paloma Cabetas; the version published here, however, was revised by the author for publication and underwent significant revisions.

2. In its June 1972 issue (Vol. 1, no. 4), the journal *Estudios Indígenas* (Indigenous Studies) of the National Center of Indigenous Pastoral Work (CENAPI) published the following three articles that illustrate the theological and historical discussion going on at that time in relation to the Indigenous people: García, "Ecclesiology and Pastoral Commitment," 3–16; Santiago Santiago, "Theology, the Bible, and Indigenous Mission," 17–36, a transcript of a conversation with Gustavo Gutiérrez and the CENAPI team of theologians that the author of this chapter coordinated; and Santiago Santiago, "Autochthonous and Foreign Indigeneity," 37–43.

3. Francis, "Letter to Cardinal Marc Ouellet."

Introduction

Pope Paul III created the Diocese of Chiapas on March 19, 1539. The diocesan territory was divided twice: first in 1957, when the Diocese of Tapachula was created, and another time in 1965, when the Diocese of Tuxtla Gutiérrez was created. After the partition, the Diocese of Chiapas changed its name to the Diocese of San Cristóbal de las Casas, which is still the current name.[4] Fray Bartolomé de las Casas arrived in these lands in 1545 as their first bishop. Although two other bishops were named before him, they were never installed and never came to Chiapas.

Bishop Samuel Ruiz García was the last bishop of Chiapas and the first of the Diocese of San Cristóbal. He was consecrated in the city of San Cristóbal on January 25, 1960, and died on January 24, 2011. He was the ordinary bishop of the diocese for forty years (1960–2000). He had a coadjutor, Bishop Raúl Vera López, from October 4, 1995 to December 29, 1999. The current bishop, Felipe Arizmendi Esquivel, took charge of the diocese on May 1, 2000. Until recently, he had a coadjutor bishop, Enrique Díaz Díaz (previously an auxiliary bishop), consecrated in San Cristóbal on July 10, 2003. On March 11, 2017, Bishop Díaz was transferred to the Diocese of Irapuato.

The majority of the diocese's population—about 63 percent—is Indigenous, belonging to five main different ethnic groups: Tzeltal, Tsotsil, Ch'ol, Tojolabal, and Mestizos. There are also communities who speak other Indigenous languages such as Lacandón, Zoque, Chuj, and Kanjobal. The Mestizo population speaks Spanish.

A Personal Note

Allow me to share my personal story of involvement in the diocese, which I believe would be helpful for understanding the breadth of this process of pastoral accompaniment, both for me personally and in the diocese. I began collaborating with the diocese as a layperson in 1969 and had previously studied theology. I participated in different ministries such as the formation of catechists, the emerging process of the Indigenous diaconate, and sometimes in the reflection sessions of the Indigenous theology groups. I have collaborated in supporting various diocesan structures since the First Diocesan Assembly of 1975, when the option for the poor was proclaimed. I also participated in activities related to the Third Diocesan Synod (1995–1999) and in the

4. The territory of the diocese of San Cristóbal covers an area of 36,821 square kilometers. The official current population of the diocese is 2,039,592.

creation of the recent Diocesan Pastoral Plan of 2016. I regularly collaborated with the analysis of reality teams and in the work of mediation over which Bishop Ruiz presided as part of the National Commission of Intermediation (CONAI) between the Mexican federal government and the Zapatista Army of National Liberation. This work began with the Dialogues of the Cathedral in 1994 and lasted until 1998, when CONAI was dissolved.

My close collaboration with Bishop Ruiz allowed me to establish a profound dialogue with him that is expressed in two published interviews I conducted with him: "Seeking Freedom" and "The Passion to Serve the People."[5] In 2010, I prepared the guide to the Museum Jtatik Samuel in San Cristóbal that was inaugurated on January 27, 2015. The museum serves as an educational and community center to remember, celebrate, and promote the legacy of Bishop Ruiz.

Since the time I was involved in the formation of catechists, I have participated in research for learning about the situation of the Indigenous peoples and understanding their history, how they were exploited, and how their identity and cultural values were denied. For a period of time, I was part of the National Center for Indigenous Pastoral Work's working team (1972–74) and also collaborated with the international meetings of the Missions Department of CELAM (Latin American Bishops' Conference). After that, I returned to the Diocese of San Cristóbal and started working in DESMI, A.C. (Social and Economic Development for Indigenous Mexicans), founded in 1969. I worked with DESMI from 1974 to 2008, first as executive secretary and then as coordinator of the organization until 2004. The work of DESMI and my experience are discussed in three published books.[6]

It has also been very important for me to accompany the experience of the *Pueblo Creyente* (the people who believe, or people of faith), a process of organizing the participation of the communities of the diocese through representatives who have a clear sense of their prophetic mission as Christians. This movement, which I will discuss below, emerged in 1991 and is now twenty-five years old. Another important moment for me was participating in founding the Commission of Support to Unity and Community Reconciliation (CORECO) in 1996; I currently serve on its board. I was also part of

5. For an edited English version of the first interview, see Andraos, *Seeking Freedom*. Both interviews will be published in the forthcoming book by Andraos, *Church with the Indigenous Peoples*.

6. DESMI, *Si Uno Come que Coman Todos. Economía Solidaria* (*If One Eats, All Should Eat: An Economy of Solidarity*); DESMI, *Cuarenta Años de DESMI* (*Forty Years of DESMI*); and Santiago Santiago, *Economía Solidaria Política* (*A Political Economy of Solidarity*).

the board of directors of the Fray Bartolomé de las Casas Center for Human Rights, founded in 1989, and also currently serve on its council.

I also came to understand the accompaniment process for approaching this dialogue-encounter with Indigenous peoples in the diocese through a profound collaborative relationship I developed with several International Agencies of Cooperation for Development. These NGOs include organizations such as Catholic Relief Services and Thousands Currents in the United States; Oxfam in England and Belgium; Novib in the Netherlands; Entraide et Fraternité in Belgium; Development and Peace, Steelworkers Humanity Fund, and Horizons of Friendship in Canada; and the Catholic Committee against Hunger and for Development (CCFD) in France. My experience working and collaborating with all of these organizations often placed me at the intersection of their work with Indigenous communities.

All of the above is to say that, in reflecting on the theme of the church and Indigenous peoples and the process of pastoral accompaniment, I cannot but think of this journey of long duration—it gives background to, and helps flesh out the meaning of, what I am going to say below.

I. Accompanying a People on a Journey

I would like to begin by citing a speech by Bishop Ruiz in 1971, which I believe reflects the church's thought about the cultures of Indigenous peoples since that time, and which has inspired our work. His speech, I believe, was like the spark that ignited the prairies. It was an address to the pastoral encounter organized by the CELAM Missions Department in Iquitos, Peru, in March 1971, entitled, "The Latin American Church in the Cultures: Pastoral Challenge and Hope."[7] Bishop Ruiz was the president of this CELAM department at the time. The following excerpts summarize the central points of his address, including the main idea that awakened our enthusiasm to go and encounter the cultures of Indigenous peoples and to put aside our eagerness to impose our ways of thinking and structures on them:

> If the dignity that the cultures carry prevents us from crushing even what is secondary in them, even more it demands that we respect their religion, which is an essential and binding element of the aboriginal cultures. The Second Vatican Council in *Dignitatis Humanae* in fact affirms: "Injury therefore is done to the human person and to the very order established by God for

---

7. Ruiz García, "La Iglesia Latinoamericana," 13–22.

human life, if the free exercise of religion is denied in society, provided just public order is observed."[8]

Therefore, our missionary action tends precisely to convert to disciples of Christ those who do not believe in him. We want paganism and mythologies to disappear ("Therefore go and make disciples of all nations, baptizing them in the name of the Father and of the Son and of the Holy Spirit, and teaching them to obey everything I have commanded you," Matt 28:19–20, NIV). To replace mythology with Christianity: does that not mean destroying the very nucleus of a culture? What does then the missionary action consist of? To be missionary, is it to merely contemplate a culture with our arms crossed, giving just an example, a witness with our own lives? Is it to build a culture archeologically, by bringing it back to its primitive splendor? All this does not sound like evangelizing. Is there, anyway, in the transcendental destiny of the human being a reason that justifies smashing a culture? If it were so, why did God allow the existence of cultural pluralism in the history of the human race? (Alfonzo Torres Laborde, *Antropología y Evangelización*. No. 1, Departamento de Misiones del Celam: Bogotá, 1969, p. 308.)

Fortunately for us, Christianity is not a mere dogmatic theology; it is not a code of moral laws; it is not an explanation of the visible world; it is not a culture, nor does it identify itself with any culture; it is not, even if this expression might seem absurd, a religion (supposing that religion is the movement, the human effort to approach the divinity through acts of purification in order to communicate with the divinity). Christianity is the movement of a God who, through the Incarnation, enters the history of the human race in order to give us an eschatological and transcendental dynamic. Christianity is an event; it is a history of salvation.

Through creation, God communicates with human beings . . . moreover, the Trinitarian family chose a different way: it became "event" in the Son and in this way the eternal "word" that expresses all that the Father is, from whom he proceeds, and by whom he is sent, became man by the action of the Holy Spirit without ceasing to be God. And the humanized Word, diluted in the sea of time, reduced to a calendar date, resounds in the whole history of the human race to the point that a natural history of humanity no longer exists; it has become a history of salvation.[9]

8. Second Vatican Council, *Dignitatis Humanae,* 3.
9. Ruiz García, "La Iglesia Latinoamericana," 16–17.

This theological reflection by Bishop Ruiz resonates very well with the accompaniment of a people who acquire awareness of their own values and rights after awakening from the lethargy of prostration, to which they have been subjected, and rebel against the structures of domination of all kinds. In the Diocese of San Cristóbal, this process has remote origins connected to significant events such as the following:

- the First Indigenous Congress, celebrated in San Cristóbal de las Casas in 1974;

- the celebration in 1992 of five hundred years of resistance and of Indigenous, black, and popular struggles;

- the emergence of EZLN (Zapatista Army of National Liberation) in 1994;

- the Agreements of San Andrés on Rights and Indigenous Culture in 1996;

- the convocation of the National Indigenous Congress in 1996;

- and finally, the long fight for the rights and the defense of territory that has mobilized the Indigenous peoples around the world.

These instances are all examples of confrontation with the power structures and strategic interests of the established system of dispossession and destruction.

On the church's side, we began to witness a deeper understanding of this history of resistance and rebellion. Since the 1970s, the church has begun to make the reality of the Indigenous peoples its own, reflecting and acting upon it and trying to understand its theological meaning and pastoral implications. For example, in 1975, the Diocese of San Cristóbal was able to publicly proclaim an option for the poor and Indigenous. A few years later, in 1993, Bishop Samuel Ruiz wrote the landmark pastoral letter, "En Esta Hora de Gracia" ["In This Hour of Grace"],[10] giving voice to the cry of the diocese's Indigenous peoples. One year later, in January of 1994, he put himself at the service of mediation to seek agreement through dialogue in the war between the Mexican Federal Government and the EZLN. In 1996, he generated the momentum needed to help create CORECO, just as he had done earlier with other diocesan organizations: DESMI, A.C., in 1969; the Fray Bartolomé de las Casas Center for Human Rights in 1989; and the Christian Committee of Support to Guatemalan Refugees in the 1980s. And in order to deepen hope, he convoked and celebrated the Third Diocesan

---

10. Ruiz García, "En Esta Hora de Gracia," 591–602.

Synod (1995–1999), which was a pastoral process of reflection on the diocesan journey of accompaniment. The synod involved all the communities,
people, and organizations of the diocese.

It is important to acknowledge that, in this dynamic process of accompaniment, the Indigenous communities were present and participating from
the beginning. The process engaged their thought, clarity, commitment,
cultural values, language, rituals, history, suffering, struggles, and rebellions,
which were all expressed in their own reading of God's presence in the concrete events of their lives. This process of accompaniment was the fruit of
work realized over many years by a multitude of catechists—both men and
women, youth and adult—committed in different ministries. The service of
the Indigenous diaconate was born precisely from the heart of this journey
of liberation as a particular ministry in the communities who were building
a church of the people on their journey searching for liberation.

During the same period, we witnessed the emergence of women's
movements which were committed to changing the situation of marginalization, mistreatment, and violence that existed within the internal structures of both the local communities and the church itself. These movements
were especially important within the context of the war of extermination in
which women became targets of war through military and police violence.
Through our pastoral work and social commitment in the diocese, we began
to understand the situation of women and their role in awakening our conscience through interpreting the word and work of God from the perspective
of their reality. At that same time, the Coordinación Diocesana de Mujeres
(CODIMUJ—in English, the Diocesan Women's Coordination) emerged; in
2016, it celebrated its twenty-fifth anniversary on this journey.[11]

On this same journey, two other significant movements were born in
1991 that were the result (in a way) of the strategic objectives of the long process of accompanying the organized people of the diocese through conflict
and war, seemingly endless and part of a larger global situation. These two
strategic movements are 1) the rise of *teología india* (Indian theology) at local
and continental levels and 2) the *Pueblo Creyente,* a movement of Christians
experiencing the reality of exclusion and exploitation who are committed
to building a reign of justice, truth, and peace. This second movement was
born from the heart of an organized, vibrant, illuminated people, relentlessly
marching with a prophetic vision toward the future.

For us in the Diocese of San Cristóbal, what I have described so far is
a summary of the initial vision of the Spirit's salvific action in creation and
the one history of salvation, in which the people of God are made up of all

11. For more information, see *Con Mirada, Mente y Corazon de Mujer.*

the peoples with their own cultures and with different forms of knowing regarding the action of the word in the life of their communities and in the world. Evangelization in this context meant discovering step by step, with the community, what God is doing among the people. It also called for a commitment to live with the people who walk seeking their liberation, which makes it possible to face the new challenges with hope.

In the same vein, in recent years the diocese has held two congresses: the Theological Pastoral Congress in 2010 and the Pastoral Congress of the Earth in 2014. These events brought together the teachings from our journey up to this point and launched us into the future. In 2016, we completed the Diocesan Pastoral Plan, which integrates the work of these two congresses.

II. The Encounter with Cultures and the Emergence of Indigenous Peoples as Subjects

To this day, I can vividly remember witnessing the birth of the *Pueblo Creyente*. I also vividly remember passionately following the unfolding of events at the time of the First Declaration of War from the Selva Lacandóna of the EZLN and all that followed: the shift of the Indigenous communities' position, announcing they would not resort to violence again; their denunciation of war as capitalist; and their efforts for building different forms of autonomy. These movements, rooted in the Indigenous communities, have not given up since. They continue to exist and resist, notwithstanding all the systemic violence exercised against them.

In the church, the teachings of the Second Vatican Council and the document entitled "Pastoral Work in the Missions of Latin America"—the final document of the First Continental Encounter of Missions in Latin America held in 1968 in Melgar, Colombia[12]—helped us to understand the concrete reality of Indigenous peoples in a new way. And they helped us become open to seeing a new dawn in the struggle and voice of the people. These teachings also help us understand the claim and denunciation contained in the January 1971 Declaration of Barbados, which analyzed the destruction of the Indigenous peoples and their cultures.[13] The Declaration

12. This meeting took place April 21–27, 1968; in Spanish, the document is titled "La Pastoral en las Misiones de América Latina."

13. The full text of the Declaration of Barbados is available online at www.lacult. unesco.org/lacult_en/docc/Barbados_1971.doc. The Declaration was a public statement that came out of a symposium on "Inter-Ethnic Conflict in South America" held January 25–30, 1971, in Barbados. A gathering of anthropologists, the symposium was sponsored jointly by the Programme to Combat Racism and the Churches Commission on International Affairs of the World Council of Churches, together with the Ethnology

of Barbados publicly called the whole world's attention to the situation of the Indigenous peoples in South America, and it was a call to responsibility for nations, religious missions, and anthropologists. It also recognized the full rights and full capability of the Indigenous peoples to create their own historic alternatives of liberation.

It is in this context that we in the diocese began to reflect on the church's control mechanisms and their role with regard to colonialism. As pastoral workers, we began to understand the mandate of dedicating ourselves to what we called the "theology of cultures." One of the theologians who elaborated on this theme in the 1970s and helped us in our work was John F. Gorski, MM. A new commitment to the study of the reality was born in the church during this period. This was the beginning of a process—which is still ongoing—of acknowledging the existence of the Indigenous peoples with their own voice. This was also the beginning of acknowledging the social, political, and economic conditions in which they lived, and learning to accompany them with their culture and their capacity to transform situations that comes from their deep core of resistance, and from their very existence as a people.

The collective experience of a church walking this path called for us to take seriously and listen to the critical thinking of Indigenous catechists and other representatives of their communities. This experience of accompaniment has also deepened the theology and the people's prophetic denunciation. We can say that this process succeeded in creating new moments of grace, intercultural dialogue, prayer, forgiveness, and we also acknowledge what remains to be done.

During this same period, it was also wonderful to enter into the new space of recognition of women, acknowledging their voice, wisdom, strength in resistance, and care for and defense of life. They did not harbor aggression in their spirit and kept their own voice, their proper language, and their capacity to organize themselves and claim justice, equality of rights, and their place as subjects in liberation history.

We had to change paradigms and understand the place and the moment of each action so as not to replace, dominate, or exclude, but to wait for the dawn. This was the fruit of the commitment and attention to the movements that were taking place throughout the world, searching for other ways of wisdom. This was also a welcome change from previous experiences—based in colonial logic—of imposition and negation of the ways of thinking.

Department of the University of Berne (Switzerland).

In order to explain my understanding of the current challenges in the Diocese of San Cristóbal, I would like to share with you a paragraph that was included in the Diocesan Pastoral Plan of 2016, which was formulated in consultation with the Indigenous communities and approved in the Diocesan Assembly of May of 2016. This particular paragraph (No. 150) is a citation from "Desafíos para el Caminar Diocesano" ["Challenges for the Diocesan Journey"], a presentation I gave at the diocese's Theological Pastoral Congress of January 2000:

> Finding alternatives at all levels definitely requires finding an alternative to submissiveness. This is the way to avoid returning to the situation which we are trying to get out of: we want to move away from domination; therefore, we undertake to follow other paths and for this, we build a new home for everyone. It is for this reason that we defend our territory, and why we seek reconciliation and dialogue. And for this reason, every day, we invent new ways to resist, to maintain unity, to integrate our past into our future, to live the present fully, and to root ourselves in our land, in our community, with our parents and our brothers and sisters. This is why we are still alive. We want to reach another place: a place of respect, of participation, of speaking the truth, of struggling to transform the relationships of submissiveness and together build the community and well-being of everyone. The result of this great effort is peace with justice and dignity. In other words, this is the way to build peace with justice and dignity.[14]

III. Key Points for Accompaniment

In this section, I would like to reflect on how the emergence of the Indigenous peoples—with their spirituality and theology—is taking place in the church. These processes in the church, if they continue with consistency, are a commitment that directly touches the deep roots of Indigenous peoples who are often threatened, defeated, and persecuted in a society that seeks to destroy their communities in pursuit of strategic resources.

It is true that the church has contributed, from a faith perspective, to the Indigenous peoples' process of emergence, taking into account the difficult history of that relationship. However, the ecclesial efforts dedicated to accompanying Indigenous peoples have not yet produced great results. Church structures resist change and still have a long way to go. They often

14. Santiago Santiago, "Desafíos para el Caminar Diocesano," para. 150.

shut themselves up in the castle of absolute truth. We need to work more from within the church, from within these structures, so that they better accompany the people in their processes of change. We seek the transformation of the local churches in light of a new consciousness of the Indigenous reality that is taking place. We seek the possibility of a reconciliation of the church with the Indigenous peoples and a dialogue along this journey of accompaniment. There are still many challenges on this journey.

As we reflect on the last fifty years, it is important to recognize, theologically, the encouragement and clarity of the Vatican II documents in relation to the pastoral mission in Latin America. In our own context, in our local history of Chiapas, we need to reflect on the systemic work we have accomplished in the Third Diocesan Synod (1995–99), the Pastoral Theological Congress of 2010, the Pastoral Congress of the Earth in 2014, and the Diocesan Pastoral Plan of 2016.

As previously mentioned, the year 2016 marked the twenty-fifth anniversary of two strategic movements: *teología india* and *Pueblo Creyente*. We are celebrating these anniversaries by remembering the historical events we lived through, so that we can responsibly assume the challenges of a new period in defense of truth, life, and liberty.

The 2016 anniversary year, however, was also a long year of mobilizations, social protests, clashes, and unrest. There are no positive signs of good governance; the government is strengthening its strategy of Indigenous territorial occupation and social control by increasing militarization and social programs for this purpose. We have not been able to open ways of communication with the government in order to reach agreements and find solutions for the fundamental demands of justice, democracy, and respect for the rights of the peoples and in defense of life against the pillaging and violence of many political and military groups who are linked to the trafficking of humans, natural resources, and drugs. The situation is serious.

At the same time, we witness the response of the people and the Indigenous communities in their resistance and their self-development. We have hope because we know that we have walked together for so long in the midst of conflicts, oppression, and suppression—more than five hundred years of exploitation and destruction.

The Indigenous communities are engaged in a process of profound decolonization and are committed to constructing alternatives to the systems of domination. They are doing this in a situation of conflict and in the face of the war of counter-insurgency that attempts to weaken and exhaust them. And this war is managed by the same systems of economic, political, and military power from which they are seeking liberation.

On the other hand, we are facing the undeniable fact that the Indigenous peoples and their communities are the subject of their own history of liberation. The ultimate goal of this journey of the people is the exercise of their autonomy. This is a practice that entails a great show of strength and concepts that are present in the geography and ecology of their resistance and rebellion. To this point, I would like to quote anthropologist Giovanna Gasparello, who studies Indigenous peoples and their movements of autonomy:

> *Autonomy*, that is, *self-governance according to one's own norms*, is an individual and collective right that implies freedom of action—economic, political, juridical, and social—of the collectivity within the Nation-State and its rights to participation and political representation. Autonomy, as an expression of self-determination, is a *right* recognized to the indigenous peoples in the international and national legislation, but it is above all a *practice* in daily life of organization, a process of resistance, and an articulated political project that proposes distinct relationships between the indigenous peoples and the State, and the transformation of the society in terms that are alternative to the neoliberal system.
>
> The discourse and the practice of autonomy, in its distinct formulations, demand the legitimacy of the forms of indigenous organizations. This implies the right to difference against exclusion; it also demands the right to equality in access to resources, to social rights, and to full civil participation.[15]

Within this reality of Indigenous autonomy, what shape will the dialogue of the Indigenous peoples and the communities take within the church? How does a new possibility for dialogue emerge from the perspective of the Indigenous peoples? These are some key questions for further reflection.

IV. What We Have Learned

By way of conclusion, I would like to list some of the key learning points in this process of accompaniment of the Indigenous peoples as pastoral agents in the church and in general. First, learning means to be present with the people and there for the long haul. We learned that the subjects are the Indigenous peoples themselves, with their proper culture and dignity, their worldview, their being, and their long historical experience of

15. Gasparello, "Indigenous Autonomies in Mexico," 84.

being colonized and exploited. We learned from them what it means to be subjects. We learned from their energy to build the future. We learned about dialogue. The result of dialogue is what we see now and what could be considered their resistance and the blossoming of their culture. We learned about interculturality, autonomy, resistance, and about how they defend the territory. We learned that these are collective and nonviolent processes. We learned to acknowledge the wisdom and strength of those who were forgotten. We also learned how to read the strategies and structures of the powerful, as well as how to read their weaknesses.

What is the role of theology in all of this? We need a theology that is committed to the struggle of Indigenous peoples and their concrete reality. A theology that acknowledges the existence of the Indigenous peoples, with their own culture, history, resistance, and faith reflection. A theology that is creative and transformative, and that is not afraid of contradicting orthodoxy, as Pope Francis is teaching us. We are on a long faith journey that seems endless and that is always getting deeper and stronger. We walk in the full light of day. We have the great certainty of faith and hope; there is no faith without hope.

*Regional Indigenous Theological Voices
and Responses*

E: The United States of America

10

Lakota-Christian Dialogue[1]

FRANCIS WHITE LANCE

My White Lance Heritage

My great-grandfather, Daniel White Lance, was one of three brothers who survived the Wounded Knee Massacre on December 29, 1890. His brothers were Joseph Horn Cloud and Iron Hail, also known as Dewey Beard. White Lance and Beard had also fought at Little Bighorn, in what is often referred to as Custer's Last Stand.

I was born Francis Charles Apple Jr. When I was a teenager, my paternal grandmother's brother, John White Lance, son of Daniel, asked me to change my name. He was the last surviving male member of the Oglala White Lance family, and he wanted me to honor the family name. In 1994, his widow and I went to the courthouse in Pine Ridge, South Dakota, to fulfill her promise and mine that I would become Francis White Lance.

Joseph Horn Cloud and Dewey Beard both converted to Catholicism, and Joseph was a catechist and prominent church member. My paternal grandfather was also a catechist in the Roman Catholic Church. I was baptized Roman Catholic, made my first communion, and had my early theological training with Jesuit priests and Franciscan sisters in Rapid City, South Dakota. My high school education was at Holy Rosary Mission, now called Red Cloud Indian School after the Oglala Chief who had asked the Jesuits to establish a mission for education on the Pine Ridge Reservation in 1925. I was and still am very much at home in the Roman Catholic Church.

---

1. This article is an edited compilation of previously published texts. See White Lance, "My Friend," 24–29; White Lance, *Why the Black Hills are Sacred*; and Barbour and Schreiter, "Plural Spiritualities," 75–90.

Roman Catholic and Episcopalian

My mother and father were considered to be in a mixed marriage, because she was Episcopalian and he was Catholic, so he joined her church and studied to become an Episcopalian priest. I had a lot of church background. My grandmother told me to stay Catholic: "No matter what happens, don't join their church." The whole family did become Episcopalian, but I always knew that I was Catholic. If I went to Mass and the priest did not know me, then I could take communion. If they knew me, I couldn't.

Grant's "Peace Policy"

In 1869, President Ulysses S. Grant established a "Peace Policy" with the stated plan to remove corrupt Indian agents who were charged with supervising reservations and replace them with Christian missionaries.

> In reality, the (peace) policy rested on the belief that Americans had the right to dispossess Native peoples of their lands, take away freedoms, and send them to reservations, where missionaries would teach them how to farm, read and write, wear Euro-American clothing, and embrace Christianity. If Indians refused to move to reservations, they would be forced off their homelands by soldiers.[2]

This resulted in the oppression of our people through the loss, not only of land and natural resources, but of our culture, language, and history. We were denied the right to practice our traditional spiritual rituals and only regained the legal right to practice them in 1978 with the passage of the American Indian Religious Freedom Act. As a result, many of us found ourselves as adults without a connection to our traditional spirituality.

The Government and Missionaries

Among the many consequences of Grant's "peace policy" was the collaboration of the US government and missionaries from different Christian denominations. Practically speaking, denominations and religious orders were allotted different reservations and/or different sections of reservations in which to establish churches and schools. Some tribes, through their chiefs, invited religious orders because of their reputation as educators. The Pine Ridge Reservation was divided up as 40 percent Roman

---

2. Trafzer, *American Indians/American Presidents*.

Catholic, 40 percent Episcopalian, 5 percent Presbyterian, and 5 percent other. Each church began boarding schools where children were removed from their homes and punished for speaking their language, forced to have their hair cut, and forced to wear Euro-American clothing. In a sense, the US government helped to determine which, if any, Christian denomination native people joined. The government sent missions from the Episcopal and Catholic churches to "Christianize the Indians." My paternal great-grandfathers and grandfathers were Roman Catholic. My mother was raised as an Episcopalian.

Renaissance of the Traditional Ways

Not everyone became Christian as a result of the intentions of Grant's peace policy and the work of Christian missionaries. However, practicing the traditional rituals and spiritual practices was forbidden. Two of my teachers, Gilbert Yellow Hawk and Tillie Black Bear, often spoke about how they and others had to practice the Sweat Lodge and other ceremonies in secret, hiding from both the police and priests. This often created division and confusion in families, with some members following the teaching of Christian churches and others following the traditional ways. In the 1970s, there was a renaissance, with more people practicing the traditional ceremonies and rituals. With the 1978 passage of the American Indian Religious Freedom Act, more and more people gradually participated in traditional ceremonies such as the Inipi (Sweat Lodge), the Sun Dance, Vision Quest, and Lowanpi, or healing ceremony. I will come back to these in the following pages.

Recovering What It Means to Be Indian

When I was young, I asked one of my grandfathers to teach me the Indian ways. He pulled out a Bible. I said "No, I want to learn the Indian ways." He said that it was in the Bible. "To be like Jesus is to be Lakota. Jesus was a good Lakota. To be like Jesus is to follow our way." As an adult, after serving in the US Air Force and obtaining a BA in philosophy, I wanted to follow my own call to become a priest. It was during my studies at Seabury-Western Theological Seminary in Evanston, Illinois, that I began a journey to learn more about the traditional ways of my people. Other Native American students at the seminary introduced me to Rev. Dr. Claude Marie Barbour, professor of world mission at Catholic Theological Union and an ordained Presbyterian minister.

Through my work with Claude Marie and her students, I began a more serious study of my own Lakota culture, traditions, and spirituality. She asked me to speak to her students about Lakota culture and spirituality. I wanted to be a good teacher and represent my people in a good way. As I prepared my presentations through reading, conversations with others, and reflecting on my own life as a Lakota, I started to gain a greater pride in my identity, culture, and spirituality.

I traveled with Claude Marie and students to the Rosebud Reservation and met the medicine man who would become my mentor, Gilbert Yellow Hawk. I worked with him until his death in 1990, learning about the spirituality, rituals, and teachings. I was already a Lakota speaker, which was important in my ability to learn from Gilbert and other traditional mentors, the majority of whom were most comfortable in Lakota. They had learned from their fathers, grandfathers, and mentors how to practice the ceremonies, sing the songs, and pray to the spirits in their native language.

Two Mentors

My theological studies at Seabury-Western Theological Seminary and the guidance I received from Gilbert, Tillie Black Bear, and others helped me on my own spiritual journey. Gilbert taught me to find spiritual lessons in everything. He encouraged me to use my education to look for truth beyond learned rules and patterns of behavior, and to be respectful toward all people. He "put me on the hill" for the first time when I went for a *hanbleciya,* or Vision Quest. During my time at Seabury-Western, I asked Gilbert to come to Evanston and help me introduce the seminary community to Lakota spirituality. I was growing in my Lakota identity even as I was studying Christian ministry. Today I am a Christian, an ordained priest in the Anglican Catholic Church in America. I am also a medicine man, a Sun Dance leader, a traditional spiritual leader, and I follow the ways of the sacred pipe. My uncle Leonard Crow Dog calls me a "scholar for the Lakota way of life."

Tillie Black Bear, a tribal leader and national leader for the struggle against domestic violence, taught me that traditional Lakota culture and spirituality emphasizes behaving in an appropriate manner toward all life. True respect is given and received when we live as if we are related to all that is. The Lakota prayer, *mitakuye oya'sin,* translates to mean "we are all related." We are related to the two-legged, the four-legged, the swimming, creeping, crawling, flying, the rocks, earth, air, water.

Christian and Traditionalist

I don't see any difference if I say I am a Christian or a Traditionalist. It is just a tradition or traditions that I am living by—two rich traditions. I don't act as a Christian when I am leading a Sun Dance. In the Sun Dance, I am following a tradition that is thousands of years old, so I don't think about Christianity at all, nor do I think about it in the sweat lodge. When I am asked to do a baptism, or last rites, then I follow the Christian tradition, and I don't mix the two. Then I am a priest, not a medicine man. I don't have a church that I am responsible for, but I am under a bishop. He is aware of what I do, and he will tell me if he thinks I am going too far. He is perfectly fine with my being a medicine man. It is the same God. The same God . . . It is the same God, and there are two different ways of worshipping God and living out that way of believing in God. They are together in me, but I do not practice them together. The other thing that is important to me is that, if I talk about Christianity, my lifestyle had better show it. So, if I say I am Christian, then I better be like a Christian. If I say I am a Traditionalist, then I better be like one, too. You won't find me in a bar or things like that. Both Christianity and a Traditionalism ask that I be a role model, that my lifestyle reflect what I preach and teach about. You are responsible to other people.

Difficulties from Within and Without

The process of becoming a priest and a Traditionalist was not always easy. The racism and oppression suffered by my people at the hands of the government and Christian churches were not always subtle during my seminary studies. That is one of the reasons that meeting Claude Marie Barbour was so important to my ability to discover and claim the traditions of my grandfathers. Claude Marie affirmed my identity and helped me to find strength in my culture. I became able to look beyond the "Indian" labels of poverty and addiction. These labels exist not only in the minds of many non-Indians, but also in the minds of many Indians as the result of internalized oppression.

When I was in my last year of seminary at Seabury-Western, my father was involved in an incident that became life-changing. An elderly Episcopalian man, Mr. Two Crow, passed away, and since his family members were devout Episcopalians, they knew all of the local priests. Rev. Lyle Noisy Hawk (who was ordained but detailed to work off the reservation in a non-Indian parish) had returned home for a vacation. The family asked Fr. Lyle to participate in the funeral of their father. Fr. Lyle is an enrolled member of our tribe. The Episcopal Diocese of South Dakota had just installed a new bishop. He reprimanded Fr. Lyle for participating in the funeral without the permission of the bishop. When this happened, Fr. Lyle asked my father, Fr. Apple, who was superintendent presbyter at the Pine Ridge Indian Reservation at the time, to accompany him to the diocesan offices to help explain about the culture. Fr. Lyle thought the problem was that the bishop hadn't worked with Indian people before. All of this went before the canonical court and articles were published in the newspaper. Because of this, my father was fired. He was later ordained by the Anglican–Catholic Church in America. I loved my father and supported him. I decided, along with Ray Takes War Bonnet and Alvin No Horse, to join my father and be ordained in the Anglican-Catholic Church. I think this story reveals some of the ongoing misunderstanding non-Indians have about our culture.

The renaissance in the 1970s, when more Lakota took part in traditional ceremonies and practices, highlighted the conflict that many Lakota Christians felt about their relatives and friends participating in the sweat lodge, the Sun Dance, and other ceremonies. The priests and catechists had always taught that these practices were evil and pagan. There is more acceptance now. In fact, many Christians can be found at ceremonies and praying outside the Sun Dance circle. Some commit to dancing themselves, a promise of dancing a total of four days each summer, over four years. While more people accept and practice the traditional ways than did before this renaissance, there are still many who do not know, understand, or practice the Lakota spirituality. At the same time, the painful memories of the boarding schools and teachings of the Christian churches have turned people away from the church. While teaching Lakota history and culture at Oglala Lakota College (in Kyle, South Dakota), at the high school, and at elementary levels on the reservation, I recognized how little people knew about their own culture and spiritual heritage. The following paragraphs give some of the teachings and descriptions of the ceremonies and rituals.

The Teachings

The ancient teachings that tell us how the Lakota should live our lives are handed down in stories. *Tokahe* (the first man) is *watogla* (wild and free). He is born from a hole in the earth and the center of the universe. From this hole, he emerges from four worlds. This is how a spirit joins the material world.

Tokahe dreams of a Bow and Seven Sacred Arrows. This dream comes from the *Pte Oyate* (Buffalo Nation). *Tokahe* is given the name *Wahinkpe*

Hoksila (Arrow Boy). This dream becomes the first *Wolakota* (Treaty of the Universe). The *Pte Oyate* sacrifice their lives so that the people who make and live this covenant will have shelter, food, and clothing. The humans of this covenant will be called *Lakota* (Peace Makers). It also means that the Lakota will live according to Seven Laws:

- *Wayuonihan* (Respect)
- *Wacante Ognaka* (Generosity)
- *Woksape* (Wisdom)
- *Wacintanka* (Fortitude)
- *Woohitika* (Courage)
- *Wowahala* (Humbleness)
- *Waunsilayapi* (Kindness)

After an eon of time, *Wahinkpe Oikpakinte* passes away. The Lakota wait for another great leader to come to them. *Inyan Hoksila* (Stone Boy) is born to them. Stone Boy brings the *Oipakinte Tipi* (Sweat Lodge) and gives instruction on how to use it to the Lakota. Stone Boy is a savior and prophet. The Lakota live an easy life with Stone Boy and soon become spoiled. They forget the Seven Laws and begin to abuse their powers.

The Buffalo Nation challenges Stone Boy and the *Lakota* people. Stone Boy tells the people, "Don't be afraid, I am with you." Stone Boy throws seven round stones into the air, and they fall down, becoming a giant stone wall around the Lakota. Stone Boy gets outside the wall and battles with the Buffalo Nation. The battle sounds like a mighty thunderstorm as the buffalo break their horns hitting Stone Boy. After nearly killing all of the buffalo, they give up and leave. In the commotion, *Wakinyan* (the Thunderbird) takes up for the buffalo and uses lightning, hail, and rain to flood the whole earth.

Stone Boy's body and great stone wall are shattered to pieces to become *He Sapa* (The Black Hills). All of the Lakota die in the flood, except one girl who is saved by a *Wambli Hoksila* (Eagle Boy). After the flood subsides, the eagle turns into a young man and marries the Lakota girl and begins the Lakota nation again.

The Seven Stones turn into the seven Sacred Sites or seven Sacred Mountains (*He Sapa*, the Black Hills):

- *Pe Sla Paha* (Bald Mountain), the geographical center of the Black Hills.

- *Inyan Kaga* (Stone Mountain), the geographical representation of the Buffalo Skull in the Black Hills which tells us when the Sun Dance is ready to take place. Also, the stars begin to line up on the horizon to give us the appropriate time for the Sun Dance ceremony.

- *Mato Tipila*, the Bear's Home (Devil's Tower). This represents the gathering of the tribes in the annual Sun Dance for the Seven Council Fires of the Great Sioux Nation.

- *Mato Paha* (Bear Butte), which represents the salvation of man in the Great Race and is the site of the annual Vision Quest.

- *Wakinyan Hohpe* (Harney Peak) or the Thunderbird's Nest, where the Thunder Beings perform their ceremony every spring.

- *Pte Oti Kinapapi* (Wind Cave), where the Lakota people emerged from the spirit world to the surface of the earth. The human beings were spirits of the buffalo below the earth. When they came up, they turned into creatures that were two-legged (humans) and four-legged (buffalo).

- *Tatanka Tatiopa* (Buffalo Gap), which represents the east gate to the *Hocokan,* or circle of red earth that surrounds the Black Hills. The sun comes through this gate to illuminate our world.

The Seven Sacred Mountains combined with the red earth circle, the Black Hills, to become a geographical medicine wheel. When photographed by satellite, the area of the Black Hills is shaped like a heart: *Wamaka Cante Ognaka* (the heart of the earth).

Star Boy and the Sun Dance

These seven Sacred Mountains will be where the Lakota can seek vision in order to restore the Seven Sacred Laws. This set the stage for the *Wicahpi Hoksila* (Star Boy) to bring the Sun Dance and for *Wicahpi Hinhpaya Win* (Falling Star Girl) to bring the Sacred Pipe.

Morning Star's son, Star Boy, was born of a star and an earth mother. One day, Star Boy dreamed of the Sun Dance as a way to bring healing from the sky to the earth. Star Boy was the circle altar on the earth, which became the Sun Dance circle. In the sky, Star Boy then saw the circle altar, which includes the Pleiades, Orion, Gemini, and Sirius (the bright star). These two altars line up on June 21, the summer solstice, the time of the Sun Dance.

Seven Ceremonies of the Sacred Pipe

1. *Wiwayang Wacipi* (Sun Dance): Translated in Lakota as Sun Dance, it should actually be translated as "observing the sun." The sun is a witness to four days of commitment to dance and fast. Other names for the Sun Dance are Sacred Circle, Mystery Circle, Sacred Hoop, and Medicine Lodge. The Lakota way of life is based on the Sun Dance.

2. *Inipi* (Sweat Lodge): This is the ceremonial wiping clean of the body while the spirit cleans your soul in the steam bath.

3. *Hanbleceyapi* (Vision Quest): This is the oldest of the Lakota sacred ceremonies in which a dream guides the individual on a spiritual path by directing him/her in four ways: *Miye* (individual), *Tiwahe* (family), *Lakota* (community), and *Oyate* (nation).

4. *Wanagi Wicauhapi* (Keeping a Ghost): Respect and remembrance of a deceased loved one is the reason we do this ceremony. We keep the "soul" of the one in honor for one complete cycle (the four seasons) and to let them leave us after this period of grief.

5. *Isnatiawicalowanpi* (Sing over a Young Girl): In this ceremony, a young girl is to spend four days alone with mentors to begin the process of adulthood. The mentors instruct her in the duties of a woman and teach her to be caretaker of the family.

6. *Topkaholyapi* (Throwing of the Ball): This ceremony expresses the value of generosity in the "giveaway" to everyone who catches the ball. This is a formal commitment by those who throw the ball in this ritual, and also by those who catch it, to live the Lakota way of life.

7. *Hunkapi* (Making of Relatives): The *Hunka* ceremony means that an individual is adopted by a family. But a deeper understanding is that the person gains the right to wear a symbol of *wakinyan oyate*, the medicine wheel with an eagle feather attached. Wearing this symbol means that your voice will be recognized in the spirit world by your name. Your prayers will be heard because you are in the Thunder Clan.

Conclusion

My concern for my people is the reason I do what I do as a Christian priest and a Traditionalist spiritual leader. Without an understanding of where we come from, our culture, and spirituality, then we are lost. Young people are growing up today without belief and spirituality, whether Christian or traditional. I hope that my work, my teaching, my prayers, and my life will serve as good guides.

11

Steps Toward Reconciliation:
The CTU-Lakota Relationship

ROGER SCHROEDER, SVD

Let me begin by stating how much I appreciate being invited to speak at the conference on "The Church and Indigenous Peoples in the Americas," cosponsored by the Catholic Theological Union (CTU) and DePaul University, and to contribute to the publication of the proceedings. First of all, I am so glad that such an event has finally been organized to bring together Indigenous and non-Indigenous peoples from across the Americas. Secondly, this allows me an opportunity to draw together my thoughts and reflections from the experience of the relationship of CTU with the Lakota people. I hope that this conference and the publication of the presentations may improve the network of understanding and action around common concerns and commitments related to the original inhabitants of the Americas.

Encounters with Indigenous Peoples: An Introduction

My encounter with Indigenous peoples actually began over forty years ago. I arrived as a seminarian with the Divine Word Missionaries (SVD), a Roman Catholic missionary order, for the first time in Papua New Guinea (PNG) in 1975, one month after the country's political independence. I would eventually spend a total of six years in PNG over several periods of time. For five of those years, I lived and worked in rural village communities that depended upon subsistence farming and a traditional cultural-religious worldview for their livelihood, and did not have access to electricity, running water, telephones, or paved roads.

One of the many things I learned fairly quickly was that the category of "religion" is a Western idea, since it seems that none of the more than seven hundred languages of the Melanesian people of PNG have a word for "religion," as there is not a sharp separation between religion and culture, or between the spiritual and material. I would learn so much about the traditional worldview of what is today often referred to as bio-cosmic religion by listening, observing, and being particularly attentive to their symbols, rituals, and sacred myths. Much of this became focused around the elaborate traditional male initiation rituals—eight stages over forty years from childhood to elderhood—which were resurfacing after being absent for about twenty years. This invitation by the people to observe and learn about this set of rites of passage provided me an opportunity to begin to appreciate and understand their worldview and spirituality, which brings meaning, order, and identity to their lives.[1] In addition, I began to understand my own worldview and that of my family, religion, and nationality much better.

However, more important than gathering knowledge and gaining insights into worlds of meaning, I began to learn how to approach another people with respect, how to be a learner, and how to acknowledge and face my own prejudices. Furthermore, this is dependent upon, slowly and appropriately, developing relationships with Indigenous people and sharing their daily life experiences, as much as it is possible and appropriate (for me as an outsider and for the insiders). This experience in Papua New Guinea provided a very important background for my future life and work.

My second major encounter with Indigenous people began in the early 1990s when, for the first time, I went to the Rosebud and Pine Ridge reservations of the Lakota in South Dakota. This journey continues today. It is an honor to be here today at this conference sitting next to Francis White Lance, whom I have known for twenty-five years. I have learned so much from Francis and his wife, Suzanne, their children, and their friends, especially Ray, who died several years ago. I have listened to the teaching of Francis on the Sun Dance ground, in a sweat lodge, in his classroom, and in his home. The focus of this essay shall be on my journey with the Lakota people—a journey which is ongoing.

Before I describe this experience, I will provide a brief overview of the relationship of the church and Indigenous peoples, particularly the Lakota. I will then describe the relationship between CTU and some Lakota people, from CTU's perspective, and finally how this has affected my/our understanding of mission theology and practice.

---

1. Schroeder, *Initiation and Religion*.

The Church and the Lakota People: Historical Context

At a conference like this, it is probably unnecessary to describe much of the history of the relationship between the church and Indigenous peoples, since we are all quite familiar with this. But let me give some background that is particularly relevant to the Lakota people, from my understanding.

The Lakota—together with the Nakota and Dakota—were inappropriately called the "Sioux" by the US government, who used the name, which means "snake," given to the Lakota by their enemies. The Lakota followed the migration of the buffalo herds across the plains. Following the massacre of the buffalo, Western diseases, violent conflicts with the US army, broken treaties, and other atrocities, a millennial "Ghost Dance" movement emerged on the plains, with the hope of restoring proper balance in Lakota life. As part of their response, the US military massacred over three hundred Lakota men, women, and children and disposed of their bodies in a mass grave in the winter of 1890 at Wounded Knee, which is situated on Pine Ridge reservation. (Francis White Lance had family members at that massacre, and the site is just ten miles from his current home.)

The US government then forbade Native Americans the right to celebrate their cultural-religious rituals. This ban would not be lifted until the second half of the 1970s—an attempt at cultural genocide. In terms of the church, on the one hand, some missionaries and other church leaders devoted their lives to what they considered "bettering" the situation of Native Americans, but at the same time, many of them blended their mission theology and practice with the manifest-destiny vision of the government. Priests and pastors on the neighboring Rosebud reservation would copy down the license plate numbers of the cars parked around homes where Lakota rituals were being performed in secret in order to provide this information to the local police and government authorities. The church was also running boarding schools where children received an education for the "new world," but they also had their traditional hair cut off and were punished for speaking their own language.

A change of consciousness began to appear in the United States in the 1960s and 1970s: the American Indian Movement (AIM) was formed in the 1960s; the best-seller *Bury My Heart at Wounded Knee* by Dee Brown was published in 1970; the Bureau of Indian Affairs (BIA) building in Washington, DC, was occupied by AIM and supporters in 1972; the "Second Wounded Knee," with a seventy-one-day siege by the FBI, occurred in 1973, and was followed by three years of what Pine Ridge residents describe as a "Reign of Terror" by a private militia known as the "goon squad"; in 1977, AIM activist Leonard Peltier was convicted, and today remains under federal custody for (allegedly) murdering two FBI agents on Pine Ridge. This was a period of great upheaval, but also an indication of changes to come.

During and after these unsettling years, some medicine persons raised their voices to alert the Lakota that the key to recovering their rights and identity was a recovery of their traditional spirituality. The American Indian Religious Freedom Act was passed by the US government in 1978. Many Lakota returned from the cities to the reservations. This was the beginning of what some Lakota call a "Native American Renaissance." In terms of the church, denominational committees and conferences on Native American ministry were started in the 1970s by the Methodists, Presbyterians, and Roman Catholics (Tekakwitha Conference). The interdenominational Protestant Native American Theological Association began in 1977, and the ecumenical Native American Project of Theology in 1978. The 1970s was a decade of new beginnings, but there was and is still a very long way to go.

CTU and the Lakota People: An Ongoing "Case Study"

The relationship of CTU with the Lakota people began within this context: In the late 1970s, Rev. Claude Marie Barbour, a French Presbyterian minister and then a CTU faculty member, was invited by some non-Lakota church personnel to speak with them on the Rosebud reservation. Several young Lakota boys heard this white missionary woman speaking differently from others and introduced her to Moses Big Crow, a blind medicine man. Conversations and relationships began. During return trips to the reservation, Claude Marie got to know and foster a mutual relationship with Tillie (Matilda) Black Bear, a Lakota woman who started the White Buffalo Calf Woman Society, which offered shelter on the Rosebud reservation for battered women, rape victims, and their children. In the 1980s, Tillie brought Claude Marie into her family circle through the *Hunka* ("Making of Relatives") ceremony, one of the seven sacred rituals of the Lakota. Tillie, who died in 2014, described the significance of this mutual and holistic relationship in this way:

> In the *Hunka* ceremony, there is great care in how the people are chosen to become *Hunka,* and when the ceremony itself is done, it is a sacred ceremony. In fact, the song they sing is sung to all six directions, so that all elements in the six directions will know that this person now belongs to this family ... The *Hunka* ceremony with Claude Marie set the foundations for how we are related and what the responsibilities are for her as the oldest

daughter in our family. The biological family also has responsibilities towards the *Hunka*.[2]

Through this important relationship, Claude Marie—and later, fellow CTU colleague Eleanor Doidge—brought one or more ecumenical groups of students from CTU and other members of the Presbyterian Church to the Rosebud every year, and eventually also to the Pine Ridge reservation. The participants were prepared to listen to and learn from Lakota teachers, including Tillie and, later, Francis White Lance and others. In the words of Tillie, her work with Claude Marie was based

> on the premise that when these people come to us, they are given an insight into themselves, not only as individuals but insight into the world that they represent to others and to themselves. If they go out into the world to work as missionaries based on what we have shared with them and what they have experienced here at Rosebud, then they can be more respectful of other cultures and other ways of thinking and doing things.[3]

One can only marvel at the significance of such a relationship between some Lakota people and some people of the church just a few years after the horrible conflicts of the 1960s and 1970s between Indigenous and non-Indigenous peoples and societies. It began, essentially, as a relationship of trust between two women, but expanded quickly through their social networks.

I was in one of these groups in the summer of 1991, after joining the CTU faculty. I was touched and surprised that the Lakota were immediately so trusting as to invite us to participate in the sweat lodge purification ritual (*inipi*, which means "to live again"), which my government had forbidden them to practice for almost nine decades. I realized this was possible due to the relationship of trust initiated and maintained by Tillie and Claude Marie.

In those years, I was also introduced to Francis White Lance when he was completing studies at Seabury-Western Seminary in Chicago. Claude Marie had invited Francis to speak about Lakota culture for a course through the First Presbyterian Church of Evanston; Francis describes the importance of this encounter with Claude Marie in his chapter in the first part of this publication.

Francis White Lance became a key Lakota teacher and friend of Claude Marie, Eleanor, and others whom they accompanied to the Rosebud and Pine Ridge reservations and who, as a collective group, became known

2. Black Bear, "Hunka," 18.
3. Black Bear, "Hunka," 22.

as "Chicago." Through my many trips to the Lakota reservation—first as a participant and later as a co-facilitator, but always as a learner—I have seen how "Chicago" persons are transformed through this experience. Before the trip, they are prepared to acknowledge their own social location and prejudices, and to *listen* to the voices and stories of the Lakota. On the reservation, they continue to learn how to understand and respect the experience and worldview of the "other" from the perspective of the "other." However, this requires "letting go" of their own agendas and of "being in control." One member of the "Chicago" group described it in this way:

> That week, I came to see that part of the answer was learning how to turn off one's own presuppositions, to shift from a frenetic future-oriented culture that rewards high-tech productivity to a slower, lower-tech culture that is more about one's presence—with other people, but also within the immense, delicate weave of God's ongoing creation. This is why our time on the reservation could not be defined as an "agenda."[4]

When the members of "Chicago" are able to be open to and vulnerable in the world of the other, they can be both enriched and challenged in many ways. First of all, many of those who are US citizens become more aware of the injustices and oppression inflicted on Native Americans by their government in the past and the ongoing racism, socioeconomic poverty, and marginalization that continues in the present. They often need to acknowledge their sense of guilt, but eventually move beyond that to proactive change. As novelist Rudy Wiebe wrote, "You repent, not by feeling bad but by *thinking different*."[5]

Secondly, some of those who traveled to the reservation have had their own experiences of colonialism (and post-colonialism) or other forms of marginalization or oppression (due to ethnicity, nationality, "race," gender, etc.). Often, they have not been fully aware of how such experiences have impacted and shaped them. They are challenged and encouraged to value and learn more about themselves—about their own culture, roots, and spirituality. As Francis White Lance often tells us, "Don't try to become Indian, but get to know your own story." When we enter the world of the "other," we need to know ourselves.

Thirdly, all those who make this "journey" to the Lakota world have the opportunity to experience deep transformations of their attitudes toward others and toward ministry/mission in general. Through this relationship between CTU and some Lakota, the "Chicago people" are

4. Montgomery-Fate, "What Are We Doing Here," 91.
5. Wiebe, *Blue Hills of China*, 258.

being prepared to minister with others in a very respectful way—crossing cultural, religious, generational, and ecumenical borders. A couple of them may continue to work with Native Americans—like Sr. Barbara Bogenschutz, OP, who continues to minister on Pine Ridge—but most will do this around the world, like Fr. Peter Tam Tran, SVD, who lived and worked for some years with aboriginals in Santa Theresa, an aboriginal community outside Alice Springs, Australia.

Years later, many trip participants still recall the words of Violet Crow Good Voice, Tillie's sister. After sharing her own story of facing the challenges of living on the reservation and working in ministry with a variety of Catholic missionaries over a period of twenty years, Violet offers those preparing to be ministers and missionaries the following advice based on her experience. She encourages them: "Go with an empty cup and let the people fill it," so that they (the trip participants) can learn and be enriched by the people. What an image for a new understanding of the relationship between the church and Indigenous people!

Reflecting on the above description of the CTU-Lakota relationship, one notes that it is based on an initial, traditional *Hunka* ritual, which formalized a mutual relationship between Tillie and Claude Marie. It then drew in Tillie's extended family circle and Claude Marie's extended family of "Chicago." Both circles were and are somehow transformed in various ways through the activities and conversations they share. This relationship, like all relationships, is dynamic—it is being challenged and reshaped by changing contexts on the reservation and at CTU, by changing personal and family circumstances, and by the changing combinations of personalities, cultures, and church backgrounds among the "Chicago" group. Tillie's death in July 2014 and Claude Marie's retirement from CTU in 2016 have certainly affected the relationship, but CTU continues to bring new groups of "Chicago" to the Rosebud and Pine Ridge reservations, based on that original *Hunka* relationship and the many subsequent trips and interactions—all grounded in mutual respect and ongoing transformation. Currently, CTU colleagues Maryellen Knuth and Jaruko Doi co-facilitate the annual trips to the reservation along with me.

Mission Theology, Practice, and Spirituality: Interplay and Development

I shall now explore how this relationship with the Lakota has both shaped and been shaped by my mission theology as a professor at CTU since 1990. While on the one hand, I do not assume to represent a uniform theology of the entire CTU faculty, on the other hand, the mission theology I will describe is situated among the shared reflections and experiences of many of my fine CTU colleagues.

My own post-Vatican II theological studies at CTU as a seminarian in the 1970s and the training I received through my missionary order of the Society of the Divine Word (both in the United States and during my two years as a seminarian in Papua New Guinea) enabled me to start with a positive attitude toward non-Western cultures, other religions, and Indigenous peoples. I also had some basic studies in anthropology and linguistics. The latter consisted of two summers of graduate studies with the Wycliffe Bible Translators (Summer Institute of Linguistics) at the University of North Dakota and gave me the understanding and tools for learning unwritten languages. However, that mission theology and practice has been challenged, nuanced, and deepened over the years through my encounters and interactions with the Lakota people.

Mission-in-Reverse and Missio Dei Theology

One of my teachers and mentors during my theological studies at CTU in 1975, Claude Marie Barbour spoke about "mission-in-reverse"—how we are to approach others and how we are touched by God's grace in our ministry with the "other." She described it in this way:

> The mission-in-reverse approach teaches that the minister can and should learn from the people ministered to—including, and perhaps especially, from the poor and marginalized people. By taking these people seriously, by listening to them and indeed learning from them, personal relationships are developed, and the dignity of the people is enhanced. Such presence to people is seen as necessarily allowing them to be the leaders in the relationship . . . Mutuality in mission cannot happen before mission-in-reverse has taken place.[6]

One can easily see how this was and continues to be the underlying theology for the CTU-Lakota relationship described above.

In his 1982 book *Christianity Rediscovered*, Spiritan missionary Vincent Donovan described how his Christian faith was enriched through his experience with the Maasai people of East Africa. My own participation in the annual four-day Sun Dance not only helped me to understand Lakota spirituality, but it also expanded my Christian understanding of the

---

6. Barbour, "Seeking Justice," 304.

symbolism of fire, the communal power of prayer, the redemptive meaning of suffering, and the role of asceticism.

With time, I have grounded the meaning of mission-in-reverse upon my deeper study of *missio Dei* theology (mission of the Trinitarian God)[7]— "that fountain of love" which generously and continuously is poured out into all people and all of creation:[8]

> God works for communion in the world because God as such *is* communion and wants to be "all in all" (1 Cor 15:28; Eph 4:7). In other words, God's very *nature* is to be in dialogue: Holy Mystery (Father), Son (Word), and Spirit in an eternal movement or flow of openness and receiving, a total giving and accepting, spilling over into creation and calling creation back into communion with Godself. Relationship, communion, and dialogue, therefore, is the ultimate goal of all existence.[9]

The *missio Dei* theology provides a profound theological basis and deep motivation for the practice of mission-in-reverse.

Reconciliation and Interculturality

My CTU colleague Robert Schreiter has contributed very much to the understanding and practice of mission as reconciliation. While the initial focus on reconciliation was the "vertical" dimension of God reconciling humanity to Godself (Rom 5:1–11), Schreiter points out that, in the 1990s, the new focus became "the deeper exploration of the 'horizontal' dimension of reconciliation: that is, reconciliation between humans, as individuals and as groups . . . [and] Christians believe that such horizontal reconciliation is possible precisely because it is rooted in God's action of reconciliation of all creation to God's own self."[10] Schreiter describes the following four practices of the ministry of reconciliation: healing, truth-telling, pursuit of justice, and forgiveness.[11]

Experience with the Lakota has deepened my understanding of these practices of reconciliation. Going to the reservation provided an opportunity for the "Chicago" group to receive, in Tillie's words, "an insight into themselves, not only as individuals, but insight into the world that they

---

7. Bevans and Schroeder, *Constants in Context*, 286–304.

8. Second Vatican Council, *Ad Gentes*, 2.

9. Bevans and Schroeder, *Prophetic Dialogue*, 25–26.

10. Schreiter, *Ministry of Reconciliation*, 235.

11. Schreiter, *Ministry of Reconciliation*, 236–38.

represent to others and to themselves."[12] For me, this meant owning and understanding the world I represent to others—as a US citizen, white man, Roman Catholic priest, and missionary. I needed to be ready to receive and absorb some of the anger, pain, and injustice that this stirs in others. I have also seen that forgiveness does not imply forgetting, but remembering in a new way that is healing and transforming for all involved.

Such reconciliation is situated within the framework of inter-culturality,[13] which moves beyond mere peaceful coexistence or adaptation "to emphasize and make more explicit the essential mutuality of the process of cultural interaction on both the personal and societal level."[14] However, such a transformation requires a deep spirituality that is based on what I now call a "second conversion." The first ongoing conversion is from selfishness to giving our lives over to Christ. The second ongoing conversion is from all forms of ethnocentrism to mutually enriching and challenging relationships with others—others who have different backgrounds and worldviews due to ethnicity, religion, nationality, social/economic status, gender, generation, sexual orientation, etc. We have to name and be converted from our prejudices, just like Peter and the early church had to acknowledge their prejudices against gentiles and the marginalized, as described by CTU biblical professor vanThanh Nguyen in his book *Peter and Cornelius: A Story of Conversion and Mission.*[15] Francis White Lance often talks about the need to overcome the racism and male chauvinism that is unfortunately still so strong in our world. The Lakota have offered me/us a "road" to such reconciliation through their forgiveness and hospitality. I recall the first time I noticed that the four "colors" of humanity were brought together in the circle of the sweat lodge in prayer and in spirit.

Right Relationships and Care of Creation

My mission theology, practice, and spirituality have been shaped by the Lakota phrase *Mitakuye Oyas'in*, which is used after every prayer and ritual action and means "all my relations"—with the living and dead; with crawling, winged, and four-legged creatures; with "mother earth." For me, this has become an image or parable for the Reign of God theology. The Reign of God is like *Mitakuye Oyas'in*. It means living in right relationships and sharing prayer and food with the living and those who have died. This is

12. Black Bear, "Hunka," 22.
13. Schroeder, "Prophetic Dialogue and Interculturality."
14. Kisala, "Formation," 335.
15. Nguyen, *Peter and Cornelius.*

done by the Lakota at gravesites, at every meal, at Wounded Knee, and in ritual and daily life. Mission theology needs to be integral, based in reality, and focused on just relationships.

Secondly, this Lakota phrase of "all my relations" expresses the theology and spirituality underlying the practice of reconciliation and interculturality described above. Barbour and Doidge describe this as the mission of accompaniment, in which the accompanier and the accompanied can alternate roles.[16] This accompaniment is more by presence than through many words.

Thirdly, *Mitakuye Oya'sin* calls me, the church, and all of humanity to a deep respect and care for "mother earth," for "father sky," for all of creation. This has become more central in mission theology and practice. "Mission witnesses to, proclaims, celebrates and works for a new way of thinking about and seeing human beings, earth's creatures and the created universe itself."[17] Ethicist Dawn Nothwehr of CTU describes this in terms of "ecojustice": "The church's ecojustice mission urgently requires a renewed understanding of the relationship between the doctrines of creation, redemption, and incarnation."[18] CTU professor Mary Frohlich makes an explicit connection with Indigenous spirituality and worldview in the following way:

> As the forces of globalization sweep more and more people away from ancestral lands and into a fast-moving struggle for survival, the urgency of rediscovering how to create and care for connection to place increases. One important place to look for clues is to the wisdom of Native Americans and other tribal peoples, many of whom exemplify an earth-oriented way of life that contrasts profoundly with the profit-focused obsession of mainstream Western culture.[19]

On the reservation, we sit on the ground in the sweat lodge, and the Lakota gather around a tree, which connects them and us with the star culture and cosmos during the Sun Dance. I am beginning to think of this ongoing transformation of our attitudes and actions toward creation as the need for a "third conversion," from consumerism to care of creation. This is another aspect of our participation in the *"missio Dei."* And I am learning this from the Lakota and other Indigenous peoples of the world.

16. Barbour and Doidge, "Mission as Accompaniment."

17. Bevans and Schroeder, *Constants in Context*, 375–76.

18. Nothwehr, "Church's Mission of Ecojustice," 88.

19. Frohlich, "Ministry to Place," 26. Frohlich, who grew up in South Dakota, taught the following courses onsite in 2012: "Spirituality Out of Doors" and "Black Hills Hiking Retreat."

Inculturation and Contextual Theology

In contrast to a negative attitude toward non-Western cultures, the Second Vatican Council affirmed that all cultures contain some "seeds of the Word"[20] and that local churches are to "borrow from the customs, traditions, wisdom, teaching, arts, and sciences of their people everything which could be used to praise the glory of the Creator."[21] In the past fifty years, many attempts have been made at what became known as inculturation, that is, bridging the gap between Christian faith and identity, on the one side, and one's culture and context on the other. More and more, I have realized how this process must be rooted within the local community. I heard an account from the Rosebud reservation about one white Catholic priest who would insist on using Lakota-looking statues of Jesus and Mary in the church, and then the next priest would move them to the basement and replace them with statues that had European features. And this continued while the pastors were often changed. Upon recounting this phenomenon, the Lakota would simply smile and say, "Whatever a priest decided and wanted." This is not inculturation.

The deeper sense of inculturation occurs within the hearts of the people. As Francis White Lance stated, "In my own journey, I find no problem being a tribal member practicing my beliefs about Sundancing and being a Christian."[22] Violet Crow Good Voice also talks often about how she has been strengthened by both the Lakota and Christian rituals and prayers. This development represents a movement toward reconciliation between two spiritualities and between the church and Indigenous peoples.[23]

Another area of inculturation that has been developed by Stephen Bevans, retired CTU faculty member, is the area of contextual theology. In his well-known work, *Models of Contextual Theology*, he describes six patterns, or models, of how inculturation efforts by the church have been applied in different circumstances around the world. From my observation and study, it appears that implicit Lakota theology and the explicit Indigenous theology of the Americas primarily draw upon two of Bevans's models: anthropological and praxis ones. The starting point for the anthropological model "is broadly speaking, present human experience, with a particular focus on human culture, secular or religious."[24] This often occurs in situations

20. Second Vatican Council, *Ad Gentes*, 11.
21. Second Vatican Council, *Ad Gentes*, 22.
22. White Lance, "My Friend," 28.
23. Barbour and Schreiter, "Plural Spiritualities."
24. Bevans, *Models of Contextual Theology*, 57.

where the culture has been disparaged over time. As its starting point, "the praxis model understands revelation as the presence of God in history—in the events of everyday life, in social and economic structures, in situations of oppression, in the experience of the poor and marginalized."[25] It is not difficult to see how the anthropological and praxis models respond to the past and present circumstances of the Lakota in relation to the church and broader society. Reflecting on my experience, obviously from my perspective, is an opportunity and privilege for me to appreciate how the Lakota, like other Indigenous people, continue to strive to integrate the gospel message within their current situation. Francis White Lance described this challenging process in this way:

> The connections I have made with my ancestors and the traditional spirituality of my people in recent years have been deepened and broadened by my study and decisions related to Church denominations. In turn, my traditional spirituality deepens my understanding of what it means to be a Christian. Each of them contributes to who I am today.[26]

The processes of inculturation and contextual theology are rooted within the local Christian community.

Concluding Remarks: Broader Perspectives and Applications

I have approached the symposium topic of "The Church and Indigenous Peoples" primarily through the lens of the particular "case study" of an almost thirty-year relationship between CTU and the Lakota. It points to the importance of a process of respectful listening, understanding the worldview and experience of the "other," naming and facing our need for conversion on various levels, addressing past and present injustice, and striving for healing and reconciliation, with a spirit of hope. This challenging process has been messy at times, marked by misunderstandings and mistakes. However, it has been an attempt to develop mutual relationships between Indigenous and non-Indigenous peoples against the backdrop of an often difficult history with the church. And, please remember that this is written from my perspective. The Lakota perspective needs to be included to complete this picture.

    I would now like to position this particular case within the bigger picture. Another CTU colleague, Michel Andraos, who has been involved

---

25. Bevans, *Models of Contextual Theology*, 75.
26. White Lance, "My Friend," 24–25.

for years with the Indigenous of Chiapas, Mexico, and more recently the First Nation peoples of Canada, summarizes some current developments under Pope Francis:

> In a landmark speech at the Second World Meeting of Popular Movements in Santa Cruz de la Sierra, Bolivia, on July 9, 2015 . . . he [Francis] spoke to the Indigenous peoples present very clearly about the impact of colonialism on the poor, past and present. He also asked for forgiveness for the sins committed against them in the name of God. "I humbly ask forgiveness, not only for the offenses of the Church herself, but also for the crimes committed against the native peoples during the so-called conquest of America . . ." In his more recent visit to San Cristobal de las Casas, Chiapas, Mexico . . . he also emphasized the important contribution of Indigenous peoples to humanity and to the Church. "You have much to teach us, much to teach humanity," he said.[27]

Indigenous Mexican theologian Eleazar López Hernández noted that the pope's presence in Chiapas "healed the wounds caused by misunderstanding and unjust accusations [by the Vatican] directed against this prophetic and martyr local church."[28] Of course, the process toward full reconciliation between Indigenous peoples and the church still has a long way to go.

In August 2016, during my participation in an "Indigenous Theology Seminar" in Alice Springs, Australia, I was enriched and challenged by the stories and reflections of Australian Aboriginal Christians and the attempts to bring together Indigenous and non-Indigenous peoples in Australia. They were also very interested in entering into more dialogue with the Indigenous peoples of the Americas.

I am very glad that we had such a symposium to bring together Indigenous and non-Indigenous voices across the Americas and that the proceedings are becoming available for others. Let the dialogue continue.

---

27. Andraos, "Church and the Indigenous Peoples," 44.

28. López Hernández, "El Papa Francisco en México." Quoted in Andraos, "Church and the Indigenous Peoples," 44.

PART TWO

Reflections and Future Perspectives

12

Reconciling Truths and Decolonizing Practices for the Head, Heart, and Hands

MARIE BATTISTE

Protocols of Place

As the conference talk which became this chapter took place in Chicago, I begin with a customary acknowledgement of the Indigenous peoples of these lands—the Potawatami peoples, a nation belonging to the larger Algonkian family of peoples of which I am a member. Algonkian peoples are a widely geographically dispersed family of linguistically similar speakers whose roots are grounded in a vast area stretching from eastern Canada's five Atlantic provinces to the far reaches of the mountains of the western prairies among the Blackfoot and Cree, south to the state of Wisconsin, and east to Michigan. By acknowledging the Potawatami as the owners and stewards of these lands, I extend my symbolic wampum in relationship with this territory and its peoples and to DePaul University and Catholic Theological Union, who have invited me to give this talk.

Introduction

I am a member of the Mi'kmaw Nation from the district of Unama'ki (Cape Breton, Novia Scotia) and from the Potlotek First Nation. I am also a member of the Houlton Band of Micmacs, with a unique status of being a federally recognized treaty with First Nations on the Canadian side of the border and a member of the federally recognized band of Micmacs in Maine. My family moved from the reserve in Canada before I was born, and it was Maine where I was born and grew up, off reserve. This occurred as the result of my family's seeking employment during the Canadian removal policies involving centralization on reserves. The government of Canada had issued its removal of families from their homelands to centralized reserves for its convenience in carrying out its treaty obligations to large numbers of Mi'kmaq in Nova Scotia. In making this move to the United States, my parents took my school-aged sister to the Indian Residential School, a place that was staffed by nuns, who they assumed would be gentle and nourishing to their daughter while they went to work in the United States. They reasoned that nuns were a kindly group of people who could care well for their child while they eked out a living in the potato farming industry as migrant laborers. Little did they know—until they returned to get her some three years later—how horrifying and traumatic that experience would be for her and others.

Colonialism and the Politics of the Church

Catholicism has been a central part of Mi'kmaw tradition dating back to 1610, when Mi'kmaq entered into a special relationship with the Holy Roman Empire. This relationship, largely political and strategic, developed into an ongoing relationship that involved the hosting of missionaries, Jesuits, and priests among Mi'kmaq for some two centuries.

The baptism of Chief Membertou in 1610 came with the baptisms of one hundred and forty other family members. A wampum belt that characteristically signifies the union of an Indigenous group and the church was found in the Vatican in 1968, and though it was reportedly of unknown origin, it has been theorized that that wampum belt was associated with the Mi'kmaq, among the first Indigenous peoples baptized in the church in the northeast lands of North America now known as Canada. That same belt was reportedly removed from the Vatican during an uprising in Rome and was not seen again until the 1990s when it was found in the Vatican once more. It continues to hold some mysteries.

Henderson has theorized that this wampum is a Mi'kmaw belt that has since been further connected to stories within Mi'kmaw oral traditions and associated with their hieroglyphic writing.[1] The connections between the symbols and also the traditions of our people being baptized have continued through the ages since that early period. While Catholicism is the main religion of Mi'kmaq, it is a religion that was reconfigured from within the Mi'kmaq cultural and iconic formations. Without priests and churches

---

1. Henderson, *Mi'kmaw Concordat.*

for many years after their removal, Mi'kmaw communities held onto the traditions of the Sunday mass, the blessings and prayers, communion when it was available, and the many sacraments that came with birth, marriage, death, and other significant stages of life. These appeared to be related to the events that Mi'kmaw people honored with their own ceremonies and prayers, and pipe, sweet grass, communal gatherings that marked significant life transitional events, and Catholicism became a fairly easy fusion of ideas and ideals of spirituality. This was especially evident when priests, in their very limited Mi'kmaw language, had little to offer but stories of God and creation. The Catholic clergy's main challenge with Mi'kmaw behavior had to do with reducing the number of wives the men would have, and reducing the number of partners the women would have. This was eventually achieved, at least at the formal level.

From the early days when missionaries and explorers were making their way throughout Mi'kma'ki (another name for the seven Mi'kmaw districts in the five Atlantic provinces of Canada) and other Indigenous peoples' territories, the political relationships of the Holy Roman empire were held in sovereign-to-sovereign agreements, concordats bound by wampum and treaties, and ceremonies that marked the events. Priests, explorers, and settlers were bound by various proclamations, established by and with their monarchs and relationships established by the Holy Roman Empire. A reportedly important discussion about the following question was held between Pope Benedict XIV (1740–58) and the monarchs regarding the discovery of Indigenous peoples in the New World: were they (the Indigenous peoples) men, beasts, or devils? The pope in 1749 eventually would hold that the native peoples in the new lands were humans who not only had human rights, but also had property rights. Thereafter, any lands found would have to be negotiated with them, and this was pronounced in the Royal Proclamation of 1763—any lands required for settlers and settlement would have to be purchased from the native peoples and with their consent. The Mi'kmaq lands have since been a terrain grounded in contesting, resisting, and colonizing settlers who have constructed a Eurocentric ideology of *terra nullius*, "empty lands," that were thus ripe for the picking and choosing as well as giving away or trading off without the consent of Mi'kmaq and other Indigenous peoples on the continent.

Mi'kmaq have thus had a long and somewhat contentious history with the colonizers of their lands and their governments, though less with their churches, who sent Jesuit priests as their parish diplomats to live among Mi'kmaq. These priests studied their languages and ways of life, leaving grammars behind, and often enlisted them as translators for the English. Their settlements often included a chapel or church, which would also be used by settlers who chose to live nearby. Eventually, given the nomadic habits of Mi'kmaq, they often would take up living on what were Mi'kmaw lands, setting up fences and other houses there. Without land being purchased, the British colonial governments established "tickets of location" that enabled these settlers to live on certain areas of land. This practice remains the major contested foundation for the loss of Mi'kmaq lands to these colonial settlers. Having initially allowed these settlements in the Treaty of 1752, Mi'kmaq did not, however, give up their lands or forfeit them by their regular hunting or fishing foraging, nor were the lands purchased. Rather, Mi'kmaw leaders agreed in the treaty that the settlers could remain in their then-established settlements with other agreements for trade, food, and tools, as well as agreements for the protection of Mi'kmaq in their usual hunting and fishing activities. The treaty also stated that any disputes between Mi'kmaq and settlers would be handled fairly by the colonial courts.

Canada and the Enactment of Eurocentrism

Canada became a self-determining nation from these settlements, which were allowed to have their own self-government, churches, schools, and other establishments that would enable them to later become a nation. However, Mi'kmaq were assured that they, too, would have their own rights and privileges on their land. The government of Canada wrote: "That the Indians shall not be molested in . . . the exercise of their Religion, Provided the Missionaries residing amongst them have leave from the Governour or Commander in chief of His Majestys Said Province of Nova Scotia or Acadie for so doing."[2]

Mi'kmaq's first relationship with colonists was likely with the Vikings, though little is left from that relationship to recover a story. On the other hand, the French colonists who probably arrived in the late fourteenth century left much behind in the form of travel literature. The explorers and missionaries that traveled with the French colonists had begun a writing campaign, both to secure more money and support for their continued travels and to maintain a historical record of their travels and of the unique and exotic peoples they met along the way. Many of the early missionaries kept records as well, detailing the sounds and words they heard; eventually, some of the adept ones discovered regularities in the local vernaculars and established early grammars of the languages they found.

---

2. United Kingdom Public Record Office, Colonial Office 217/5:3r–5r, Elikawake Treaty.

Abbé Maillard was one such French Jesuit priest who was able to develop a relationship with the Mi'kmaq; he lived among them, mainly among the women and children when the men would hunt. His solitude and his writing of Mi'kmaw language would later be important to his being appointed by the English to work on their behalf, negotiating several treaties and other agreements. Although the British expelled French Acadians from Acadie in 1758, Abbé Maillard was able to remain to translate for the British until his death in 1762. Even though the Catholic priest was an asset to the English, they sought ways to turn Mi'kmaq from the Catholic faith to their own. The British planted a Protestant pastor, Reverend Thomas Wood (a medical doctor and Anglican minister) to work beside the priest and learn the language of Mi'kmaq, and when Maillard passed away in 1762, Wood acclaimed himself the Jesuit's next protégé. Yet, despite crossing himself and saying some prayers, Wood did not fool Mi'kmaq into adopting the English religion or entering into any further covenants with the British. Left without priests for one hundred years, Mi'kmaq retained their spirituality and some of the rituals and prayers of their revered Catholic priest Maillard; they largely held onto their own spiritual beliefs and practices until the time when priests were allowed once again to return to their communities.

The nineteenth century brought with it new and growing settlements of English and eastern Europeans. Mi'kmaq were no longer the larger population; they had been decimated by the diseases that the Europeans brought and had been pushed into the forests where they built their homes, supported in part by government rations, subsidies, and trade goods. Mi'kmaq continued to urge their priests to write on their behalf to the king: about the trespassing of settlers onto their lands, the fences that halted the migrations of the animals on which they fed themselves, and the lawless nature of these colonial people who had little respect for Mi'kmaq and the treaties.

The land was still largely populated by Mi'kmaq, and they fed on fish and game in their land and the waters, their daily livelihood one of survival and enjoyment. The missionaries who lived among them could do little to support themselves, and so the Mi'kmaq supported them generously with their food and rations. In return, they hoped that the missionaries would enact fair deals in their negotiations with the British. However, when the Mi'kmaq questioned Abbé Maillard as to why he would not translate as they told him to, his response was that he had to be "loyal" to his sovereign, the king. This led to Mi'kmaq's having to learn more of the language of the local Basque settlers, and thus, in some parts of Port Royal, a combined Basque-Mi'kmaq dialect began as a local vernacular.[3]

---

3. Upton, *Micmacs and the Colonists*, 23.

The westward push of settlements and explorations led to a renewed treaty-making period in the western provinces, which focused on new kinds of settlements, called "reserves," for Indigenous peoples. The inducements to the "Indians" to leave their migratory lifestyle and settle on these reserves included support for their new livelihood of farming and other domestic pursuits in the form of cows, seeds, subsidies, and farming tools, as well as medical supplies, clothing, money, ammunition, and/or food rations for each family member or band. Schools and salaried teachers were also often included in the western Numbered Treaties, but under various conditions (as noted in each treaty), such as when the Indigenous peoples had settled and wanted a school, or when they were ready for a school, or when the Queen deemed it time for them to have a school. One such provision is as follows: "Her Majesty agrees to maintain schools for instruction . . . as to Her Government of the Dominion of Canada may seem advisable, whenever the Indians of the reserve shall desire it."[4]

Churches were not included (nor probably desired in many cases) as provisions in these treaties. However, churches were constructed by the priests and other religious people who followed the Indigenous peoples' migrations, hoping to capture their souls and the monies from their homeland colonial churches and parishes. The growth of an organization called the Propagation of the Gospel hinged largely on how much money could be raised to support the missionaries and priests in the new land.

The treaties and their obligations are part of what is understood and has been affirmed by the courts as the "honor of the Crown." The Crown is to ensure that the treaty obligations are fulfilled as part of the constitution of Canada. The treaties and the Proclamation of 1762 created the Canadian government's constitutional responsibility "for Indians and lands reserved for Indians." In the implementation of the same treaties, the honor of the Crown thus provided for schools, teachers, health provisions, housing, and tools for farming and other activities on the land, while the Indigenous peoples continued to assert the transmission of their own language and cultural knowledge on the land through their communities and family. This transmission of language and culture remains a constitutional right and an aboriginal right aimed at their continued survival as a people, a nation with a spiritual connection to all things, and distinctive languages and identities connected to their ecology.

The Indigenous peoples embraced lifelong learning that was holistic, experiential, and communally activated. This learning was also spiritually enhanced and culturally based in Indigenous knowledge and pedagogies

---

4. Assembly of First Nations, "Numbered Treaty Education Provisions," Treaty 5.

that built learning from place and territory, from stories and teachings and families and land, learning that would eventually go beyond the family into the schools. The domestication of the Indians, however, did not go as well as hoped by the government. The reserve lands were poorly suited for the farm tools the Indians received, and the limited supplies did little to enable them to start a new livelihood. The starvation of the people that resulted from the eradication of the buffalo hardly induced the Indians to live productively and quietly out of sight. Much has been written about the starvation, the lack of animals for the people to live off of, the health consequences of poor diets, and the poorly stored food rations that rotted before they reached the people. James Daschuk offers a horrific account of this food scarcity, and the callous disregard the settlers had for the Indians they had displaced for their own land and food needs.[5]

Schools fared less well as inducements for Indigenous parents and families. As the Indigenous family and community unit was the source of the best learning for children for their continued survival, the people had little need for either the language or the domesticated habits of the English, and farming the land made little sense when the game was plenty. In the Indian Commissioner reports of the eastern territory, there were often comments that Indian children could be good at reading and writing if they had put more time into these skills. But the people's seasonal migrations with the animals and the seasons for berry picking, moss gathering, fishing, and other necessary food and fun pursuits often left schools without many children. Eventually, the commissioners and local folk began to think of other ways to encourage the Indians to become more settled, and less transient and migratory. Schools came to be seen as places where all children should go to be weaned off their migratory habits, and thus, more domestication could take place by requiring parents to send their children to school. Compulsory schooling could not be achieved in the large settlements, however, without force, fear, and the withholding of rations. Thus, parents were allowed to starve long enough to force them to give up their children to the schools in exchange for these rations and subsidies; those parents who refused lost their money rations and were also threatened with prison.[6]

From 1870 onward, despite British Crown treaties that would be negotiated across Canada, the colonial government continued to encourage and increase British settlements throughout the prairies, issuing what was called "free" land to settlers through a homesteaders' program. The "whitening" and clearing of the prairies evolved through the subjugation of the Indians

5. Daschuk, *Clearing the Plains*.

6. Daschuk, *Clearing the Plains*. See also Battiste, "Micmac Literacy."

on reserves, the forced deportation of children to residential schools, and the induced Chinese labor on the railroads.

Perceived Justice and Eurocentric Blame Frames

Using several frames of injustice, Eurocentrism rationalized the subjugation of the Chinese, black Africans, and Indigenous people. Hanson and Hanson offer several ideological blame frames as to how injustice is rationalized and tolerated based on justifications that hold up other unjust ideals or even just the perception of justice.[7] These blame frames ensure that, despite all good ideas of self and others, injustice can still be served with the certainty that individuals or societies remain just and that inequalities do not happen on their own watch but rather, by these frames. This is how it goes!

The first of these frames is the God blame frame. The God frame, along with a similar nature frame, excused the Europeans (as they held a divine plan as God's servants) and blamed injustice on the Indigenous peoples themselves. The European colonists originally viewed themselves as complying with divine forces. God had given them the right, and perhaps duty, to Christianize the world and all its inhabitants. They were merely following God's apparent larger plan, and the Indigenous peoples were not playing their own part in the grand scheme of things. The settlers had a further storehouse of reasons for their greedy thrust forward. Among these reasons was the inevitably uncivilized dispositional behaviors of Indians and other non-Europeans, viewed as nomadic savages who did not need the land but who *did* need the tutelage of the better, more informed peoples of God to learn how to use the land. The Indians' blatant lack of skill and vulnerability to disease seemed to reaffirm their savage dispositions for the Europeans, who believed that it was God's will to shower these problems upon them as punishment for the sins of their past. Their odd languages and cultures were justification enough that they were ignorant and inferior. In the eighteenth and nineteenth centuries, the European colonists adopted the concept of race as a natural frame. This frame further excused their unjust actions on the basis of the presumed racial inferiority of the natives, justifying the need to domesticate the lands of America according to God's covenant and their superior tools and dispositions. These two elements—(1) perceiving the victim as deserving (blaming the victim) and (2) perceiving bystanders or beneficiaries as innocent (excusing the nonvictim)—combine to create the perception of, and satisfy the craving for, justice.[8]

---

7. Hanson and Hanson, "Blame Frame."

8. Hanson and Hanson, "Blame Frame," 423.

However, the Indians did not eschew the domesticated habits of the colonial settlers and their governments; in fact, they rather enjoyed the lifestyle of living off the land and the animals that were often abundant in uncleared forests. Their habits were seen by the Europeans as further evidence that they must be converted to Christianity, domestic tilling of the soil for vegetables, and living in the solitary patriarchal homes that Indians thought too large to heat effectively. Stereotypes played out both ways, although it would be the stereotypes of the Indians that would be used to usher in new programs to induce Indigenous children into forced farm labor. As early as 1815, the colonial governments would engage in a program called "planting out," whereby farmers would receive a year's salary for taking in an Indian child and teaching them the habits of homemaking and farming. "Planting out" continued until the next iteration of programs was implemented to take all Indian children from their families and put them into residential schools to receive the full training in labor skills and Christianization, as well as their first introduction to physical, mental, and sexual abuse.

Indian Residential Schools were proposed well before Confederation (1867), but were instituted in 1870. From then on, more than one hundred and fifty schools were built throughout Canada to which over 150,000 children were sent to live. Some were able to return home at least a couple of times a year, while others attended continuously throughout the years until the end of their mandatory ages for schooling. In 1920, the government of Canada revised the Indian Act, extending compulsory schooling from sixteen to eighteen years of age. In 1920, the deputy superintendent general of Indian Affairs, Duncan Campbell Scott, assured Parliament that "I want to get rid of the Indian problem . . . Our objective is to continue until there is not a single Indian in Canada that has not been absorbed into the body politic and there is no Indian question, and no Indian Department; that is the whole object of this Bill."[9]

The commissioner added that it was the government's intention to "kill the Indian in the child" by removing children from their family and communities. This concerted effort—from 1870 to 1999—would also kill the parent in the adult. It dissolved families and relationships, discontinued the spiritual and holistic learning children had in their families, eradicated the Indians' livelihood on the land, forcing them to sit and wait for everything the government wanted to issue them; it killed the spirit in them as individuals and communities. The testimonies of these students—now grandparents and elders in their communities—reveal the horrors and tragedies of their youth. Their languages were eradicated or eroded, and their

9. *Final Report*, 172.

lives as children stolen from them, replaced with abuses of all kinds, largely at the hands of Christian personnel who ran the schools. The schools were cold, damp, and moldy—diseased, infested incubators. As many as thirty thousand children were known to have died in these schools or immediately after returning home.[10] In many cases, there is no trace left behind of these children, no burial grounds and no memorials—only dark stories of mental, emotional, physical, and sexual abuse told by their classmates and reverberating across Canada and beyond.

The schools were run by many of the churches, both Catholic and Protestant—and share the same stories. While not all of the students who attended those schools have testified, some brave ones have accepted the invitation to speak in the Truth and Reconciliation Commission (TRC) hearings of the atrocities that took place in those schools. Those stories are now resounding throughout Canada as important testimonies that we must share, for they identify complicities that we must connect to religious and political organizations, churches, policies, and individuals of this government. However, this experience is not unique to Canada. The United States shares in the same policies and practices revealed in the histories written about Indian Industrial Schools and boarding schools.

The result of these travesties for Indigenous peoples on both sides of the border is evidence of the litany of statistics that yield a narrative of uneducated, unemployed, incarcerated, unhealthy peoples, the silent faces of poverty and racism who have lost knowledge and languages and are victims of nihilism, despair, addictions, trauma. Yet, these statistics tell a growing story of Indigenous Canada that is but one additional measure of the distance that separates the First Nations, Inuit, and Métis peoples from the center of power, privilege, control, and agency that has exercised colonial privilege and superiority over them. Whiteness as power and control has represented that agency center for over four hundred years; it is represented in the foundation of Eurocentrism that has racialized the "other" as inferior.

Eurocentrism is a European "center" characterized by superiority, progress, hegemony, and monopoly over all other knowledge systems, and the Christian knowledge system is foundational to the Eurocentric system. Characterized as a singular center with universal applications and diffused to the periphery for its perceived value, Eurocentrism is a dominant theory legitimized in scientific, educational, and public institutions, publications/print, government policy, and practice. It is the foundation of conventional educational curricula, of heroes past and present, and it is the foundation for our understanding of the one hundred and fifty years of a colonial

10. Truth and Reconciliation Commission of Canada, *Honouring the Truth*, 61–71.

government that only in 1982 gained its independence from the British monarchy and government.[11]

Today, this forced assimilation to Eurocentrism is understood as cultural imperialism and the cultural genocide of Indigenous peoples. The government and churches have conspired with demeaning discourses, ideologies of superiority, that enacted policies and practices against Indigenous peoples. As Chief Justice Beverly McLachlin said, "The most glaring blemish on the Canadian historic record relates to our treatment of the First Nations that lived here at the time of colonization . . . Starvation and disease were rampant. Indians were denied the right to vote. Religion and social traditions, like the Potlatch and the Sun Dance, were outlawed."[12]

The Indigenous peoples have had to learn to adjust to displacement from their lands and homes and forced segregation on reservations. They have had to learn to adjust to starvation and disease that resulted from the decimation of the buffalo and their way of life and living. They have had to learn to adjust to the forced assimilation of their children to languages that wiped out their cognitive connections to community and cultural life, killing their spiritual connections to the land and to themselves. And finally, they have had to adjust to the introduction of violence and trauma as ways of inducing amnesia and dissonance. Such learning has come with many costs to themselves and their communities.

Today, the largest population in Canada is Aboriginal peoples, growing at the rate of 45 percent each decade. Without employment and other needed services, they are moving to urban areas and having to live in poverty, in racially charged and violent environments. While Canada has ranked between sixth and eighth on the UN Human Development Index, the First Nations fall between sixty-third and seventy-eighth. The federal government's Community Well-Being Index shows that the gap has not changed at all since 1981. While there is now a growing call for change and for an understanding of that past colonial mentality and its effects on Indigenous peoples, it is clear that there is also no one who has been privileged with the knowledge of how to achieve a decolonized education, because every person—every one of us—has been both a victim and beneficiary of the same educational system. This realization affirms that we must become critical learners and healers within a wounded space. In that space—in elementary and high schools, curricula, and institutions of higher learning; government decision-making; media, books, and publishing firms; and pop

11. For a fuller description of Eurocentrism, see Blaut, *Colonizer's Model of the World*.

12. Fine, "Chief Justice," para. 4.

culture—there is a superior and inferior notion of peoples, which refuses to allow Indigenous peoples to exist in the totality of their being.

Decolonization and Cognitive Justice

As they come into their own awareness, the Indigenous peoples must be engaged with decolonization in order for the diversity of their knowledges/languages/capacities, as well as holistic spiritual and learning practices, to survive. The TRC has issued ninety-four calls to action to Canada that are aimed at addressing and remedying the Indian Residential School experience specifically, but overall, they aim to address the historical legacy of Eurocentrism, cognitive imperialism, racism and racialization, forced assimilation to Christianity, trauma and violence, and cultural genocide. Going back to the colonial government of Canada's Royal Proclamation of 1763—the provision that all land must be purchased by the settlers—affirms that Canada has its own reconciliation to do.

Today, Canada is on a reconciling path supported by the federal government, some churches, and most schools, universities, and municipalities. The TRC's Calls to Action are a platform for raising the national consciousness and a justification for a new strategy in Canada with needed actions to remedy and reconcile the Indigenous peoples' experiences in Canada and with Canadians. They also constitute a history of the policies, practices, ideologies, and complicities among Canadians and the Canadian professions in the subjugation of Aboriginal peoples—for example, through education. There is overwhelming evidence of the planned national cognitive assimilation of Aboriginal peoples. Multiple generations of Indigenous peoples continue to live out deeply subjugated traumatized experiences, and they continue to experience poverty, ethnostress, undereducation, and overrepresentation in various social systems, childcare, and prisons and detention centers, as well as gangs and street violence. This framework is beginning to find groundswells of people willing to listen, learn, share, and be moved to do something to ensure that the past histories of violence to Indigenous peoples be understood, comprehended, and laid bare for all to witness. According to Justice Murray Sinclair, chair of the TRC, reconciliation "is about ensuring that everything we do today is aimed at that high standard of restoring balance between Aboriginal and non-Aboriginal people."[13] Such a reconciliation has also been noted by the Catholic Church, as Pope John Paul II said in his address to Indigenous peoples:

13. Bernstein, "We Must All Put First Nations Children First," para. 10.

Over the centuries, dear Amerindian and Inuit peoples, you have gradually discovered in your cultures special ways of living your relationship with God and with the world while remaining loyal to Jesus and to the Gospel.

Continue to develop these moral and spiritual values . . . Guard this wisdom preciously. To let it become impoverished would be to impoverish the people around you . . . To live the spiritual values in a new way requires on your part maturity, interiority, a deepening of the Christian message, a concern for the dignity of the human being, and a pride in being Amerindian . . . Your encounter with the Gospel has not only enriched you, it has enriched the Church . . . We are well aware that this has not taken place without its difficulties and, occasionally, its blunders. However, and you are experiencing this today, the Gospel does not destroy what is best in you.[14]

You do not have to be people divided into two parts, as though an aboriginal had to borrow the faith and life of Christianity, like a hat or a pair of shoes, from someone else who owns them.[15]

The TRC defines reconciliation as an ongoing process of establishing and maintaining respectful relationships under the supreme law of Canada and human rights. It is important that all Canadians understand how traditional Indigenous approaches to resolving conflict, repairing harm, and restoring relationships can and must inform the reconciliation process. Churches cannot signal symbolic changes by appropriating cultural symbols and icons, as if to pacify Indigenous peoples into cognitive imperialism. They must be willing to change the ideologies associated with oppression.

Christian Eurocentrism has demonstrated its rejection of nature for its immanence and transcendence based on human soul theory. Indigenous peoples, on the other hand, have taken as their own ideology a respect of Indigenous relationships with the earth and all living beings as part of constitutional reconciliation. If human beings resolve problems only between themselves but continue to destroy the natural world, then reconciliation remains incomplete. Indigenous peoples are seeking the holistic reconnection to themselves, to each other, and to their lands and the animate world in which they live.

There is a call to both personal and collective action toward reconciliation. It is not enough that each individual listens to, contemplates,

14. John Paul II, "Meeting with Native Peoples," paras. 6, 7.
15. John Paul II, "Address to the Aborigines," para. 26.

and accepts the revisionist colonial history of the church and his or her complicities within that history. It may and should affect people's views and beliefs, as well as perhaps require them to unlearn old ideas and learn new ones about people not of their own kind, in order to understand and reconcile negative views of Indigenous peoples. They need to rethink their privileges, their safety nets, and their complicities in the losses Indigenous peoples have experienced and how those losses came with many of their gains. It might mean that they need to consider their territorial relationships to the treaties, aboriginal rights, and principles of the United Nations Declaration on the Rights of Indigenous Peoples. In Canada, the collective aspects involve implementing organizational and community efforts to make commitments to change; developing coalitions and consensus; and working together to monitor efforts and adjust accordingly in order to ensure that the Indigenous Nations have an opportunity to be addressed as a collective and not only as individuals.

Finally, churches today must take responsibility for the role they and their parishes played in the destruction of Indigenous peoples' lands, lives, and potentialities. As Indigenous peoples work through their own understandings of their past and their lives, they are coming to the realization that it was not their spirituality, their languages, their cultures, or their teachings that were the problem, as they have been told over and over again. Rather, the problem is the destructive effects of ideologies—both Christian and secular—that are born out of cultural histories and enhanced and strengthened by the hand of power, control, and deceit within the destructive legacies of colonization that have wreaked such havoc in their lives. Churches must now inspire Indigenous and non-Indigenous people to transform their societies, so that their children and grandchildren can live together in dignity, peace, and prosperity on these lands we now share.

Congregations might consider how their histories, complicities with colonization, assumptions about Indigenous peoples, and internalized oppression have created the losses to the collective peoples' cultures, communities, and families, and how these have contributed to nihilism and trauma. They might consider how internalized dominance has emerged and how knowledge is socially produced with all the biases of the group who has distributed that knowledge. They must give up the privileging of one kind of spirituality and accept that Indigenous peoples' worldviews can be morally affirming and equally contribute to goodness, health, and well-being. Finally, congregations must respect and honor Indigenous peoples' rights to their own knowledge systems, which include their languages, their worldviews and spirituality, and their right to engage the widest Indigenous community participation, considering their interest, impact, and benefit in reconciliation and decolonization; congregations must understand how traditional First Nations, Inuit, and Métis approaches to resolving conflict, repairing harm, and restoring relationships can inform the reconciliation process.

Not all churches, parishes, or citizens—on either side of the border— believe that they need to change. As Sensoy and DiAngelo assert, "The most subtle yet powerful way we resist knowing is by simply being uninterested."[16] This remains, perhaps, one of the ways that many continue to assert their superiority and enact the other justice blame frames. They assume that the reason why many Indigenous peoples today are incarcerated or are not employed, educated, and living in abundance is that God deemed that to be their fate, or that it is their inferior dispositions that influence their behavior and lead to this ill fate, or that their need for equality is well-fed by equity-seeking programs aimed at improving their literacy, education, employment or a number of other aspects of their culture, languages, motivation, or incentives to continue to go to Eurocentric schools or institutions. Many equity programs continue to pathologize Indigenous students as lacking capacities of all kinds, requiring the tutelage of the more superior peoples; they dismiss their need to consider the languages and youth stolen from them, the territories and lands that have been appropriated, or the important teachings and stored knowledge that comes from the rich cultural heritage of their peoples living in place, in territory, in their own languages.

Cognitive justice, then, is—in part—a frame for reconciliation. Reconciliation is rooted in the educational choice of First Nations parents, in Aboriginal and treaty rights, and the transfer of jurisdiction of land to the Crown provides the means and framework to implement educational rights for First Nations, Inuit, and Métis peoples. The Supreme Court of Canada has identified several constitutional purposes that include determining the historical rights of Aboriginal peoples and giving Aboriginal and treaty rights constitutional force to protect them against legislative powers;[17] sanctioning challenges to social and economic policy objectives embodied in legislation to the extent that Aboriginal and treaty rights are affected;[18] and committing to recognize, value, protect, and enhance their distinctive cultures.[19] To ensure the continuity of Aboriginal customs and traditions, the Supreme Court has determined that every substantive constitutional right will normally include the incidental constitutional right to teach such

16. Sensoy and DiAngelo, *Is Everyone Really Equal*, 33.

17. *R. v. Sparrow* (1990) 1 SCR 1075, para. 65.

18. *R. v. Sparrow* (1990) 1 SCR 1075, para. 64.

19. *R. v. Powley* (2003) 2 SCR 207, paras. 13 and 18.

a practice, custom, and tradition to a younger generation.[20] Current education systems have not implemented these constitutional reforms in the education of Aboriginal peoples. The constitutional framework and court decisions generate an emerging reconciliation of Indigenous knowledge and culture in learning and pedagogy that must be translated into policy, practice, and impact on all public forms of education. The constitutional framework affirming aboriginal and treaty rights creates the context for systemic educational reform to include Indigenous science, humanities, visual arts, and languages, as well as existing educational philosophy, pedagogy, teacher education, and practice.

To some degree within the emerging Indigenous renaissance, Aboriginal educators have begun the reconciliation in their academic and social justice activist agendas, which are now developing new avenues, empowering Aboriginal people to realize their educational goals and join various professions. However, this is not the responsibility of Aboriginal peoples alone. The federal and the provincial Crown must reconcile these constitutional rights to education. At present, they have not done so, as evidenced by the lack of negotiation for these constitutional rights within provincial and territorial education systems. Thus, the task is great to sensitize Canadian politicians, policy-makers, and educators to be more responsive and proactive in order to reconcile the national and provincial curricula and displace the persistent educational failures among Aboriginal peoples in the diverse educational systems across Canada. I conclude with this last word from a survivor of the Indian Residential school, Chief Robert Joseph, who is also Ambassador for Reconciliation Canada and a TRC honorary witness: "To reconcile is to weave a stronger and more vibrant social fabric, based on the unique and diverse strengths of Canadians and their communities."

20. *R. v. Coté* (1996) 3 SCR 139.

13

Witness and Practice of Living Memory

JOANNE DOI, MM

A single bright star in the predawn sky over Lake Michigan carries me back to a different stretch of this same sky south of the equator. Up at twelve thousand feet in the southern Andes of Peru, the stars are so numerous in the rarified air far from city lights that there are names for the dark spaces in the midst of the Milky Way. The *Llama Niwa* (mother llama and offspring) journey patiently across the night sky, illuminated by the principal constellation of the Southern Cross, which is seen only in the southern hemisphere.[1] Both the stars and the dark spaces orient the living and have guided the Andean peoples in their agricultural cycle (which is their life) for centuries. Yet more than an astronomical almanac, it is expressive of a *telúrica-cósmica* religion, or *cosmovisión* (worldview), that holds sacred the interrelationships among people with the earth, sun, moon, stars, and all of nature.[2]

When journeying by foot through this distinct *altiplano* bioregion surrounding Lake Titicaca, one encounters many *apachetas*, or crossroads, distinguished by the small pile of stones at the high point of the path, marking a turning point on the way. Pausing briefly at the *apacheta*, one places a stone there, which signifies an interchange of energies with those who have gone before and with the earth itself. One continues on the journey with renewed *ánimo* and energy. In the context of several theological gatherings of Indigenous peoples of Latin America, Stephen Judd interprets this ordinary ritual gesture metaphorically, noting that "*apachetas* as crossroads mark the turning points in the journeys of a people to greater self-understanding and awareness of their place in history according to cyclical patterns," with new

1. Huarachi, "Economía Comunitaria Aymara," 160.
2. Acarapi, "La Cruz Cuadrada," 263.

emerging paradigms for intercultural dialogue.[3] "The Church and Indigenous Peoples in the Americas" conference in Chicago marks a new crossroads of encounter, of "memory, resistance, and hope," gathering Indigenous speakers and allies from across the Americas, north and south.

The witness and practice of living memory in the simple ritual gesture of placing a stone at the *apacheta* acknowledges a sacred presence with ancestors and earth, carried forward in those who journey. The land holds memory. Upon reflection over time, I am convinced that the land in which we abide, from which we live and are recreated, *is* sacred. As Valencia notes, it is where we encounter mystery, restorative hope, and deep joy.[4] Yet there are signs that we have often lost our way. Practices of living memory reorient our living for the *buen vivir,* fullness of life for all creation. This essay is an exploration of crossroads, resonances, and living memory in my shared journey as a Maryknoll Sister among Indigenous peoples, mainly with the Aymara of the southern Andes, where I lived and served for eleven years and, more recently, with the Lakota people of Pine Ridge and Rose Bud in South Dakota through participation in a praxis course at Catholic Theological Union (CTU) over three years. I share this journey as a third generation (Sansei) Japanese American woman religious.

Recently, there have been vital interconnections and solidarities occurring in the struggle for water, the earth, and Indigenous peoples. There had been a call out to clergy and religious leaders the day before this conference began—with six hundred responding—to stand with the Standing Rock Sioux to resist the Dakota Access Pipeline. The oil pipeline had been rerouted from Bismarck, North Dakota, crossing the Missouri River half a mile from the Standing Rock Sioux Reservation. It had been rerouted for the same reason that the resistance began: the threat of an oil spill contaminating the water sources. However, for the tribe, the construction of the pipeline would also desecrate sacred ground along its route. Ladonna Bravebull, founder of the Standing Rock Sioux camp, asserts the following:

> The U.S. government is wiping out our most important cultural and spiritual areas. And as it erases our footprint from the world, it erases us as a people. These sites must be protected, or our world will end; it is that simple. Our young people have a right to know who they are. They have a right to language, to culture, to tradition. The way they learn these things is through connection to our lands and our history.

---

3. Judd, "Indigenous Theology Movement," 211. This interpretation is based on the Andean myth of "Two Brothers."

4. Valencia Parisaca, *La Pachamama,* 83.

If we allow an oil company to dig through and destroy our histories, our ancestors, our hearts and souls as a people, is that not genocide?[5]

In September 2016, Yolanda Flores, an Aymara woman who works for DHUMA (Derechos Humanos y Medioambiente; in English, the Association of Human Rights and the Environment), had come to Washington, DC. She and other members of her team—Aymara lawyer Cristobal Yugra and Maryknoll Sister Pat Ryan—came at the invitation of an international court established within the World Bank to arbitrate grievances concerning trade deals. Specifically, the Canadian Bear Creek Mining Corporation was suing the government of Peru after their mining permit was revoked in Puno, Peru—the *altiplano*. Companies mining for silver, lead, copper, and other minerals are devastating the earth and water, considered sacred by the people for centuries. There had been a massive campaign of nonviolent resistance with more than fifteen thousand Indigenous peoples participating, blocking roads in and around Puno for nearly six months. Transportation was immobilized, markets closed, and tourism halted. The government took the surprising step of revoking the mining company's permit.[6] The international court accepted DHUMA's amicus brief, which refutes many of the company's arguments and invited them to attend the hearing in order to call on them to respond immediately to requests for additional evidence. On September 14, 2016, their one day off from the weeklong hearing, the DHUMA team was able to join the Dakota Access Pipeline protest in front of the White House, asserting together that "Water is Life" across the Americas, across the earth.[7] In December 2016, during a large interfaith service, Chief Arvol Looking Horse, a Lakota spiritual leader, spoke of the threat to clean water at Standing Rock as only one of millions of attacks on the integrity of the earth's elements. Fighting back would take a particular kind of power, he said: "We will be victorious through tireless, prayer-filled, and fearless nonviolent struggle. Standing Rock is everywhere."[8]

The rerouting of the pipeline near Lakota tribal land echoes back to the idea of a national sacrifice area. The following quote is from the Proclamation written during the Alcatraz Island occupation from November 1969 to June 1970:

5. Allard, "Founder of Standing Rock," paras. 12–13.

6. Maryknoll Office for Global Concerns, "Trade." See also Radio Mundo Real, "Six Years."

7. Maryknoll Office for Global Concerns, "Trade."

8. Markey, "How Standing Rock Became a Spiritual Pilgrimage," para 4.

Right now, today, we who live on the Pine Ridge Reservation are living in what white society has designated a "National Sacrifice Area." What this means is that we have a lot of uranium deposits here, and white culture (not us) needs this uranium as energy production material. The cheapest, most efficient way for industry to extract and deal with the processing of this uranium is to dump the waste by-products right here at the digging sites. Right here where we live. This waste is radioactive and will make the entire region uninhabitable forever. This is considered by industry, and by the white society that created this industry, to be an "acceptable" price to pay for energy resource development. Along the way, they also plan to drain the water table under this part of South Dakota as part of the industrial process, so that the region becomes doubly uninhabitable. The same sort of thing is happening down in the land of the Navajo and Hopi, up in the land of the Northern Cheyenne and Crow, and elsewhere . . . We are resisting being turned into a National Sacrifice Area. We are resisting being turned into a national sacrifice people. The costs of this industrial process are not acceptable to us. It is genocide to dig uranium here and drain the water table—no more, no less.[9]

Since the 1970s, the ecological movement and the new cosmology supported by the fields of science have gained momentum. However, I have often asked myself: "From whose perspective is the 'new' cosmology new?" The new cosmology sounds very similar to the Aymara *cosmovisión* of interdependence and interaffection within the cosmos of earth (*Pachamama*), her people and living beings, and the cosmos itself, most symbolically imagined as the night sky in all its constellations. Is the term "new" used in a similar fashion the way America was "discovered" by Columbus? A decolonial/postcolonial critique is undoubtedly needed here. The purpose and necessity of such a critique is for a truly mutual collaboration and solidarity—even reconciliation—among those of the "new cosmology" and those whose similar ancient cosmologies have been suppressed. Perhaps the moment is arriving when liberatory mediation from both perspectives will enable a convergence of positive energy for the healing and nurturing of the earth and its interdependent reality with all living beings. Those who stand with Standing Rock are realizing this today.

This is a new moment in history. The global ecological crisis is of emergency proportions. Those who live and work in Latin America and other Two-Thirds World countries and contexts witness the effects of the capitalist-consumerist development complex in what Brazilian liberation theologian

9. Ojibway, "Call to Native Americans," 49.

Leonardo Boff has identified as the two great wounds: increasing inhumane poverty and ecological devastation. Destitute persons often find themselves amidst diminished ecosystems of contaminated water, fouled air, soil erosion, pesticide, agrochemical contamination, as well as land and whole ecosystems (such as rainforests) that have been lost. The McDonald's Corporation and other fast food chains have contributed to the "hamburgerization" of Central America where, between 1960 and 1980, 50 percent of the 400,000 kilometers of rainforests were depleted in order to graze cattle.[10] In the Philippines, toxic waste has been dumped through US military bases. As noted above, nuclear toxic waste from energy and military complexes are dumped in the Third World of the US Southwest, often on Native American land. Twin violence exists: ecological violence against the environment and social violence, often against Indigenous peoples and those who are in solidarity with them. Among the victims of this twin violence are several who spoke out against it: Chico Mendes, a rainforest rubber tapper activist in Brazil; Dorothy Stang, a Notre Dame sister who lived in Brazil; and Berta Caceres of Honduras. Ecological devastation is often a result of economic exploitation; poverty is an environmental dilemma as well as a sociopolitical one. At the second meeting of World Popular Movements in July 2015 in Santa Cruz, Bolivia, Pope Francis called for urgent change to humanity as a whole. A global system, he said, "has imposed the mentality of profit at any price, with no concern for social exclusion or the destruction of nature . . . We want a change which can affect the entire world, since global interdependence calls for global answers to local problems. The globalization of hope, a hope which springs up from peoples and takes root among the poor, must replace the globalization of exclusion and indifference!"[11]

Ivone Gebara, the Brazilian ecofeminist theologian (or, as she calls herself, a Samba feminist theologian), notes that we discover our interconnectedness in our suffering. The water is polluted, food is tainted from the lakes and rivers, and sickness comes from eating tainted fish. Instead of being over creation, we are the earth's thought and reflection of itself, echoing the influence of Teilhard de Chardin. Matter and consciousness are not two different "things," as with Descartes. On the contrary, in the very "stuff of the universe," even in the tiniest atom or cell, there is a force calling it to consciousness. It may well be that the suffering of the earth and its marginal peoples may awaken us all to this necessary consciousness, rather than

10. Hedström, "Latin American," 120. See also Myers, "Hamburger Connection" and Caufield, *In the Rainforest*, 109–10.

11. Shriver, *Pilgrimage*, 251–52.

the New Age individualism that often superficially borrows (or robs) from deeper Indigenous ritual and vision.

Gebara brings in an epistemological critique to what may still be an anthropocentric emphasis of humans alone as cocreators or copilots, a concept that does not adequately reflect human interdependence with nonhuman nature. Her delineation of an ecofeminist epistemology recovers a knowing that reveals not simply an amazing cosmos, thought of as a fully formed and static entity, but an awesome cosmogenesis, an emerging, dynamic, and integral living phenomenon. The ongoing narrative of this unfolding cosmogenesis is what Thomas Berry describes as the universe story.[12] The universe is the context for doing theology and, as Teilhard de Chardin has developed, cosmogenesis becomes Christogenesis as the perfect incarnation (God coming to matter) of sacred and human nature, or rather, the highest point of communion. Gebara proposes that we come to this knowing through our experience, which cannot always be expressed in words. To recover our human experience permits the meaning of our deepest beliefs to develop in our minds and bodies.

Vine Deloria Jr. of Standing Rock—activist, author, educator, and lawyer—also wrote about understanding through experience: "Our task is to live in such a way that the information we receive through analysis becomes—over the passage of time and through grace and good fortune—our experience also." Yet, he is referring to tribal wisdom, which is communal wisdom, "the distilled experiences of the community and not the aesthetic conclusions of sensitive individuals or the poetic conclusions of personal preferences."[13] This wisdom has been tested by uncounted generations in a variety of settings. It is communal wisdom about what it means to be a human being as part of the earth. The sacredness of the land is foremost an emotional experience and names an important distinction, of two fundamental categories of emotional responses to sacred places, reflective and revelatory:

> This distinction between reflective and revelatory places is not intended to downgrade the validity of reflective experiences of lands. It is the ability to reflect that creates the awareness and sensitivity of peoples to the qualitative intensity of revelatory places. But the distinction is necessary because revelatory places are known only through the experience of prolonged occupation of land.[14]

12. See Swimme and Berry, *Universe Story*, and Berry and Tucker, *Sacred Universe*.
13. Deloria and Treat, *For This Land*, 251.
14. Deloria and Treat, *For This Land*, 251–52.

A "prolonged intimacy with the land" has stories, tribal histories, which are connected with geographic features and places. With the bones and dust of previous generations as part of the earth, the first dimension of Indian feeling about the land is, therefore, an admission that we are part and parcel of it physically. However, our physical contribution makes sense only because our memory of land is a memory of ourselves and our deeds and experiences: "When asked where his lands were, Crazy Horse replied that his lands were where his dead lay buried . . . Luther Standing Bear once remarked that a people had to be born, and reborn again, on a piece of land before beginning to come to grips with its rhythms . . . people must have freely given of themselves to the land at specific places in order to understand it."[15] From my limited experience at Pine Ridge and Rose Bud and through the generosity of our Lakota teachers there, I understand that much of the learning of communal wisdom is passed on through ceremony and deep-time sharing of stories, such as the star knowledge and Milky Way, which illuminates a Life Path of a People. How the stars align in a certain way indicates the time for a certain ceremony.

Popular religious practice among the Aymara relates profoundly with the earth. This no doubt strengthened their resistance and hope during centuries of colonization. As in many areas around the world, many are migrating to the urban centers out of necessity to find work. However, they return annually to their *fiesta principal* to reconnect to their people and land, feeling *Pachamama's* and God's embrace of them once again. The *Fiesta de la Cruz* (Feast of the Cross) involves reaching the summit of the mountains around the community, in some places requiring an overnight vigil of prayer and trust until dawn. The land holds memory, *is* memory embedded with spiritual resonance through regular pilgrimages, prayer, and rituals.

Even as I was in pastoral ministry in Peru from 1983 to 1994, the ways in which I found resonance and affinity with the unknown world of the Aymara began to challenge and encourage me to enter into my own unknown world as a Sansei Japanese American woman, to enter into our "underside of history." I reconnected with my own heritage by participating in the Manzanar Pilgrimage, a return to the WWII Japanese American internment or detention camp, where my father, grandfather, and extended family were held. Such pilgrimages revisit shadowed ground, uncovering sacred traces of suffering and hope. The land holds memory. The cemetery obelisk at Manzanar expresses the message, "This is the place of consolation for all of humanity." It is about reconnection with each other, with the "bones and dust of our previous generations," with mystery and the depth of life. It is

15. Deloria and Treat, *For This Land*, 253.

not an escape, like tourism, but a return to the center of pivotal events that have marked us and to narratives implanted in the land itself. The pilgrim's journey seeks a restoration of wholeness through a recentering, a reentering, and recovery of history—and recovering *from* history. It is a rediscovery that we are part of a living and vital collective memory.

The imprinting of historical memory on the American landscape, as explored by cultural geographer Kenneth Foote, gives evidence that the tendency to forget simply obscures rather than breaks with the past. Foote asserts that the sites of violence and tragedy themselves force people to face the naming of the events, that the inscriptions in the landscape are a sort of "earth writing."[16] Lisa Yoneyama agrees that mnemonic sites, or "memoryscapes," interrupt the process of amnesia; she holds that the power of such spaces and the accompanying spatial strategies of corresponding testimonies and storytelling produce new subjectivities.[17] Land holds memory; land is memory and, thus, is sacred.

The imprinting of historical memory on the American landscape indicates that the places and sites themselves are resources for our engagement, welcoming our attentive presence in the same way as that which seemed absent beckons our embrace. Through such spatial knowings and "memoryscapes," the pilgrimages to former internment camp sites are efforts that contribute to overcoming the general US characteristic of collective amnesia, to restoring our *anamnesis* (remembering) and our solidarity of memory that gives opportunity for compassion, communion, and commitment instead of antagonisms within our intercultural reality. The Greeks had two words—*mneme* and *anamnesis*—to designate memory. *Mneme* is memory as a noun ("the popping into mind of a memory"), while *anamnesis* is the process of remembering—the search, recall, or recollection. The *ana* of the Greek word *anamnesis* signifies returning to and recovering what had earlier been experienced or learned; the search for memory is directed against forgetting.[18]

The depth of meaning often arrives in the inconclusive absence, precisely by sitting with it. The cross of our Christian faith insists on God's presence at this moment when we are contemplating the mystery of God's grace in absence, in rupture, in betrayal and shock, in physical hardship, in psychological scars and denial. These forces of rupture would rather have us forget about the "infinite horizon of love"[19] in which we live. Thus,

16. Foote, *Shadowed Ground*, 5, 33.

17. Yoneyama, *Hiroshima Traces*, 34.

18. Ricoeur, *Memory, History, Forgetting*, 4.

19. Schreiter, *Ministry of Reconciliation*, 57.

our Christian *anamnesis* returns us to the experience of "love and mercy in the very desire and effort to bring about that love and mercy where it is absent."[20] The narratives of others in the land also beckon. Many of the internment camp sites were on what once was Native American land, and to some degree, I believe that their communal wisdom has affected our spirits and understanding in subtle and profound ways. My gratitude spans the Americas for many reasons. The question of identity formation in recovering the past and recovering from history is not identity for its own sake, as much as this is cause for celebration, but rather for compassionate relatedness and action with and toward other human beings of this earth who are threatened by similar conditions: Arab Americans in a post 9/11 world. Undocumented immigrants. Families in detention centers. Syrian refugees. African Americans. Native Americans. The earth herself.

During an autumn dawn in the forests of Yosemite Valley, I witnessed the twinkling stars greet the first rays of the morning sun as the giant sequoias seemed to erupt in birdsong. A large black raven seemed to guide me to a soft forest path with a great swoosh of its long iridescent wings. As I felt the earth cradling my morning footsteps in the presence of ancient time evoked by the sequoias, I wondered: is there a deep America? The United States is such a young country yet with ancient memories in the land. Is there a deep United States of America? A similar phrase is often uttered amidst the poverty of the *pueblos jóvenes* (shantytowns) in the urban capital of Lima, invoking *Peru profundo,* or deep Peru. (I've recently learned that this is invoked in Mexico as well, as *Mexico profundo.*) Even as the inhospitable economic and political conditions marginalize Indigenous peoples, forcing displacement and migration to the urban centers, the invoking of the consciousness of *Peru profundo* yields a defiant hope and tenacity for life as it reclaims Peru as home deep within identity, a deep rootedness in the land and cosmos as home, that reverberates in a deep rootedness in each other. The prayerful presence, resistance, and solidarity at Standing Rock is perhaps a hopeful sign for a deep America.

Dark spaces birth new stars. The dark space of the Aymara cosmology which is named *Llama Niwa*, mentioned earlier, holds deeper significance in Andean mythology. The mother llama and her offspring were the sacrificed animals during the first destruction of the world sometime after it was first created. In the night sky, the dancing stars of the Milky Way are their tears streaming profusely from their shadowy faces. The *Llama Niwa* appeared on the horizon for the first time at the beginning of a deluge, the first rainy season that initiated a new age. As Lawrence Sullivan noted,

20. Morrill, *Anamnesis as Dangerous Memory*, 190.

"the symbolism of weeping is coinvolved here with the material reality of flooding rainwaters and a new quality of time."[21] In closing, I remember Rev. Narciso Valencia Parisaca, Aymara diocesan priest of the Prelature of Juli, Peru, and Mr. Alejo Choque Chipana, lay pastoral agent of the town of Zepita, also of the Prelature. In April 2017, they were involved in a transit accident as they were returning from an Andean theology gathering in La Paz; neither survived. To these men who gave themselves to the land and people of the *altiplano* in life and in death: *Jilatanaka yuspagarpuni.*[22]

---

21. Sullivan, "Seeking an End to the Primary Text," 52–53.

22. "Brothers, we are profoundly grateful" (my translation).

14

Horizons of Memory and Hope: Some Concluding Reflections

ROBERT J. SCHREITER, CPPS

Indigenous Voices

The final session of the conference brought together four of the Indigenous voices that had spoken and given presentations: those of Eva Solomon, Marie Battiste, Roberto Tomichá Charupá, and Pedro (jPetul) Gutiérrez Jiménez. Eva Solomon noted the many similarities of the struggles and the common features of the journeys that Indigenous people in Canada and Latin America have made. She showed special appreciation for the careful elaboration of the outlines of a truly Indigenous Church that Tomichá had proposed. For her part, Marie Battiste drew attention to the common themes of how Indigenous lives had been disrupted by colonialism and violence. She pointed once again to the resources of Indigenous knowledge as a means for healing those profound wounds, and also to the need to repatriate the lands and waters that the colonizers had taken from the Indigenous. She called for a greater dialogue between Indigenous and Western cultures that would empower Indigenous cultures to speak and act; this could lead, however gradually, to a global reconciliation.

Roberto Tomichá Charupá noted, too, the common features of the struggles of the Indigenous peoples of America, but called attention at the same time to the fact that no single person can speak on behalf of the entirety of these peoples. As a theologian, he focused on the need to retrieve a genuinely Indigenous Church, along the lines of what has been happening in Chiapas in Mexico and in his native Bolivia. Here, primacy is given to the lives of Indigenous peoples and to the very principle of life as a source of theology. Viewed through this lens, that commitment to the primacy of life must ensure the recovery of all voices, including those often not allowed to speak—such as women and children—but also the voices of the earth itself. These voices together must become the protagonists of a truly autochthonous church, creating an eco-theology that brings together all the voices. JPetul Gutiérrez echoed many of these same themes, noting the presentation of Jorge Santiago Santiago, who had made a particularly eloquent appeal for developing and sustaining autochthonous voices in his review of the *pastoral indígena* developed under the auspices of CELAM over the past fifty years, and especially as articulated in the ministry and teaching of Don Samuel Ruiz, the longtime bishop of San Cristóbal de las Casas and a foremost defender of the rights of Indigenous peoples. Theology itself must be firmly grounded in a spirituality. Indeed, a spirituality may be a more comprehensive term than theology for embracing what must be articulated: the importance of beginning with the lived experience of Indigenous people; the realization that all persons and things are deeply interconnected; that this reality is enacted and performed, and not just thought about; and that it is out of this holistic vision that a new way of being the church will be discovered. To that end, he reiterated a theme that ran through all of the presenters' reflections: the importance of a sustained dialogue between Indigenous peoples and the larger church if Christian faith is to be truly incarnated in Indigenous lives and in the world church.

For this non-Indigenous participant and listener, three consolidating themes emerged from the reflections of these Indigenous speakers, as well as from the other presentations and discussions throughout the conference. These themes were presented to the four speakers in the final session for their reflection and comment. What follows includes their responses and my own further reflections on the rest of the presentations and discussion. The three themes are (1) carrying the wounds of a colonized people, (2) a renewed spirituality in the face of globalization, and (3) developing an integral eco-theology.

I then want to conclude with some reflections on the dialogue for which all the speakers were calling, and then also suggest what all of this might mean for the larger church if it is to acknowledge its own history with Indigenous peoples and allow itself to be moved forward by the challenges that they are presenting.

Healing the Wounds of a Colonized People

It is hard to find language that can encompass the pain and suffering that the Indigenous peoples of the Americas have undergone at the hands of the European colonizers over the past half millennium. The list of violations and depredations continues in a long trail of tears: the violent invasion of the native peoples; their being dispossessed of their lands and subjected to forced removals from their ancestral territories; the betrayal and negation of treaties into which Indigenous leaders had entered in good faith; the introduction of diseases to which Indigenous peoples had no resistance or immunity and which decimated whole peoples; the outright massacre of whole populations, at times focusing upon women, children, and the elderly; the deliberate destruction of their languages, cultures, ways of life, and family bonds; the use of boarding schools to extinguish Indigenous cultures among the young, with their attendant patterns of physical and sexual abuse; and the ongoing discrimination against Indigenous peoples by the colonizers.

There is no abstract concept that can begin to hold together this painful history, which is not only part of the past, but continues down to the present day in active discrimination and transmitted trauma. The language of the "violation of human rights," used by the United Nations in its Declaration on the Rights of Indigenous Peoples, is intended to place these violations in the language of international law, which all the countries of the earth are pledged to implement. As such, it is a useful way of entering into this discussion. But this language of an objective, impartial process does not capture the centuries of pain that this history carries. In view of that, the language of "wound," used by several of the speakers, comes closer to expressing the experience.

The wound spoken of here is not a wound treated in a single event. It speaks rather of a continuing and compounding wounding, an enduring and constantly recurring wounding over generations. Some of the speakers tried to express this profound reality. Stephen Judd spoke of a "colonial wound," echoing many decolonial thinkers. By this is meant that the entire colonial process continues to wound: it is not just a matter of a one-time invasion, but an ongoing (and usually deliberate) policy of colonizing. Roberto Tomichá Charupá expanded upon the colonial wound by distinguishing between "colonialism" (*colonialismo*) and "coloniality" (*colonialidad*). Colonialism is the act of violently subjugating a people by military force. Such colonialism, he suggested, can be overcome by resistance and eventual liberation. Coloniality, on the other hand, is a colonizing of the mind and its capacity to imagine. This makes a people into victims long after the colonizers have withdrawn, inasmuch as the colonial mindset is internalized and even transmitted to subsequent generations. In this way, the colonizers never actually withdraw; the effects of colonization continue to oppress. In places like North America, the colonizers indeed have not actually withdrawn, and even still control the spaces that are supposed to be accorded to Indigenous peoples.

Archbishop Sylvain Lavoie spoke of the "original wound," echoing the Christian doctrine of original sin. This doctrine holds that original sin is not just the first action of the primeval couple, but is also an originating event that in turn displaces and skews everything that follows it. The image of a wound is one of sundering the integrity and wholeness of the body (be it an individual body or the social body), threatening the well-being of the entire body. It is a festering reality that, in turn, can poison all that is around it, a disabling event that keeps a body from being restored to its full dignity and agency. As such, it calls us to remember what has been done in such viola-tion, to be attentive to its ongoing toxic character, and to look toward ways of healing that will restore the body to some measure of integrity.

Finding the means to claim, name, and explore those multiple vio-lations is a journey that many Indigenous people have embarked upon. Rather than expressing it in Western medicine's abstract and analytic lan-guage of "healing," the words "struggle" and "journey"—used by nearly all the participants—better captures the dynamic process that must be engaged to come to terms with this wound.

It is a process of recovery. In English, "recovery" can mean both getting back what has been lost as well as being restored to full health. The Spanish *recuperar* and *recuperarse* capture the same set of meanings. "Recovery" was a word heard frequently during the conference. It tries to track both the memory of what has happened as it is being recovered and the horizon of hope that the struggle for healing entails.

That struggle, that journey, is best captured in the personal narratives that played such an important role in the conference. The narratives of Francis White Lance, Eva Solomon, and Rosa Isolde Reuque Paillalef were all striking in this regard. Their narratives of growing up and living with this wound—and their own struggles to come to terms with it—are not just examples of different approaches. Rather, they are living testimonies to how the wounding has taken place, how the wounds have been con-fronted, and how lives are reconstructed in this journey. The narratives *are* the recovery. Roberto Tomichá Charupá and jPetul Gutiérrez, speak-ing from a more general perspective, put it clearly and simply: this whole recovery—both in terms of getting back and moving ahead—has to start from the experience of life itself. In places where Indigenous people speak as the majority of the population (as in the cases of Tomichá Charupá's

Bolivian example and the Mexican examples of Gutiérrez and Santiago), one can speak of developing a *teología india* that encompasses much of Central America and the Andean region, and which can lead to a genuinely autochthonous church. For Indigenous peoples that are beleaguered minorities in a larger population, the approach might appear more localized, as it is for the Mapuche in Chile, the Lakota in the United States, or the Anishinaabe in Canada. This does not make the contributions of the North Americans less significant; it only points to the additional challenges that exist when one has to work from limitations, such as having been dislocated onto reservations or scattered into urban venues.

Recovering memory, then, is an important dimension of healing. It brings together the fragments of a once integral worldview and way of living (what the Lakota seer Black Elk called the "hoop of the world") to reclaim dignity and identity. Marie Battiste presented this eloquently in the language of "frames"—especially the frames imposed by European colonizers to break and subjugate Indigenous ways of knowing. Being able to reweave these fragments into a narrative, to reclaim language that has been suppressed, and to reengage in rituals that affirm the place of the people within the purview of Mother Earth and its Creator are all part of this double act of recovery. Giving voice to these narratives, attending closely to what is said, and imagining what different kind of future might emerge out of these stories is the process by which recovering happens.

A Renewed Spirituality in the Face of Globalization

A common theme running through the conference was the need for recovering an Indigenous spirituality. "Spirituality," in this sense, meant both a recovery of each Indigenous people's life ways, as well as an integration of both theology and spirituality in the Christian sense so as to live a holistic life of faith, true both to Indigenous traditions and Catholic faith.

Marie Battiste spoke particularly insistently about the importance of recovering "Indigenous knowledge." Much of what shaped the life ways of many Indigenous groups has been lost in the violent and unequal encounter with the colonizers. Institutions, such as the boarding schools used in North America, had as an explicit goal the destruction of Indigenous knowledge. Nonetheless, fragments remain. Indigenous peoples have also been borrowing from their neighbors' Indigenous knowledge and practices to reshape and invigorate their own traditions.

An important factor to keep in mind here is that Indigenous knowledge arises out of an oral culture and not a literate one. For a long time, this issue has been approached only from the side of the colonizers: "oral cultures" represented an earlier, underdeveloped form of "literate cultures." Indeed, oral cultures were often called "illiterate" because they lacked writing (or used systems of writing in only a limited way).

This is one of the colonizers' "frames" that must be acknowledged and overcome in the recovery of Indigenous knowledge. Oral cultures organize knowledge in different ways than do literate ones. Oral cultures rely on memory and personal transmission of knowledge. Images and metaphors carry knowledge more effectively than abstract concepts. Those images and metaphors in narratives serve as *aide-mémoires* and also preserve the complexity of the teachings involved. For literate cultures, on the other hand, knowledge can be preserved in written texts. These can be engaged and transmitted irrespective of specific places and times. As a result, written texts can be read beyond the immediate context and even be given new meanings. The value of such a move is that they can speak to people in vastly different situations and over long periods of time. This is the source of the great power of the so-called "world religions" such as Christianity and Islam. But reliance on texts can also mean an alienation from the wellsprings of knowledge that brought them forth. They can be utilized by people of quite different emotional and spiritual dispositions by placing preference on the cognitive dimensions of knowledge.

As distance grows between the origins of the text and the world of their current readers, the texts can become alienated from the sources that gave them life. The results of this alienation can result in the cognitive eclipsing of the other dimensions of the human being—the embodied, the emotional, the relational, and the spiritual.

Knowledge in oral cultures is embedded in places and bodies that allow it to be both particular and cosmic at the same time. That all things are interconnected was a recurring theme throughout the conference. Stephen Judd drew attention to the *apachetas*, or sites of intersections in the dense world of symbolic meaning in Aymara cultures. Interconnection, rather than analysis, gives a holism to Indigenous spirituality. Being embedded in the land, in a specific place, does not mean that it cannot communicate with other spiritualities. Commonalities abound among Indigenous traditions. But one can only get to know the really cosmic dimensions through immersion and abiding in specific traditions.

The recovery of spirituality, in the sense of both reclaiming the past and healing for the sake of a different kind of future, does not happen in a vacuum. Reclaiming the past does not mean a return to the past as though there is some kind of inviolate zone that we can reenter. What has happened since colonization is also an undeniable part of a people's memory and history. To ignore or deny that is a new victimization: it says that either colonization was not important, or that Indigenous peoples are not important enough for the rest of the world to take notice of what has happened to them. Recovering memory and reorienting one's story has to engage the contemporary environment in which we now find ourselves.

As a number of speakers pointed out, that environment today is one of globalization. Globalization is a complex reality with many dimensions and is fraught with tensions and contradictions. The compression of time and space that marks the technological force of globalization can obliterate local cultures on the one hand, but can also strengthen them in their acts of resistance to globalization's overriding power. In approaching globalization from the perspective of Indigenous peoples, it is clear, first of all, that globalization is the heir to the European colonial adventures of the past half millennium. Globalization and colonialism are not coterminous, but globalization owes its expansive momentum to its colonial forbears. Its tendencies to homogenize whatever it touches flow from the ideologies of racism that propelled *conquistadores* and merchants in an earlier era and that continue to exist today. Its economic forms are more complex than those of the colonial-era European trading companies, but the impact on local economies has been equally devastating. Globalization's promises of interconnectedness and a cosmopolitan worldview are contradicted by the profound dislocations that so often follow in its wake.

The processes of globalization are often presented as the antithesis of Indigenous ways of life, and rightly so. In many ways, globalization is the cumulative result of the assault on Indigenous cultures. Indigenous cultures cannot isolate themselves from the impact of globalization, but must seek ways to resist its blandishments and cultivate resilience out of their own spiritual resources. The sense of connection and interrelation (captured especially in the Lakota *Mitakuye Oyasin*—"all my relations"—noted by Roger Schroeder and Eleanor Doidge in their remarks) speaks in contrast to globalization's celebration of the postmodern with its fragmentation.

Indeed, the fragmentation brought on by globalizing forces has deepened the yearning of many non-Indigenous people for the cosmic vision of Indigenous peoples. The quest of those refugees from globalization has produced a special challenge for the recovery of Indigenous cultures, especially in North America, where young non-Indigenous seekers come and try to appropriate Indigenous ways without committing themselves to the holism that those ways bespeak. But that such a problem even exists hints at possibilities for Indigenous ways to heal the fragmentation and alienation that accompany globalization's impact on societies.

Developing an Integral Eco-Theology

What Indigenous spiritual ways can contribute to the larger world found special expression among many speakers in the matter of the ecological destruction that threatens the survival of the planet itself. Indigenous peoples learned to live *with* the land they inhabited, not just *on* the land, as though it were an accidental place where they found themselves. This is obvious, among other things, in the fate of agricultural products taken from the Americas and introduced into Europe and Asia. Take, for example, the expropriation of the potato from the Andean region. Potatoes served as a food staple in the Andes and were carefully cultivated there. When introduced into Europe, without the careful husbandry of the Indigenous, they become subject to periodic blight, with disastrous consequences for the populations that had come to depend upon them.

Responding to the threats against the earth will require more than conservation (more careful use of resources) and preservation (setting up reserves). It will take a holistic approach that has much to learn from Indigenous peoples. Pope Francis's encyclical, *Laudato Si': On the Care of Our Common Home*, was cited again and again throughout the conference. In that document, Pope Francis appeals especially to the wisdom of Indigenous peoples as one of the most important guides to attaining a genuine eco-theology that both corrects some of the previous theology about creation (especially about human domination of the environment) and charts a way into the future that is built on genuinely integral human and social development.

It is noteworthy that the pope's namesake, Saint Francis of Assisi, was a forerunner of the church's current concerns about the environment. His capacity to communicate with animals (as in the stories of his encounters with Brother Wolf and with the birds) shows that he understood a central aspect of Indigenous spirituality, i.e., the capacity to communicate with our four-legged and winged fellow creatures. We "two-leggeds" must recover our bonds with the other beings around us.

The Importance of Dialogue

The Catholic Church's commitment to dialogue as a way of engaging the world is one that has only come about in the last half-century. There were always individuals and groups committed to dialogue in the church's history, but it never held the kind of high endorsement it now enjoys. It should not be surprising, then, that Catholics are still finding their way in dialogue.

This conference dwelt on a special aspect of dialogue. Alongside the many calls to engage in further and deeper dialogue, the space was opened to think about dialogue in a more fundamental way. What dialogue means is also shaped by culture. Frequently church people in the West have taken up dialogue along the lines of their culture. Dialogue is seen there as an amicable encounter marked by sincerity and hospitality. It tends to be occasional, that is, focused upon events of encounter. Such an approach, while having genuinely human qualities, can become instrumentalist in its practices. For many traditional cultures, dialogue is not about occasional meeting, but about a commitment to a relationship. In that relationship, it is about more than getting to know each other or exchanging information. It is about building and deepening ongoing bonds that transform those engaged in it.

Marie Battiste made this point especially clearly. Dialogue is not just a space where the colonizers can get to know Indigenous ways better, or come to understand the devastation that has been wrought on Indigenous peoples or the need to build more just relationships. Dialogue should also result in colonizers' coming to know themselves better—how their frames of knowledge led to the destruction of the Indigenous peoples' life ways and how those frames of knowledge continue to shape colonizers' attitudes and relationships with native peoples. There has to be a shift in the asymmetries of power, away from the continuing domination of colonizers and their church toward empowering Indigenous communities. Without this shifting of power, there will be no acknowledgement by the colonizers of how coloniality continues to distort relationships. There will be no undoing of the ideology of "discovery" or of the *terra nullius* that formed the foundation for the colonizing narrative.

In this light, the calls for working toward reconciliation come into clearer focus. The healing of memories is not just an issue for victims who carry a history that is still toxic to this day; it is also an issue for the victimizers who must come to name, accept, and examine their complicity in the destruction of Indigenous life ways and move to seek forgiveness from those whom they have harmed. Only when this is done are victims and colonizers on the way to healing memories. As memories are thus acknowledged and owned, the contours of pursuing justice come into clearer focus. What will count for a genuine restorative justice? What will real restitution look like? What can be the future of life together?

Forgiveness is built on healed memories and justice. Forgiveness was not a major motif in this conference. That was no surprise, since so much has to be done before any talk about forgiveness will have genuine substance. But two speakers—Eva Solomon and jPetul Gutiérrez—spoke of the need for Indigenous peoples to forgive themselves for abandoning or not following their own traditions. The theme of self-forgiveness does not come up much in talk about forgiveness and reconciliation. More often, emphasis is put on the fact that wrongdoers cannot forgive themselves for what they have done to others. This is true. But there is an important strain of forgiveness that involves the self which Solomon and Gutiérrez recognized. Such an appeal for self-forgiveness can free other victims to create the space necessary to rebuild their relationship to their heritage. For wrongdoers to hear such appeals for self-forgiveness can give them deeper insight into the damage they have done to the very capacity of victims to regain agency as subjects of their own history. I have encountered this same sentiment in places where I have worked, where people struggle to rebuild their lives after armed conflict and cultural devastation. It is important learning for the continuing engagement between Indigenous and colonizers.

The Church and Its Future Relationship with Indigenous Peoples

In this process of recovery, the tasks before the church are manifold. There is both a need to help Indigenous peoples recover the traditional ways of life, as well as to recover how the church contributed to and even promoted what has amounted in many places to cultural genocide. As was already noted, "recovery" has a forward-looking dimension as well. How can what we do to heal and restore memory build a horizon of hope in which Indigenous peoples and the rest of the church can work together, so that such destruction does not happen again and we can ensure the future of Earth itself?

Here, the speakers' narratives showed the different pathways that are being pursued in different parts of the Americas. They all, in varying ways, captured this twofold task of recovery. Eva Solomon spoke of how Anishinaabe ritual had been integrated into the celebration of baptism so that the sacrament could exhibit the two roots of identity for her people. JPetul Gutiérrez and Jorge Santiago spoke of the development of the autochthonous church among the various Mayan peoples of southern Mexico, and Rosa Isolda Reuque addressed this clearly in her presentation of Mapuche prayer and ritual.

Institutional efforts on the part of the church were also outlined. Roger Schroeder spoke of the Catholic Theological Union's long relationship with the Lakota peoples in South Dakota and how this has shaped the missionary vision of so many of its students, now working all around the world. Jaime Bascuñán presented what the University of San José de Temuco has been developing with the Mapuche people in southern Chile to support and sustain Mapuche culture in that region. Stephen Judd reflected on the efforts of the Maryknoll missionaries in their decades of work among the Aymara peoples of Peru and Bolivia.

Within those institutional efforts, the commitment and solidarity of individuals cannot be overestimated. Maria Clara Bingemer's presentation of the film *Two Persons, One Cause,* which documents the work of two Dorothys—Dorothy Day and Sister Dorothy Stang—highlighted Sister Stang's work among the Indigenous of northern Brazil, a commitment that ended in her murder. Such commitment reminds us that solidarity is not a concept, but a program of action for the sake of justice.

At another level, the church's engagement with the Truth and Reconciliation Commission (TRC) of Canada represented both the church's effort to support such an examination of how Indigenous peoples had been treated in the past and also to accept a charge to the churches to implement the recommendations resulting from the TRC. Both Marie Battiste and Michel Andraos elaborated upon this event and its hoped-for outcomes in great detail.

All of these helped to show the many avenues of approach in which the church must engage if it is to be a partner on the long road to reconciliation and also in promoting an integral eco-theology for the sake of the planet's future. As an international and intercultural religious body, it has to acknowledge its own wrongdoing in the past, accompany the victims in their tasks of recovery, and help shape and guide a movement toward a sustainable future within a horizon of hope. The church's own sacramental sensibility will then be able to align itself with the Lakota prayer *Mikuye Oyasin*—"all my relations."

Bibliography

Aboriginal Affairs and Northern Development Canada. "Treaty 1 between Her Majesty the Queen and the Chippewa and Cree Indians of Manitoba and Country Adjacent with Adhesions." http://www.trcm.ca/treaties/treaties-in-manitoba/treaty-no-1/.

——. "Treaty 2 between Her Majesty the Queen and the Chippewa and Cree Indians of Manitoba and Country Adjacent with Adhesions." http://www.trcm.ca/treaties/treaties-in-manitoba/treaty-no-2/.

Acarapi, Valentin Mejillones. "La Cruz Cuadrada." In *La Cruz Escalonada Andina*, edited by Centro de Cultura, Arquitectura y Arte Taipinquiri, 259–76. La Paz: Centro de Cultura, Arquitectura y Arte Taipinquiri, 1994.

Adam, Lucien, and Victor Henry, eds. *Arte y Vocabulario de la Lengua Chiquita: Con Algunos Textos Traducidos y Explicado*. Paris: Maisonneuve, 1880.

Aguiar, William, and Regine Halseth. "Aboriginal Peoples and Historic Trauma: The Process of Intergenerational Transmission." http://www.nccah-ccnsa.ca/Publications/Lists/Publications/Attachments/142/2015-04-28-AguiarHalseth-RPT-IntergenTraumaHistory-EN-Web.pdf.

Alfred, Geral Taiaiake. "Restitution is the Real Pathway to Justice for Indigenous Peoples." In *Response, Responsibility, and Renewal*, edited by Greg Younging et al., 163–70. Ottawa: Aboriginal Healing Foundation, 2011.

——. *Wasáse: Indigenous Pathways of Action and Freedom*. Peterborough, Ontario: University of Toronto Press, 2005.

Allard, LaDonna Brave Bull. "Why the Founder of Standing Rock Sioux Camp Can't Forget the Whitestone Massacre." *Yes! Magazine*, September 3, 2016. http://www.yesmagazine.org/people-power/why-the-founder-of-standing-rock-sioux-camp-cant-forget-the-whitestone-massacre-20160903.

Andraos, Michel. "Bishop Samuel Ruiz's Early Theological Insights." *Journal of Hispanic/Latino Theology* 19.1 (November 2013) 9–22.

——. "The Church and the Indigenous Peoples of the Americas: In-Between Colonization and Reconciliation." *New Theology Review* 29.1 (September 2016) 42–45.

——. *A Church with the Indigenous Peoples: The Intercultural Theology of Bishop Samuel Ruiz*. Eugene, OR: Cascade, forthcoming.

——. "March of the Pueblo Creyente, January 24, 2015: Commemorating the Fourth Anniversary of the Death of Bishop Samuel Ruiz." https://vimeo.com/151265932.

————. "Pope Francis and the Indigenous Peoples: Why a Visit to Chiapas?" *The Ecumenist* 53.4 (Fall 2016) 1–5.

Andraos, Michel, ed and trans. *Seeking Freedom: Bishop Samuel Ruiz in Conversation with Jorge S. Santiago on Time and History, Prophecy, Faith and Politics, and Peace.* Toronto: Toronto Council, Canadian Catholic Organization for Development and Peace, 1999.

Anglican Church of Canada. "The Apology—English." https://www.anglican.ca/tr/apology/english/.

Asch, Michael, et al. *Resurgence and Reconciliation: Indigenous-Settler Relations and Earth Teachings.* Toronto: University of Toronto Press, 2018.

Assembly of First Nations. "Numbered Treaty Education Provisions." http://www.afn.ca/uploads/files/education/26._numbered_treaty_education_provisions.pdf.

Barbour, Claude Marie. "Seeking Justice and Shalom in the City." *International Review of Mission* 73 (1984) 303–9.

Barbour, Claude Marie, and Eleanor Doidge. "Mission as Accompaniment." In *A Century of Catholic Mission,* edited by Stephen Bevans, 275–83. Regnum Edinburgh Centenary Series 15. Oxford: Regnum, 2013.

Barbour, Claude Marie, and Robert Schreiter. "Plural Spiritualities in Dual Religious Belonging." In *Plural Spiritualities: North American Experiences,* edited by Robert Schreiter, 75–90. Christian Philosophical Studies 14. Washington, DC: Council for Research in Values and Philosophy, 2015.

Battiste, Jaime Youngmedicine, ed. *Honouring 400 Years, Kepmite'tmne.* Eskasoni, NS: Mi'kmaq Grand Council, Eskasoni First Nation (Culture/Recreation and Youth), Nova Scotia Tripartite Forum on Education, 2010.

Battiste, Marie. "Micmac Literacy and Cognitive Assimilation." In *Indian Education in Canada: The Legacy,* edited by Jean Barman et al., 1:23–44. Vancouver: University of British Columbia Press, 1986.

Bear Clan Patrol. "History." https://www.bearclanpatrolinc.com/.

Benedict XVI, Pope. "Inaugural Session of the Fifth General Conference of Bishops of Latin America and the Caribbean." http://w2.vatican.va/content/benedict-xvi/en/speeches/2007/may/documents/hf_ben-xvi_spe_20070513_conference-aparecida.html.

Bernabé, Vicenta Mamani. *Identidad y Espiritualidad de la Mujer Aymara.* La Paz: Fundación Shi-Holanda, 2000.

————. *Mujer Aymara Migrante: Hermana, Ponte Derecha y Anda.* Colección Misión y Diálogo 8. Cochabamba: Instituto Latinoamericano de Misionología UCB, 2007.

Bernabé, Vicenta Mamani, and Calixto Quispe Huanca. *Pacha-Jaqi-Runa.* Espiritualidades Originarias 2. Cochabamba: Verbo Divino, 2007.

Bernabé, Vicenta Mamani, et al. *Pacha, Jiwasan QWamawisa: Nuestras Vivencias.* Espiritualidades Originarias 6. Cochabamba: Verbo Divino, 2010.

————. *Pacha, Suma Qamaña: Vivir Bien.* Espiritualidades Originarias 8. Cochabamba: Verbo Divino, 2012.

Bernstein, Marv. "We Must All Put First Nations Children First." *The Hill Times,* March 7, 2017. https://www.hilltimes.com/2017/03/07/must-put-first-nations-children-first/98905.

Berry, Thomas, and Mary Evelyn Tucker. *The Sacred Universe: Earth, Spirituality, and Religion in the Twenty-First Century.* New York: Columbia University Press, 2009.

Bevans, Stephen, and Roger Schroeder. *Constants in Context: A Theology of Mission for Today*. Maryknoll: Orbis, 2004.

———. *Prophetic Dialogue: Reflections on Christian Mission Today*. Maryknoll: Orbis, 2011.

Bevans, Stephen, et al. *The Healing Circle: Essays in Cross-Cultural Mission*. Chicago: CCGM, 2000.

———. *Models of Contextual Theology*. Rev. ed. Maryknoll: Orbis, 2002.

Binger, Carl. *Thomas Jefferson, a Well-Tempered Mind*. New York: Norton, 1970.

Black Bear, Matilda (Tillie). "Hunka, The Making of Relatives." In *The Healing Circle: Essays in Cross-Cultural Mission*, edited by Stephen Bevans et al., 17–23. Chicago: Chicago Center for Global Ministries, 2000.

Blais-Morin, Madeleine. "Comment Faire Revivire une Langue qui n'Était plus Parlée depuis un Siècle?" http://ici.radio-canada.ca/nouvelles/societe/2015/12/15/001-enseignement-langue-huron-wendat-wendake-quebec-cpe.shtml.

"Blanket Exercise." http://justicepaix.org/wp-content/uploads/2016/02/Blanket-Exercise.-B.McD_.pdf.

Blaut, James M. *The Colonizer's Model of the World: Geographical Diffusionism and Eurocentric History*. New York: Guilford, 1993.

Boff, Leonardo. *Trinity and Society*. New York: Orbis, 1988.

"Books of Chilam Balam: Mayan Literature." https://www.britannica.com/topic/Books-of-Chilam-Balam.

"Brothers and Sisters to Us: U.S. Bishops' Pastoral Letter on Racism in Our Day." Washington, DC: US Conference of Catholic Bishops, 1979.

Brown, Dee. *Bury My Heart at Wounded Knee*. New York: Pocket, 1970.

Canadian Conference of Catholic Bishops, et al. "A Catholic Response to Call to Action 48 of the Truth and Reconciliation Commission (On Adopting and Implementing the *United Nations Declaration on the Rights of Indigenous Peoples*)." http://www.cccb.ca/site/images/stories/pdf/catholic%20response%20call%20to%20action%2048.pdf.

———. "The 'Doctrine of Discovery' and *Terra Nullius*: A Catholic Response." http://www.cccb.ca/site/images/stories/pdf/catholic%20response%20to%20doctrine%20of%20discovery%20and%20tn.pdf.

Canadian Press. "Text of Stephen Harper's Residential Schools Apology." http://www.ctvnews.ca/text-of-stephen-harper-s-residential-schools-apology-1.301820.

Caufield, Catherine. *In the Rainforest*. Chicago: University of Chicago Press, 1985.

CBC News. "Shoal Lake 40 and Winnipeg's Drinking Water: What's at Stake?" *CBC News*, August 10, 2015. http://www.cbc.ca/news/canada/manitoba/shoal-lake-40-and-winnipeg-s-drinking-water-what-s-at-stake-1.3185733.

Celano, Thomas. "Vita Prima Sancti Francisci." In *Fontes Franciscani*, 273–424. Medioevo Francescano Testi 2. Assisi: Porziuncola, 1995.

Chalco, Efraín Cáceres. "El Zorro y la Ética Andina: Representaciones y Recomendaciones Simbólicas para Ser '*Allin Runa*' (Buena Persona)." *Volveré* 4.28 (November 2007). http://iecta.uta.cl/revistas/volvere_28/articulos.htm#c.

Chipana Quispe, Sofía. "Desafíos y Tareas de la Teología en la Región Andina: Desafíos y Tareas desde la Teología India." Presentation at Jornadas Teológicas Andinas, Bogotá, October 21, 2011. http://www.redescristianas.net/desafios-y-tareas-de-la-teologia-en-la-region-andina-desafios-y-tareas-desde-la-teologia-indiasofia-chipna-quispe.

Churchill, Ward. *Kill the Indian, Save the Man: The Genocidal Impact of American Indian Residential Schools*. San Francisco: City Lights, 2004.

Comisión de Pueblo Creyente. *Venticinco Años Del Pueblo Creyente: Caminando con Voz Profética: Diócesis de San Cristóbal de Las Casas, 1991–2016*. San Cristóbal de Las Casas, Chiapas, Mexico: Centro de Derechos Humanos Fray Bartolomé de Las Casas, 2017.

Conferencia General del Episcopado Latinoamericano y del Caribe. *Concluding Document: Aparecida, May 13–31, 2007*. Bogotá: Consejo Episcopal Latino americano, 2008.

Con Mirada, Mente y Corazon de Mujer. Chiapas, Mexico: Coordinación Diocesana de Mujeres, 1999.

Coordinación Ecuménica de Teología India Mayense. *El Aroma de las Flores en la Milpa Mayense: Ofrenda de Nuestro Caminar Teológico. Veinticinco Años de los Encuentros Ecuménicos de Teología India Mayense*. San Cristóbal de Las Casas, Chiapas, Mexico: Coordinación Euménica de Teología India Mayense, 2016.

Cormie, Lee. "Another Theology Is Possible: Exploring Decolonial Pathways." *Toronto Journal of Theology* 33.2 (Fall 2017) 262–78.

Crosby, Doug. "An Apology to the First Nations of Canada by the Oblate Conference of Canada." http://www.cccb.ca/site/images/stories/pdf/oblate_apology_english.pdf.

Curivil, Ramón. *La Fuerza de la Religión de la Tierra: Una Herencia de Nuestros Antepasados*. Santiago: Universidad Católica Silva Henríquez, 2007.

Dalarun, Jacques. *La Vita Ritrovata del Beatissimo Francesco: La Leggenda Sconosciuta di Tommaso da Celano*. Milan: Biblioteca Francescana, 2015.

———. "Thome Celanensis Vita Beati Patris Nostri Francisci (*Vita Brevior*): Présentation et Édition Critique." *Analecta Bollandiana* 133 (2015) 23–86.

Daschuk, James W. *Clearing the Plains: Disease, Politics of Starvation, and the Loss of Aboriginal Life*. Regina, SK: University of Regina Press, 2013.

Davenport, Frances G., and Charles Oscar Paullin. *European Treaties Bearing on the History of the United States and Its Dependencies to 1648*. Washington, DC: Carnegie Institute of Washington, 1917–37.

Deloria, Vine, Jr., and James Treat. *For This Land: Writings on Religion in America*. New York: Routledge, 1999.

DESMI. *Cuarenta Años de DESMI*. San Cristóbal de las Casas, Chiapas, Mexico: DESMI, 2012.

———. *Si Uno Come que Coman Todos: Economía Solidaria*. Mexico City: Grafía, 2001.

Díaz Fernández, José Fernando. *Misión y Pueblo Mapuche: Lectura Crítica desde un Horizonte no Sacrificial*. Temuco, Chile: Universidad Católica de Temuco, 2012.

Diocese of Santa Cruz del Quiché. *Padre Guillermo Woods*. 2nd ed. Ixcán, Quiché, Guatemala: Misioneros Maryknoll, 2006.

Donovan, Vincent. *Christianity Rediscovered*. Maryknoll: Orbis, 1982.

Dussel, Enrique. *Desintegración de la Cristiandad Colonial y Liberación: Perspectiva Latinoamericana*. Salamanca: Sígueme, 1978.

Estermann, Joseph. *Compendio de la Filosofía Occidental en Perspectiva Intercultural— Tomo IV: Filosofía Contemporánea*. 5 vols. La Paz: Instituto Superior Ecuménico Andino de Teología, 2011.

———. *Si el Sur fuera el Norte: Chakanas Interculturales entre Andes y Occidente*. La Paz: Instituto Superior Ecuménico Andino de Teología, 2008.

Falkinger, Sieglinde, and Roberto Tomichá. *Gramática y Vocabulario de los Chiquitos (Ss. XVIII)*. Cochabamba: Itinerarios, 2012.

Final Report, Vol. 1: Looking Forward, Looking Back. Ottawa: Royal Commission on Aboriginal Peoples, 1996. http://data2.archives.ca/e/e448/e011188230-01.pdf.

Fine, Sean. "Chief Justice Says Canada Attempted 'Cultural Genocide' on Aboriginals." *Globe and Mail*, May 28, 2015. https://www.theglobeandmail.com/news/national/chief-justice-says-canada-attempted-cultural-genocide-on-aboriginals/article24688854/.

Fontaine, Tim. "Canada Discriminates Against Children on Reserves, Tribunal Rules." *CBC News*, August 2, 2016. http://www.cbc.ca/news/indigenous/canada-discriminates-against-children-on-reserves-tribunal-rules-1.3419480.

Foote, Kenneth E. *Shadowed Ground: America's Landscapes of Violence and Tragedy*. Austin: University of Texas Press, 1997.

Ford, Stephen John. "Sovereignty: Do First Nations Need It?" http://www.idlenomore.ca/sovereignty_do_firstnations_need_it.

Francis, Pope. *Amoris Laetitia: The Joy of Love—On Love in the Family*. Frederick, MD: Word Among Us, 2016. https://w2.vatican.va/content/dam/francesco/pdf/apost_exhortations/documents/papa-francesco_esortazione-ap_20160319_amoris-laetitia_en.pdf.

———. *Evangelii Gaudium*. Frederick, MD: Word Among Us, 2013. http://w2.vatican.va/content/francesco/en/apost_exhortations/documents/papa-francesco_esortazione-ap_20131124_evangelii-gaudium.html.

———. *Laudato Si': On Care for our Common Home*. Washington, DC: USCCB Communications, 2015. http://w2.vatican.va/content/francesco/en/encyclicals/documents/papa-francesco_20150524_enciclica-laudato-si.html.

———. "Letter to Cardinal Marc Ouellet, President of the Pontifical Commission for Latin America." https://w2.vatican.va/content/francesco/en/letters/2016/documents/papa-francesco_20160319_pont-comm-america-latina.html.

———. "Meeting with Government Authorities and the Diplomatic Corps." http://w2.vatican.va/content/francesco/en/speeches/2015/july/documents/papa-francesco_20150710_paraguay-autorita.html.

———. "Meeting with Indigenous Peoples of Amazonia." http://w2.vatican.va/content/francesco/en/speeches/2018/january/documents/papa-francesco_20180119_peru-puertomaldonado-popoliamazzonia.html.

———. "Participation at the Second World Meeting of Popular Movements." http://w2.vatican.va/content/francesco/en/speeches/2015/july/documents/papa-francesco_20150709_bolivia-movimenti-popolari.html.

Francis of Assisi. *Primera Regla*. Translated by Paul Schwarz and Paul Lachance. In *The Birth of a Movement: A Study of the First Rule of St. Francis*, edited by David Flood et al., 63–85. Chicago: Franciscan Herald, 1975.

———. *Scritti: Testo Latino e Traduzione*. Padua: Editrici Francescane, 2002.

Frohlich, Mary. "Ministry to Place and Placelessness in a Globalized World." *New Theology Review* 16.1 (2003) 21–30.

Gasparello, Giovanna. "Indigenous Autonomies in Mexico: Building Peace in Violent Contexts." *Quaderns-e de l'Institut Català d'Antropologia* 21.1 (2016) 81–97. www.raco.cat/index.php/QuadernseICA/article/view/317136/407205.

Gastant Aucoin, Duane. "Residential Schools: A Reflection." *Mission* 2 (1995) 23–29.

Geertz, Clifford. *After the Fact: Two Countries, Four Decades, One Anthropologist.* Cambridge: Harvard University Press, 1996.

Gerhart, Mary. "Bernard Lonergan's Law of the Cross: Transforming the Sources and the Effects of Violence." *Theological Studies* 77.1 (2016) 77–95.

Gorski, Juan, and Roberto Tomichá. *Semillas del Verbo: Consideraciones Teológicas.* Cochabamba: Verbo Divino-Instituto de Misionología, 2006.

Grosfoguel, Ramón. "The Epistemic Decolonial Turn." *Cultural Studies* 21.2/3 (March 2007) 211–23.

Gutiérrez, Gustavo. *A Theology of Liberation: History, Politics, and Salvation.* Maryknoll: Orbis, 2004.

Hall, Suzanne E. *The People: Reflections of Native Peoples on the Catholic Experience in North America.* Washington, DC: National Catholic Educational Association, 1992.

Hanson, Jon, and Kathleen Hanson. "The Blame Frame: Justifying (Racial) Injustice in America." *Harvard Civil Rights-Civil Liberties Law Review* 41 (2006) 414–80.

Harper, Stephen. "Statement of Apology to Former Students of Indian Residential Schools." http://www.aadnc-aandc.gc.ca/eng/1100100015644/1100100015649.

Hedström, Ingemar. "Latin America and the Need for a Life-Liberating Theology." In *Liberating Life: Contemporary Approaches in Ecological Theology*, edited by Charles Birch et al., 111–22. Maryknoll: Orbis, 1990.

Henderson, James (Sa'ke'j) Youngblood. *Mi'kmaw Concordat.* Halifax: Fernwood, 1997.

Hicks, Savannah. "Buen Vivir: An Old, but Fresh Perspective on Global Development." *Thousand Currents* (blog), September 14, 2016. https://thousandcurrents.org/buen-vivir-an-old-but-fresh-perspective-on-global-development.

Hornbeck Tanner, Helen. "Treaties." *Encyclopedia of Chicago.* Chicago: Newberry Library, 2004. http://www.encyclopedia.chicagohistory.org/pages/1270.html.

Huanacuni, Fernando. "Buen Vivir-Vivir Bien." YouTube. Posted by Caoi Andina, June 22, 2012. https://www.youtube.com/watch?v=90ZHJMTcfOE.

Huarachi, Simón Yampara. "Economía Comunitaria Aymara." In *La Cosmovision Aymara*, edited by Hans van den Berg et al., 143–86. La Paz: HISBOL, 1992.

Huel, Raymond J. A. *Proclaiming the Gospel to the Indians and the Metis.* Edmonton: University of Alberta Press, 1996.

"Idle No More is Founded by Four Women." http://www.idlenomore.ca/idle_no_more_is_founded_by_4_women.

"Impact on Indigenous Peoples of the International Legal construct known as the Doctrine of Discovery, which has served as the Foundation of the Violation of their Human Rights." https://www.un.org/esa/socdev/unpfii/documents/E.C.19.2010.13%20EN.pdf.

International Theological Commission and Pope John Paul II. *Memory and Reconciliation: The Church and the Faults of the Past.* Boston: Pauline, 2000.

Irarrázaval, Diego. *Un Cristianismo Andino.* Quito: Abya Yala, 1999.

John Paul II, Pope. "Address to the Aborigines and Torres Strait Islanders in Blatherskite Park." http://w2.vatican.va/content/john-paul-ii/en/speeches/1986/november/documents/hf_jp-ii_spe_19861129_aborigeni-alice-springs-australia.html.

———. "Carta Apostólica a los Religiosos y Religiosas de América Latina con Motivo del V Centenario de la Evangelización del Nuevo Mundo." https://w2.vatican.va/content/john-paul-ii/es/apost_letters/1990/documents/hf_jp-ii_apl_29061990_v-centenary-evang-new-world.html.

———. "Celebración de la Palabra con los Campesinos y los Indígenas." https://w2.vatican.va/content/john-paul-ii/es/homilies/1987/documents/hf_jp-ii_hom_19870405_campesinos-indigeni.html.

———. *Fides et Ratio: To the Bishops of the Catholic Church on the Relationship between Faith and Reason.* Washington, DC: US Catholic Conference, 1998. http://w2.vatican.va/content/john-paul-ii/en/encyclicals/documents/hf_jp-ii_enc_14091998_fides-et-ratio.html.

———. "Meeting with Native Peoples: Sainte-Anne de Beaupre." http://www.cccb.ca/site/Files/1984-09-10_Amerindians_Inuuit.html.

———. *Novo Millennio Ineunte: To the Bishops, Clergy, and Lay Faithful at the Close of the Great Jubilee of the Year 2000.* Boston: Pauline, 2001. https://w2.vatican.va/content/john-paul-ii/en/apost_letters/2001/documents/hf_jp-ii_apl_20010106_novo-millennio-ineunte.html.

———. *Salvifici Doloris: On the Christian Meaning of Human Suffering.* Boston: Pauline, 1984. https://w2.vatican.va/content/john-paul-ii/en/apost_letters/1984/documents/hf_jp-ii_apl_11021984_salvifici-doloris.html.

———. *Sollicitudo Rei Socialis: To the Bishops, Priests, Religious Families, Son and Daughters of the Church and All People of Good Will for the Twentieth Anniversary of* Populorum Progressio. Washington, DC: US Catholic Conference, 1988. http://w2.vatican.va/content/john-paul-ii/en/encyclicals/documents/hf_jp-ii_enc_30121987_sollicitudo-rei-socialis.html.

———. *Ut Unum Sint: On Commitment to Ecumenism.* Vatican City: Libreria Editrice Vaticana, 1995. http://w2.vatican.va/content/john-paul-ii/en/encyclicals/documents/hf_jp-ii_enc_25051995_ut-unum-sint.html.

Johnston, Angus Anthony. *A History of the Catholic Church in Eastern Nova Scotia.* Antigonish, NS: St. Francis Xavier University Press, 1960.

Jordá, Enrique. "Aporte Región Andina: Quechua-Aymara." In *IV Simposio Latinoamericano de Teología India (Lima, 28 marzo-abril 2 de 2011): El Sueño de Dios en la Creación Humana y en el Cosmos,* 93–94. Bogotá: Consejo Episcopal Latinoamericano, 2012.

Judd, Stephen P. *De Apacheta en Apacheta: Testimonio de Fe en el Sur Andino Peruano.* Cochabamba: Verbo Divino, 2016.

———. "From Lamentation to Project: The Emergence of an Indigenous Theological Movement in Latin America." In *Santo Domingo and Beyond: Documents and Commentaries from the Historic Meeting of the Latin American Bishops' Conference,* edited by Alfred T. Hennelly, 226–35. Maryknoll: Orbis, 1993.

———. "The Indigenous Theological Movement in Latin America: Encounters of Memory, Resistance, and Hope at the Crossroads." In *Resurgent Voices in Latin America: Indigenous Peoples, Political Mobilization, and Religious Change,* edited by Edward L. Cleary and Timothy J. Steigenga, 210–30. New Brunswick: Rutgers University Press, 2004.

King, Thomas. *The Inconvenient Indian: A Curious Account of Native People in North America.* Minneapolis: University of Minnesota Press, 2013.

Kisala, Robert. "Formation for Intercultural Life and Mission." *Verbum SVD* 50.3 (2009) 331–45.

Klaiber, Jeffrey. *The Jesuits in Latin America, 1549–2000: Four Hundred and Fifty Years of Inculturation, Defense of Human Rights, and Prophetic Witness.* St. Louis: St. Louis University Press, 2009.

Knitter, Paul F. "El Diálogo Interreligioso." Conference paper given at Pontificia Universidad Javeriana, Bogotá, Colombia, August 25, 2011. http://servicioskoinonia.org/relat/416.htm.

Knockwood Shay, Isabelle, and Gillian Thomas. *Out of the Depths: The Experiences of Mi'kmaw Children at the Indian Residential School at Shubenacadie, Nova Scotia.* Lockporte, NS: Roseway, 1992.

Labaca Ugarte, Alejandro. *Crónica Huaorani.* Quito: CICAME and Vicariato Apostólico de Aguarico, 2003.

Lescarbot, Marc. *History of New France, 1618.* Translated by W. L. Grant. 3 vols. Toronto: Champlain Society, 1907–14.

Llanque, Domingo. *Ritos y Espiritualidad Aymara.* La Paz: ASETT, IDEA, and CTP, 1995.

López Hernández, Eleazar. "América: Diálogo de la Iglesia con el Mundo Indígena—Flores y Espinas." In *Segunda Asamblea Mundial de Misionólogos Católicos—Compartir la Diversidad en la Misionología: Cuestiones de Lenguaje Teológico,* edited by Juan Gorski and Roberto Tomichá, 49–62. Evangelio y Culturas 8. Cochabamba: Verbo Divino-Instituto de Misionología, 2006.

———. "El Papa Francisco en México: Análisis de los Textos y Contextos de la Visita desde la Perspectiva Indígena." *Observatorio Eclesial,* February 28, 2016. https://observatorioeclesial.org.mx/2016/02/28/persectiva-indigena-de-la-visita-del-papa-francisco-en-mexico.

———. *Teología India: Antología.* Cochabamba: Verbo Divino, 2000.

———. "Teologías Indígenas en las Iglesias Cristianas: ¿Podemos los Indígenas Ganar en Ellas el Lugar que Merecemos?" In *La Teología de la Liberación en Prospectiva: Congreso Continental de Teología, São Leopoldo, Brazil, October 7–11, 2012,* 2:293–306. Montevideo: Fundación Amerindia, 2012. http://www.elpuente.org.mx/wp-content/uploads/2013/01/Libro-II-Congreso-Continental-de-Teolog%C3%ADa-San-Leopoldo-Brasil2.pdf.

López Hernandez, Eleazar, et al. *Caminos de Herradura Veinticinco Años de Teología India.* Cochabamba: Verbo Divino, 2016.

López, José Luis. "*Aparecida*, Globalización, y Cambio Cultural: Una Lectura para Bolivia." In *Y Después de Aparecida, ¿Qué? Comentarios al Documento de Aparecida,* edited by Roberto Tomichá, 155–66. Cochabamba: Verbo Divino, 2007.

———. *Derechos de los Pueblos Indígenas.* Cochabamba: Centros de Culturas Originarias, 2005.

Malone, Dumas. *Jefferson and His Time: Jefferson the Virginian.* Boston: Little, Brown & Co., 1948.

Malone, Kelly. "'It's Everything for Us': Shoal Lake 40 Celebrates Start of Freedom Road Construction." *CBC News,* July 1, 2017. http://www.cbc.ca/news/canada/manitoba/shoal-lake-40-starts-construction-1.4187464.

Manuel, Arthur. "Until Canada Gives Indigenous People Their Land Back, There Can Be No Reconciliation." *Rabble* (blog), January 18, 2017. http://rabble.ca/blogs/bloggers/views-expressed/2017/01/until-canada-gives-indigenous-people-their-land-back-there-ca#.WIAw9l1F2Ko.twitter.

Markey, Eileen. "How Standing Rock Became a Spiritual Pilgrimage for Activists." *America,* June 14, 2017. https://www.americamagazine.org/faith/2017/06/14/how-standing-rock-became-spiritual-pilgrimage-activists.

Maryknoll Office for Global Concerns. "Trade: Indigenous Peoples Say 'Water is Life.'" *NewsNotes* 41.6 (November–December 2016) 9–10. http://maryknollogc.org/ sites/default/files/newsnotes/attachments/NovDec2016NewsNotes.pdf.

Marzal, Manuel María, et al. *The Indian Face of God in Latin America*. Maryknoll: Orbis, 1996.

Mayer, Enrique. "Las Reglas de Juego en la Reciprocidad Andina." In *Reciprocidad e Intercambio en los Andes Peruanos*, edited by Giorgio Alberti and Enrique Mayer, 37–65. Lima: IEP, 1974.

McGrory, Barry. "Membertou Speaks: What Happened on June 24, 1610?" In *Honouring 400 Years, Kepmite'tmne*, edited by Jaime Youngmedicine Battiste, 16–65. Eskasoni, NS: Mi'kmaq Grand Council, Eskasoni First Nation (Culture/ Recreation and Youth), Nova Scotia Tripartite Forum on Education, 2010.

Medina, Néstor. "A Decolonial Primer." *Toronto Journal of Theology* 33.2 (Fall 2017) 279–87.

Menesto, Enrico, and Stefano Brufani. *Fontes Franciscani*. Medioevo Francescano Testi 2. Assisi: Porziuncola, 1995.

Migne, Jacques-Paul. *Patrologiae Cursus Completus, Seu Bibliotheca Universalis, Integra, Uniformis, Commoda, Oeconomica, Omnium Ss. Patrum, Doctorum Scriptorumque Ecclesiasticorum, Series Graeca*. Vol. 37. Paris: Migne, 1862.

Mignolo, Walter D. *The Idea of Latin America*. Malden: Blackwell, 2005.

Miller, Jim. "Denominational Rivalry in Indian Residential Education." *Western Oblate Studies* 2 (1992) 139–55.

Montgomery-Fate, Tom. "What Are We Doing Here?" In *The Healing Circle: Essays in Cross-Cultural Mission*, edited by Stephen Bevans et al., 89–93. Chicago: Chicago Center for Global Ministries, 2000.

Montoya Upegui, Laura. *Autobiografía*. Medellín: Congregación de Misioneras de María Inmaculada y Santa Catalina de Siena, 2008.

Morrill, Bruce T. *Anamnesis as Dangerous Memory: Political and Liturgical Theology in Dialogue*. Collegeville: Liturgical, 2000.

Myers, Norman. "The Hamburger Connection: How Central America's Forests Become North America's Hamburgers." *Ambio* 10.1 (1981) 2–8.

The Newberry. "Popol Vuh." https://www.newberry.org/popol-vuh.

Newcomb, Steven. "Five Hundred Years of Injustice: The Legacy of Fifteenth-Century Religious Prejudice." *Shaman's Drum* (Fall 1992) 18–20. http://ili.nativeweb.org/ sdrm_art.html.

Nguyen, VanThanh. *Peter and Cornelius: A Story of Conversion and Mission*. Eugene, OR: Pickwick, 2012.

Nothwehr, Dawn. "The Church's Mission of Ecojustice: A Prophetic Dialogue Approach." In *Mission on the Road to Emmaus: Constants, Context and Prophetic Dialogue*, edited by Cathy Ross and Stephen Bevans, 87–105. London: SCM, 2015.

Obispos Católicos del Sur de Chile. "Al Servicio de un Nuevo Trato con el Pueblo Mapuche." http://documentos.iglesia.cl/documento.php?id=44.

Obispos de Concepción, Los Ángeles, Temuco, La Araucanía, Valdivia y Osorno. "Carta Pastoral: Evangelización del Pueblo Mapuche." Temuco, Chile. May 4, 1979.

Ojibway, Paul. "A Call to Native Americans." In *The People: Reflections of Native Peoples on the Catholic Experience in North America*, edited by Suzanne E. Hall, 39–54. Washington, DC: National Catholic Educational Association, 1992.

Otto, Rudolf. *Lo Santo: Lo Racional y lo Irracional en la Idea de Dios*. Madrid: Alianza, 1996.

Oyarce, Ana María, and Fabiana Del Popolo. "Hogar y Familia Indígenas en Bolivia, Chile y Panamá: Algunos Hallazgos y su Aporte a la Recolección de la Información Censal." *Notas de Población* 35.87 (2009) 121–49. https://repositorio.cepal.org/bitstream/handle/11362/12843/np87121149_es.pdf?sequence=1&isAllowed=y.

Panikkar, Raimon. *Ecosofía: Para una Espiritualidad de la Tierra*. Madrid: San Pablo, 1994.

Panikkar, Raimon, et al. *La Trinidad y la Experiencia Religiosa*. Barcelona: Obelisco, 1989.

Paul VI, Pope. *Gaudium et Spes: Pastoral Constitution on the Church in the Modern World*. Washington, DC: National Catholic Welfare Conference, 1965. http://www.vatican.va/archive/hist_councils/ii_vatican_council/documents/vat-ii_const_19651207_gaudium-et-spes_en.html.

Peelman, Achiel. *Christ Is a Native American*. Ottawa: Novalis, 1995.

———. *La Communion des Saints: Approche Chrétienne et Aamérindienne*. Montreal: Médiaspaul, 2016.

Potente, Antoinetta. *Una Vita Religiosa per Tutti*. Milan: Paoline, 2015.

Presbyterian Church. "The Confession of the Presbyterian Church." http://caid.ca/PresChuApo1994.pdf.

Radio Mundo Real. "Six Years after the 'Aymarazo' Protests in Peru." *Bilaterals*, June 27, 2017. http://www.bilaterals.org/?six-years-after-the-aymarazo.

Ricoeur, Paul. *Memory, History, Forgetting*. Translated by Kathleen Blamey and David Pellauer. Chicago: University of Chicago Press, 2004.

Roberto, Claude. "Les Relations des Autochtones avec les Communautés Religieuses dans l'École Résidentielle d'Onion Lake (Alberta)." *Études Oblates de l'Ouest* 5 (2000) 249–74.

Ruiz García, Samuel. "Ecclesiology and Pastoral Commitment." *Estudios Indígenas* 1.4 (1972) 3–16.

———. "En Esta Hora de Gracia." *Origins* 23.34 (February 10, 1994) 591–602.

———. "La Iglesia Latinoamericana en las Culturas, Reto y Esperanza para la Pastoral." *Estudios Indígenas* 1.2 (1972) 13–22.

Santiago Santiago, José Jorge. "Autochthonous and Foreign Indigeneity." *Estudios Indígenas* 1.4 (1972) 37–43.

———. "Desafíos para el Caminar Diocesano." Presentation given at Diocese of San Cristóbal's Theological Pastoral Congress, San Cristóbal de las Casas, Chiapas, Mexico, January 20–23, 2000. http://dicesisdesancristbaldelascasaschiapas.blogspot.com/p/la-memoria-de-nuestro-caminar-nos.html.

———. *Economía Solidaria Política: Construyendo Alternativas*. Colección Rebeldías. Mexico City: Eón, 2017.

———. "Theology, the Bible, and Indigenous Mission." *Estudios Indígenas* 1.4 (1972) 17–36.

Sarmiento Tupayupanqui, Nicanor. *Un Arco Iris de Voces Teológicas: La Trilogía Andina desde la Experiencia Quechua y Aymara*. Cochabamba: Itinerarios, 2016.

Schreiter, Robert. *The Ministry of Reconciliation: Spirituality and Strategies*. Maryknoll: Orbis, 1998.

———. "Reconciliation as a Model of Mission." In *A Century of Catholic Mission*, edited by Stephen Bevans, 232–38. Regnum Edinburgh Centenary Series 15. Oxford: Regnum, 2013.

———. *Reconciliation: Mission and Ministry in a Changing Social Order*. Maryknoll: Orbis, 1992.

Schroeder, Roger. *Initiation and Religion: A Case Study from the Wosera of Papua New Guinea*. Studia Instituti Anthropos 46. Fribourg: University Press, 1992.

———. "Prophetic Dialogue and Interculturality." In *Mission on the Road to Emmaus: Constants, Context and Prophetic Dialogue*, edited by Cathy Ross and Stephen Bevans, 215–26. London: SCM, 2015.

Second Vatican Council. *Ad Gentes: Decree on the Missionary Activity of the Church*. London: Catholic Truth Society, 1966. http://www.vatican.va/archive/hist_councils/ii_vatican_council/documents/vat-ii_decree_19651207_ad-gentes_en.html.

———. *Dignitatis Humanae: Declaration on Religious Freedom*. Washington, DC: National Catholic Welfare Council, 1965. http://www.vatican.va/archive/hist_councils/ii_vatican_council/documents/vat-ii_decl_19651207_dignitatis-humanae_en.html.

Sensoy, Özlem, and Robin DiAngelo. *Is Everyone Really Equal? An Introduction to Key Concepts in Social Justice Education*. New York: Teachers College Press, 2012.

Shriver, Mark K. *Pilgrimage: My Search for the Real Pope Francis*. New York: Random House, 2016.

Simpson, Leanne Betasamosake. *As We Have Always Done: Indigenous Freedom through Radical Resistance*. Minneapolis: University of Minnesota Press, 2017.

———. *Dancing On Our Turtle's Back: Stories of Nishnaabeg Re-Creation, Resurgence, and a New Emergence*. Winnipeg: Arbeiter Ring, 2011.

Smithsonian National Museum of the American Indian. "The Calendar System." https://maya.nmai.si.edu/calendar/calendar-system.

"Statement by the National Meeting on Indian Residential Schools." http://www.cccb.ca/site/images/stories/pdf/apology_saskatoon.pdf.

Stogre, Michael. *That the World May Believe: The Development of Papal Social Thought on Aboriginal Rights*. Sherbrook, QC: Paulines, 1992.

Sullivan, Lawrence E. "Seeking an End to the Primary Text." In *Beyond the Classics? Essays in Religious Studies and Liberal Education*, edited by Sheryl Burkhalter and Frank E. Reynolds, 41–59. Atlanta: Scholars, 2006.

Swimme, Brian, and Thomas Berry. *The Universe Story: From the Primordial Flaring Forth to the Ecozoic Era—A Celebration of the Unfolding of the Cosmos*. New York: HarperCollins, 1992.

Taylor, Alan. *American Colonies: The Settling of North America*. New York: Penguin, 2002.

Thomson, Bob. "*Pachakuti*: Indigenous Perspectives, Degrowth, and Ecosocialism." *Climate and Capitalism*, October 6, 2010. http://climateandcapitalism.com/2010/10/06/pachakuti-indigenous-perspectives-degrowth-and-ecosocialism.

Thwaites, Ruben Gold. "A Letter Missive in Regard to the Conversion and Baptism of the Grand Sagamore of New France, 28 June 1610." In *The Jesuit Relations and Allied Documents: Travels and Explorations of the Jesuit Missionaries in New France, 1610–1791*, 1:121–23. New York: Pageant, 1959.

Titley, Brian. "Hayter Reed and Indian Administration in the West." In *Swords and Ploughshares: War and Agriculture in Western Canada*, edited by R. C. Macleod, 109–48. Edmonton: University of Alberta Press, 1993.

Tomichá, Roberto. "Inculturación e Interculturalidad en Alejandro Labaka e Inés Arango." In *La Aventura Misionera de Inés Arango y Alejandro Labaka*, edited by Miguel Ángel Cabodevilla, 153–205. Coca, Ecuador: CICAME and Fundación Alejandro Labaka, 2012.

———. *La Primera Evangelización en las Reducciones de Chiquitos, Bolivia, 1691–1767: Protagonistas y Metodología Misional*. Cochabamba: Verbo Divino, 2002.

———. "Teilhard de Chardin y los Pueblos Indígenas: Una Lectura Preliminar." *ITER: Revista de Teología* 67 (2015) 159–70.

———. *Trinidad y Relacionalidad: Apuntes desde los Pueblos Originarios*. Bogotá: Consejo Episcopal Latinoamericano, 2016.

Tovar, Cecilia. *Ser Iglesia en Tiempos de Violencia*. Lima: CEP Instituto Bartolomé de Las Casas, 2006.

Trafzer, Clifford, ed. *American Indians/American Presidents: A History*. New York: Collins, 2009.

Truth and Reconciliation Commission of Canada. *Canada's Residential Schools: Reconciliation: The Final Report of the Truth and Reconciliation Commission of Canada, Volume 6*. Montreal: McGill-Queen's University Press for the Truth and Reconciliation Commission of Canada, 2015. http://www.myrobust.com/websites/trcinstitution/File/Reports/Volume_6_Reconciliation_English_Web.pdf.

———. *Honouring the Truth, Reconciling for the Future: Summary of the Final Report of the Truth and Reconciliation Commission of Canada*. Winnipeg: Truth and Reconciliation Commission of Canada, 2015. http://www.trc.ca/websites/trcinstitution/File/2015/Honouring_the_Truth_Reconciling_for_the_Future_July_23_2015.pdf.

———. *The Survivors Speak: A Report of the Truth and Reconciliation Commission of Canada*. Winnipeg: Truth and Reconciliation Commission of Canada, 2015. http://nctr.ca/assets/reports/Final%20Reports/Survivors_Speak_English_Web.pdf.

———. *They Came for the Children: Canada, Aboriginal Peoples, and Residential Schools*. Winnipeg: Truth and Reconciliation Commission of Canada, 2012.

Truth and Reconciliation Commission of Canada and Phil Fontaine. *A Knock at the Door: The Essential History of Residential Schools*. Winnipeg: University of Manitoba Press, 2016.

Turner, Victor. *The Ritual Process: Structure and Anti-Structure*. Chicago: Aldine, 1969.

United Church. "The Apologies." http://www.united-church.ca/social-action/justice-initiatives/apologies.

United Nations Declaration on the Rights of Indigenous Peoples. http://www.un.org/esa/socdev/unpfii/documents/DRIPS_en.pdf.

Upton, Leslie. *Micmacs and the Colonists: Indian-White Relations in the Maritimes, 1713–1867*. Vancouver: University of British Columbia Press, 1979.

Valencia Parisaca, Narciso. *La Pachamama: Revelacion del Dios Creador*. Quito, Ecuador: Ediciones ABYA-YALA, 1999.

Vitoria, Franciso de. *De Indis et de Ivre Belli Reflectiones: Being Parts of Reflectiones Theologicae XII.* Edited by Ernest Nys. Washington: Carnegie Institute of Washington, 1917.

Vitoria, Francisco de, et al., eds. *Political Writings.* Cambridge: Cambridge University Press, 1991.

Volf, Miroslav. *Exclusion and Embrace: A Theological Exploration of Identity, Otherness, and Reconciliation.* Nashville: Abingdon, 1996.

White Lance, Francis. "My Friend, the Reverend Doctor Claude Marie Barbour." In *The Healing Circle: Essays in Cross-Cultural Mission,* edited by Stephen Bevans et al., 24–29. Chicago: CCGM, 2000.

———. *Why the Black Hills are Sacred: A Unified Theory of the Lakota Sundance.* Rapid City, SD: Ancestors, 2004.

"The White Paper 1969." http://indigenousfoundations.arts.ubc.ca/the_white_paper_1969.

Wiebe, Rudy. *The Blue Hills of China.* Toronto: McClelland & Stewart, 1995.

Wilken, Robert Louis. *The Spirit of Early Christian Thought: Seeking the Face of God.* New Haven: Yale University Press, 2003.

Yoneyama, Lisa. *Hiroshima Traces: Time, Space, and the Dialectics of Memory.* Berkeley: University of California Press, 1999.

Zarazaga, Gonzalo J. *Dios es Comunión: El Nuevo Paradigma Trinitario—Homenaje a Karl Rahner, 1904-2004.* Salamanca: Salamanca Secretariado Trinitario, 2004.

Zorich, Zach. "The Maya Sense of Time." *Archaeology* 65.6 (2012) 25–29.

BIBLIOGRAPHY

Index

Aboriginal and non-Aboriginal
Relations Community
(ANARC), 96
Aboriginal vs. Indigenous, 51
Abraham (Old Testament), 23
accompaniment, 8, 138–42, 144–47, 170
Agreements of San Andrés on Rights
and Indigenous Culture (1996),
140
agricultural exports, 210
ajayu (spirit, soul), 24
Albó, Xavier, 35, 39
Alcatraz Island occupation (1969–
1970), 195–96
Alexander VI, Pope, 90n13
Alfred, Gerald Taiaiake, 3, 72–73
Algonkian people, 177
alienation, 3–4
ama llulla (do not be a liar), 26
ama qhella (idleness), 25
American Indian Movement (AIM),
162–63
American Indian Religious Freedom
Act (1978), 152, 153, 163
anamnesis (remembering), 200–201
Andean people
cosmic spirituality, 17, 19–21, 127n6
Indigenous theological movement,
30–41
Maryknoll experience, 31–34
"non-duality" of reality, 17

relatedness and, 17–18, 17n19, 113,
116, 154
See also Bolivia; Peru
Andraos, Michael, 172–73
Anishinaabe rituals, 70, 212
anthropological model, 171–72
Aparecida Brazil Conference (2007), 38
apologies, 3, 4, 61, 66, 88
Apple, Fr., 156
Apple, Francis Charles, Jr., 151
apprentices, in dialogue, 111
Archambault, David, 9n7
Arizmendi Esquivel, Felipe, 136
Arnold, Simón Pedro, 39
Assembly of First Nations, 87
Assembly of Western Catholic Bishops
(AWCB), 50–51
assimilation, 48, 48n4, 56, 61, 87, 109n2
Association of Human Rights and the
Environment, 195
Aucoin, Duane Gastant, 71
Australia, 60, 166
Australian Aboriginal Christians, 173
autochthonous church, 14, 128, 132
autonomy, 146
awareness, 78–82
ayllu and *ayni* reciprocally, 25
Aymara cosmology, 193, 201

Bald Mountain (*Pe Sla Paha*), 157
Barbour, Claude Marie, 153–54, 155,
163–64, 166, 167, 170

Barco Huerta, Maria Estela, 40n21
"barefoot theologians," 40
Bascuñán, Jaime, 7, 107
Battiste, Marie, 8, 177–78, 203, 207, 211
Bear Butte (*Mato Paha*), 158
Beauval Indian Residential High School
    (BIRHS), 81
"Becoming a Warrior" program, 96
"being universal," as a Catholic, 113–14
Benedict XIV, Pope, 179
Berry, Thomas, 198
Bevans, Stephen, 171
Big Crow, Moses, 163
Black Bear, Tillie, 153, 154, 163, 166,
    168–69
Black Hills, 157–58
"Blanket Exercise," 68n35, 95, 96
Blondin-Andrew, Ethel, 76n58
Boff, Leonardo, 197
Bogenschutz, Barbara, 166
Bohan, Daniel, 79
Bolivia
    agricultural cycle, 193
    Buen Vivir, 38–41, 38n16
    church with an Indigenous face,
        13–29
    communitarian space, 24–26
    connections principle, 16–18
    cosmic spirituality, 17, 19–21
    creative and cosmic spirituality,
        19–21
    decolonize minds, 21–24
    extended family, 25–26
    historical memory, 21–24
    nomadic hospitality, 26–29
    renewal process, 36–38
    systematic understanding of
        encounters, 34–36
    "Tale of Two Brothers" myth, 30–31
    theological movement, 39
    transcultural content, 14–16
Bonaventure, Saint, 16
"borderland co-existence," 40
Bravebull, Ladonna, 194
"Breaking New Ground Together"
    program, 96
British North America Act (1867), 90
Brown, Dee, 162

Buen Vivir, 38–41, 38n16, 132
Buffalo Gap (*Tatanka Tatiopa*), 158
Buffalo Nation (Pte Oyate), 157–58
Building Bridges Project, 7, 50–51, 83n6
Bureau of Indian Affairs (BIA), 162
burial grounds, 46, 78
Bury My Heart at Wounded Knee
    (Brown), 162

Caceres, Berta, 197
Cáceres Chalco, Efraín, 26
Caminos de Herradura (Andraos), 39
Canada
    caste system, 85
    church responsibilities in, 62–66
    colonization, 45–52, 81, 90–92
    Eurocentrism and, 180–84
    Mi'kmaw Nation, 177–78
    reconciliation, 52–55, 65, 93–97,
        188 (*see also* Truth and
        Reconciliation Commission of
        Canada)
    social reconciliation, 55
Canadian Bear Creek Mining
    Corporation, 195
Canadian Catholic Aboriginal Council,
    94
Canadian Catholic Organization for
    Development and Peace, 68–69
Canadian Conference of Catholic
    Bishops, 65, 65n25, 68–69
Canadian Human Rights Tribunal
    (2016), 66–67
Canadian Religious Conference, 68–69
Carrasco, Bartolomé, 36
Carter, Maryann, 79
caste system, in Canada, 85
Catholic Indigenous Elders' Dialogue,
    with Catholic theologians, 51
Catholic Theological Union (CTU), 3, 8,
    32, 160, 163–66
Catholic University of Temuco, Chile,
    107–8
cemetery grounds, 46, 78
CENAMI (National Center for
    Assistance to Indigenous
    Missions), 36–37, 36n12, 37n13

Center for World Catholicism and
Intercultural Theology
(CWCIT), 3, 9
Chiapas, Diocese of, 136
"Chicago" group, 164–65, 166
Chilam Balam Books, 127n8, 131
Chile. *See* Mapuche people
Chipana Quispe, Sofía, 19, 21–22
Choque Chipana, Alejo, 202
Christian tradition, Traditionalist and,
155
"Christianity of the Indies" (Mogrovejo),
14
Christianity Rediscovered (Donovan),
167
Christopher Columbus, 90
church
on accompaniment, 144–46
Calls to Action response, 94–96
Christianity, 139
colonialism, 178–180
control mechanism and role in
colonialism, 143
on dialogue, 210–12
diocesan-level initiatives, 95–96
future relationship, 212–13
Indigenous faces in, 13–29
inter-diocesan initiative, 96
Lakota relationship, history of,
162–63
in Mapuche culture, 103–4
meaning of being universal, 113–14
papal bulls, medieval period, 90
reconciliation, 93, 189–191
religion and, 139
responsibilities in Canada, 62–66
views on Indigenous theology, 131
"The Church and Indigenous Peoples
in the Americas" (2016
conference), 3–4
church-affiliated pastoral institute, 37,
37n13
circle, as symbol of mutuality and
equality, 109
*The Clash of Civilizations and the
Remaking of World Order*
(Huntington), 40

clear-cutting, for commercial use, 92
cognitive justice, 188–92
collective grief, 81
colonial Christendom, 14
colonial mindset, 23n49
colonial wound, 33–34, 33n6
colonialism, 143, 178–80, 205
coloniality, 205–6
colonization
accepting the reality of, 54–54
in Canada, 45–52, 81, 90–92
church politics and, 178–80
church's reflection on, 143
defined, 90
healing wounds of, 205–7
Common Experience Payment (CEP),
88–89
communal wisdom, 198–99
communitarian reductionism, 19
communitarian space, 24–26
community, 101, 114, 129–30, 133
Community Well-Being Index, 187
compensation for past wrongs, 88–89
complementary values, 105
connections principle, 16–18, 73n49
Constitution of the Plurinational State
of Bolivia (2008), 40
contextual theology, 171–72
Convention on the Prevention and
Punishment of the Crime of
Genocide (1948), 59n7
convivencia (living together), 14, 15
cosmic spirituality, 17, 19–21, 127n6
cosmic upheaval (*Pachakuti*), 31
cosmology, 193, 196, 201
cosmology movement, 196
"The Council of Three Fires," 45
courage (*qamasa*), 24
courage (*woohitika*), 157
Couture, Joe, 81, 81n3
Crazy Horse, 199
creation, care for, 169–170
creative spirituality, 19–21
criminal justice system, 69, 69n36
Crow Dog, Leonard, 154
Crow Good Voice, Violet, 166, 171
Crowshoe, Reg, 75n54

cultural genocide, 59–60, 162
culture
    as dynamic development, 116
    internalized, 80
Custer's Last Stand, 151

Dakota Access Pipeline, 73n47, 194–95
    See also Standing Rock Reservation,
        North Dakota
Dalle, Luis, 36
dancing, in a circle, 109
Daschuk, James, 183
Day, Dorothy, 213
Declaration of Barbados (1971), 142–
    43, 142n13
decolonial ecclesiology, (iglesia
    autoctona), 8
decolonization, 33–34, 92, 134, 145,
    188–92
decolonize minds, 22–24
"Decolonizing Our Hearts and Minds"
    program, 96
"decolonizing the heart" (jPetul), 8
deep places, 201
Delmas (priest), 79
Deloria, Vine Jr., 198
DePaul University. See Catholic
    Theological Union (CTU)
Devil's Tower (Mato Tipila), 158
Dewey Beard (Iron Hale), 151
diaconate program, 141
dialogue
    Catholic Indigenous Elders
        Dialogue, 51
    "Elder's Dialogue" program, 97
    importance of, 210–12
    intercultural (see intercultural
        dialogue)
    interreligious dialogue, 114–15
    mission encounter and, 111–14
    symbols and gestures in, 109–10
dialogue roundtable symposium, Chile,
    108–10, 114
DiAngelo, Robin, 191
Díaz Díaz, Enrique, 136
Diego, Juan, 94
Dignitatis Humanae (Vatican Council II
    document), 65n25, 138–39

dignity, 82
Diocesan Pastoral Plan (2016), 137, 142,
    144, 145
Diocese of Chiapas, 136
Diocese of San Cristóbal de las Casas
    accompaniment, lessons learned,
        146–47
    Call to Action initiatives, 96–97
    confrontation events, 140–41
    description of, 136–38, 136n4
    Indigenous theology, 128–29
    Pastoral Plan (2016), 144
Directions for Indigenous Ministry
        program
    2013 conferences, 52
    2016 conference, 51
    formation of, 83, 83n6
    social justice tour, 96
Directions in Aboriginal Ministry
        program, 97
discipleship, 23
disposition, interior, 110, 110n4
diversity, 113, 115
Divine Word Missionaries (SVD), 160,
    166
Doctrine of Discovery, 49–51, 90–91,
    91n14, 94
Doi, Joanne, 8, 166, 193
Doidge, Eleanor, 164, 170
domination, move away from, 144, 145
Donovan, Vincent, 167
dreams, 121–23, 132
Durocher, Paul-André, 65

earth, protection of, 75, 75n54
ecofeminist theologian, 197–98
ecojustice, 170
ecological devastation, 196–97
eco-theology, 210
"Elder's Dialogue" program, 97
empowerment, 80, 132
encounters
    with cultures, 142–44
    with Indigenous people, 160–61
    Indigenous theology, 133
    Maryknoll missionaries, 31–34
    systematic understanding of, 34–36
Eurocentrism, 186–87

Evangelii Gaudium (Francis, Pope), 13, 41

evangelization, 114, 142

exclusion, 3–4

experiences shared, outcomes, 84

extermination, war of, 141

EZLN (Zapatista Army of National Liberation), 140, 142

Falling Star Girl (*Wicahpi Hinhpaya Win*), 158

family, 24–25

Fides et Ratio (John Paul II, Pope), 13

Fiesta de la Cruz (Feast of the Cross), 199

First Continental Encounter of Missions in Latin America (1968), 142

First Indigenous Congress (1974), 140

First Latin American Meeting of *Teología India*, 1990, Mexico City, 123–24

First Nations, Inuit, and Métis (FNIM) committee, 95

Flores, Yolanda, 195

Fontaine, Phil, 88

Foote, Kenneth, 200

Ford, Stephen John, 51

forgiveness, 26, 53–55, 125, 211–12

Forster, Ken, 88

Fort Black trading post, 85

fortitude (*wacintanka*), 157

Fourth Latin American Episcopal Conference, Santo Domingo, 37

Francis, Pope
   on accompaniment, 135
   Amazonia peoples, 2018 meeting, 5, 8
   apologies, 4, 67, 67n32, 173
   on apostles, 22
   Evangelii Gaudium, 13, 41
   historical memory, 22
   hospitality, 29
   humanity, call for change to, 197
   Laudato Si, 18, 41, 75n55, 92–93, 210
   missionary discipleship, 41
   on repeal of Doctrine of Discovery, 91

theology as creative and transformative, 147

Francis of Assisi, Saint, 20–21, 210

Franciscan missionaries, 127n6

French colonists, 180

Frog Lake Massacre, Alberta (1885), 86

Frohlich, Mary, 170, 170n19

Funk, Jack, 79

fur trade, in Canada, 85

Gaudium et Spes (Vatican II document), 16

Gebara, Ivone, 197–98

Geez (magazine), 93

generational impacts of Residential Schools, 57–59, 75n56

generosity (*wacante ognaka*), 157

Ghost Dance movement, 162

Girardi, Juan, 38

globalization, 207–9

The Go-Between (Hartley), 63n17

God
   image of, 53, 70–71, 112, 114
   as kenosis, 116
   listening to heart of, 130
   in nature, 21, 104
   response from, 130

God Mystery, 19–20

Gorski, John F., 143

gospel insights, in intercultural dialogue, 111–14

Gosselin, Rose-Anne, 56n1

government
   missionaries and, 152–53
   resistance, Mexico, 145
   See also Indian Residential Schools, Canada

Grandin College, Fort Smith, Northwest Territories, 76n58

Grant, Ulysses S., 152

grief, 47, 81

Grief to Grace program, 94

Guatemala, 34–35, 34–35n8, 38

guillatún (religious ceremony), 102, 102n5

Gutiérrez, Gustavo, 34, 135

Gutiérrez Jiménez, Pedro (jPetul), 7–8, 121, 204, 206, 211–12

Hanbleceyapi (Vision Quest), 159
Hanson, Jon, 184
Hanson, Kathleen, 184
harmony, 40n21
Harney Peak (*Wakinyan Hohpe*), 158
Harper, Stephen, 59n7, 61, 65
Hartley, L. P., 63n17
healing, 22
Henderson, James, 178
historical memory, 21–24, 74n51
Hodgson, Maggie, 94
Holy Rosary Mission, 151
Holy Spirit, 16, 22, 29, 104
honor, 49, 69
Horn Cloud, Joseph, 151
hospitality, nomadic, 26–29
Houlton Band of Micmacs, 177
Huanacuni, Fernando, 18
human being (*jaqi*), 17–18
humbleness (*wowahala*), 157
Hunka ceremony, 163–64
Hunkapi (Making of Relatives), 159
Huntington, Samuel, 40
Huron-Wendat ancestral language,
     76n59

IDEA (Instituto de Estudios Aymaras),
     37
IDECA (Instituto de Culura Andina), 37
Idle No More (peace movement), 52
idleness (*ama qhella*), 25
iglesia autoctona (decolonial
     ecclesiology), 8
"In This Hour of Grace" (Ruiz), 140
incarnation, 13, 15–16, 15n11
inculturation, 15, 171–72
Independent Assessment Process (IAP),
     89
Indian Act of Canada (1876), 56n2, 91
Indian Residential School Settlement
     Agreement of 2006 (IRSSA)
     activism, beginning od, 88
     Truth and Reconciliation
          Commission, 57n3
Indian Residential Schools, Canada
     as assimilation strategy, 48–49
     Beauval Indian Residential High
          School, 81

generational impacts, 57–59, 75n56
Image of God and, 70–71
Indian Act of Canada (1876), 56n2
instituted, 185
"killing the Indian in the child,"
     48–49, 48n4, 185–86
positive experiences, 76–77, 89
Returning to Spirit program, 55–59
survivor testimony, 75n56, 86
Truth and Reconciliation
     Commission, 7
See also Truth and Reconciliation
     Commission of Canada
Indian Residential Schools Settlement
     Agreement (2006), 61–62, 88
Indigenous knowledge, 74n51, 207–8
Indigenous languages, 74, 74n53, 76n58,
     76n59, 77n60, 128, 179, 181
Indigenous peoples, current status,
     187–88
Indigenous theology movement
     (*teología india*), 6, 30–41
Indigenous theology (*teología india
     maya*)
     as axes of building local Catholic
          church, 8
     challenges ahead, 133–34
     concepts of, 125–28
     current situation, 131–32
     emergence in Mexico, 123–25
     fruits of, 132–33
     methodology, 129–31
     in San Cristóbal diocese, 123–25,
          128–29
     themes reflected on, 129
Indigenous voices, 203–4
Indigenous-led movements, 82–83
Inipi (Sweat Lodge), 159
"integral ecology" (Francis, Pope), 41
Inter Caetera (Alexander VI, Pope), 90
interconnectedness, 197–98, 204, 208
intercultural challenges, 3, 9, 103, 106
intercultural dialogue
     apprentices, 111
     gospel insights, 111–14
     interior disposition, 110
     interreligious dialogue, 114–15
     overview, 107–8

questions and challenges, 115–17
safe environment, 110–11
symposium, 108–10, 114
See also dialogue
interculturality, 168–69
internalized culture, 80
interreligious dialogue, 114–15
Inyan Hoksila (Stone Boy) story, 157–58
Inyan Kaga (Stone Mountain), 158
IPA (Instituto de Pastoral Andina),
    36–37
Irarrázaval, Diego, 35, 39
Iron Hale (aka Dewey Beard), 151
Iskay Hermanonimanta myth, 30–31
Isnatiawicalowanpi (Sing over a Young
    Girl), 159

Japanese American internment camp,
    199–201
jaqi (human being), 17–18
Jesuit missionaries
    Albó, Xavier, 35
    Huron-Wendat ancestral language,
        76n59
    Mi'kmaq mission, 179–81
    model of the Reductions, 33
    Velásquez, Alberto, 123
John Paul II, Pope
    apologies, 67n31
    apology, 4
    Fides et Ratio, 13
    on missionaries, 14
    reconciliation, 188–89
    Sollicitudo Rei Socialis, 62n14
    support of Mapuche people, 105
Johnson v. McIntosh (1823) US Supreme
    Court, 91
Joseph, Robert, 192
jPetul, meaning of, 122n2
Judd, Stephen, 6, 30, 193, 205, 208
justice
    cognitive justice, 188–92
    ecojustice, 170
    embrace and, 73, 73n49
    perceived justice, 184–88
    social justice tour, 96

Kagan, David Dennis, 9n7
Kairos Canada, 68n35, 95, 96
kairos moment, 6
Kakfwi, Stephen, 58n5
Keeping a Ghost (*Wanagi Wicauhapi*),
    159
Killarney, Ontario, 45–46
"killing the Indian in the child," 48–49,
    48n4, 185–86
kimün (wisdom/knowledge), 112
kindness (*waunsilayapi*), 157
King, Thomas, 93
Knitter, Paul, 115
Knuth, Maryellen, 166
kultrun tailfe (drum instrumentalist),
    102, 102–3n6

Labaka, Alejandro, 24–25
Lafond, Harry, 79–80, 91–92, 91n15, 94
Lakota Nation
    church relationship, history of,
        162–63
    CTU relationship, 163–66
    CTU-Lakota relationship, 160
    mentors, 154
    Peace Policy, 152
    reservations, changes to, 152
    seven ceremonies, 159
    teachings, origins of, 156–57
    traditional ways of Lakota, 153–54
    traditional ways, renaissance of,
        153, 156
    White Lance heritage, 151–52
land
    clear-cutting, for commercial use, 92
    confiscation of, 45–46, 73n47, 79,
        107–8, 180
    National Sacrifice Area designation,
        195–96
    Royal Proclamation (1763), 85
    sacred grounds, destruction of, 9,
        194–95
language issues for Indigenous people.
    See Indigenous languages
language learning, for non-Indigenous
    people, 79, 82–83, 93
Las Casas, Bartolomé de, 36, 36n11, 136

Laudato Si' (Francis, Pope), 18, 41,
    75n55, 92–93, 210
Lavoie, Sylvain, 7, 52, 78, 206
law of plenary power, 91
learning styles, 104
Lebret Task Force (LTF), 83
liar, do not be (*ama llulla*), 26
liberation theology, 34, 39
life
    principles of, 17, 17n19
    sharing problems and pleasures, 130
    symbolic-religious concept of, 26
liminality, 31
literate cultures, 208
Little Bighorn, 151
living together (*convivencia*), 14, 15
"living well" (*Buen Vivir*), 40
Llama Niwa, 193, 201
Llanque, Domingo, 35
llellipun (personal prayer), 102, 102n4
"logical exclusivity" principles, 17
"Long Ago Parenting" program, 96
lonko (community chief), 101, 101n1
Looking Horse, Arvol, 195
Loon Lake battle, Saskatchewan (1885),
    86
López Hernández, Eleazar
    CENAMI's pioneering work, 36,
        37n13
    ecclesial structures, 23
    on living well, 40
    on nomadism, 26
    official statements vs. ecclesial
        realities, 4
    on pope's presence in Chiapas, 173
    published reflections, 39
    reflections in *Caminos de Herradura*,
        39
    workshops/conferences, 35
lumber industry, 92

Maasai people, East Africa, 167
Macdonald, John A., 60, 91
Mackay, Stan, 73
Madden, James, 34
Maillard, Abbé, 181
Making of Relatives (*Hunkapi*), 159
male initiation rituals, 161

Mamani, Vicenta, 35
Manuel, Arthur, 90
Manzanar Pilgrimage, 199
Mapuche people
    childhood experience, 101–3
    dialogue (*see* intercultural dialogue)
    educational challenges, 103
    identity as Catholic woman, 103–4
    intercultural challenges, 106
    personal prayers, 102, 104
    spirituality, 104–5
Maqque, Victor, 39
Martin, Paul, 60
martyrs, in Guatemala, 34–35, 34–35n8,
    38
Mary Magdalene, 23, 55
Maryknoll Mission Center,
        Cochabamba, Bolivia, 37
Maryknoll missionaries
    conferences, 32n4, 35
    encounter with Indigenous world,
        31–34
    IDEA and IDECA, founding of,
        37n13
    martyr, in Guatemala, 34–35
    as witnesses at U.N. hearing, 39
Mato Paha (Bear Butte), 158
Mato Tipila (Devil's Tower), 158
Maya Codices, 127n6
Mayan Calendars, 127n9, 133
McAdam, Sylvia, 93
McDonald's Corporation, 197
McDonough, Brian, 7, 9n7, 56
McLachlin, Beverly, 187
McLean, Sheelas, 93
Membertou, Chief, 178
memory, historical, 21–24, 74n51
memory, living
    communal wisdom, 198–99
    cosmology movement, 196
    ecological devastation, 196–97
    interconnectedness, 197–98
    land as sacred, 193–96, 199–200
    National Sacrifice Area designation,
        195–96
    sacred places, 198–99
Menchú, Rigoberta, 37
Mendes, Chico, 197

Méndez Arceo, Sergio, 36
Mexico. *See* Indigenous theology
    (*teología india maya*)
Mignolo, Walter, 33–34, 40
Mi'kmaq Treaty (1752), 180
Mi'kmaw Nation
    colonization, 178–80
    compulsory schooling, 183, 185
    Eurocentrism and, 180–84
    injustice imposed on, 184–88
    Potlotek First Nation, 177–78
    "reserves," settlements, 182–84
    schools, 182–84
    treaty-making period, 182
mining industry, 75n56, 95, 195
missio Dei theology, 168
Missiological Institute, Catholic
    University, Bolivia, 37
mission
    as encounter and dialogue, 111–14
    as theology, 112, 166–72
missionaries
    American Indians and, 152–53
    Divine Word Missionaries (SVD),
      160, 166
    Jesuit (*see* Jesuit missionaries)
    living with Indigenous people, 14,
      24–25, 62–63, 63n16
    Maryknoll (*see* Maryknoll
      missionaries)
    Oblates of Marie Immaculate,
      62–63, 66, 77, 83, 96
    in San Cristóbal diocese, 139
missionary call out of poverty (Latin
    America), 37
Missionary Oblates of Marie
    Immaculate, 62–63, 66, 77, 83,
    96
mission-in-reverse, 167–68
Mitakuye Oya'sin (all my relations),
    169–70, 209, 213
Models of Contextual Theology (Bevans),
    171
Mogrovejo, Toribio de, 14
Montoya Upegui, Laura, Saint, 21
Mullin, Margaret, 70
Murdered and Missing Indigenous
    Women (MMIW), 52, 94

mythologies, 139

Náhuatl philosophy, 17
National Aboriginal Day, Canada, 94
National Center for Assistance
    to Indigenous Missions
    (CENAMI), 36–37, 36n12,
    37n13
National Center of Indigenous Pastoral
    Work (CENAPI), 135n2
National Day of Prayer in Solidarity
    with Indigenous Peoples, 94
National Day of Reconciliation in
    Canada (2009), 65
National Indian Brotherhood, 87
National Indigenous Congress (1996),
    140
National Inquiry into Missing and
    Murdered Indigenous Women
    and Girls (Winnipeg), 52
National Sacrifice Area, 195–96
Native American Project of Theology,
    163
Native American Renaissance, 163
natural resources, exploitation of, 75,
    75n54
new cosmology, 196
new evangelization, 114
Newcomb, Steven, 91, 93
newen, defined, 104, 104n7
Nguenechen (God), 101n2, 104
Nguyen, vanThanh, 169
Nicholas V, Pope, 90n13
No Horse, Alvin, 156
Noisy Hawk, Lyle, 155–56
nomadic hospitality, 26–29
"non-duality" of reality, 17
Nothwehr, Dawn, 9m7, 170

Oblate Star of the North Retreat Centre,
    96
oil industry, 73n47, 95, 194–95
option for the poor and Indigenous, 140
oral cultures, 207–8
original sin, doctrine of, 53, 206
Our Lady of Guadalupe, 94, 96
Our Lady of Guadalupe Circle, 93–94
Outside, the Women Cried (Funk), 79

Pacha (Trinity), 26
Pachakuti (cosmic upheaval), 31, 31n3, 41
paganism, 139
pampachanakuy (forgiveness), 26
Papua New Guinea (PNG), 160–61
Pastoral Congress of the Earth (2014), 142, 145
Pastoral Theological Congress (2016), 145
"Pastoral Work in the Missions of Latin America" (Vatican II document), 142
Paul, Elsie, 96
Paul III, Pope, 136
Pe Sla Paha (Bald Mountain), 157
Peace Policy (Grant, Ulysses S.), 152
Peelman, Achiel, 71n41
Peltier, Leonard, 162–63
Pérez Quispe, Julio, 25
perichoresis, 16, 20, 20n32
Perrier, Christine, 39
personal narratives, 206
Peru, 38–39, 195, 201
Peter and Cornelius (Nguyen), 169
Phélan, Mauricio, 40n21
Philippines, toxic waste disposal, 197
Pine Ridge Reservation, 151–53, 156, 161–62, 164, 166
plenary power, law of, 91
Plourde, Omer, 64
poor and Indigenous, option for, 140
poos (meaning of), 27–28
Popol Vuh ("Book of the Community"), 127n7, 131
positive experiences, residential schools, 76–77, 89
Potawatomi Indigenous people, 45, 177
Potlotek First Nation, 177
power
    in the community, 114
    transfer of, 80
praxis model, 172
prayers and prayer spaces, 102, 104, 122, 132
Prince, Rose, Saint, 70, 70n40
Proaño, Leonidas, 36

Protestant Native American Theological Association, 163
Pte Oti Kinapapi (Wind Cave), 158
Pte Oyate (Buffalo Nation), 157–58
Puebla, Santo Domingo, 37
Pueblo Creyente, 8, 10, 137, 141, 145
pueblos originarios (way of living as original people), 112, 114–15, 116

qamasa (courage, self-esteem), 24
Quispe, Calixto, 17, 25, 35

Rabbit-Proof Fence (movie), 93
racism, 46–47, 81, 85, 111, 112
rainforest depletion, 197
reality, building a new, 130–31
reciprocity, 25
reconciliation, 22, 72n45, 76n57, 82–84, 168–69
    See also Truth and Reconciliation Commission of Canada
recovery, 206–9
Red Cloud Indian School, 151
Redsky, Erwin, 47
Reed, Hayter, 64
refugees, Guatemala, 35
relatedness
    diversity and, 113
    of life and identity, 116
    principle of, 17–18, 17n19, 154
relationships
    Canadian stories, 50–52, 78, 84–87
    with churches, 3–4, 36–38
    with cosmos, 17
    cultural/religious, 105
    with dominant societies, 3–4
    between faith and cultures, 13
    interrelationship of everything, 18
    between justice and embrace, 73, 73n49
    Mexican personal stories, 121–23
    in nomadic culture, 27–28
    right relationships, 169–170
    social relationship, 25
    United States stories, 151–52
    See also Buen Vivir
religion

defined, 139
in Papua New Guinea, 161
See also church
remembering (anamnesis), 200–201
renewal process, 36–38
repentance, 54
resistance and rebellion movements, 140
respect (*wayuonihan*), 157
restitution, 72–74
Resurgent Voices in Latin America
(Andraos), 39
Returning to Spirit (RTS) program,
53–54, 55, 68, 94
Reuque Paillalef, Rosa Isolde, 7, 101,
206
revelatory place, 198–99
Riel rebellion, Saskatchewan (1885), 86
right relationships, 169–70
Romanus Pontifex (Nicholas V, Pope),
90
Roosevelt, Franklin D., 45
Rosebud reservation, 161–64, 166, 171
Royal Commission on the Aboriginal
Peoples (RCAP), 48n5, 87–88
Royal Proclamation (1763), 85, 91, 179
Ruah (Spirit), 24
Ruiz, Samuel (jTatic Samuel), 36, 37n13,
79, 96, 123–24, 123n3, 136, 204
Ruiz García, Samuel, 136, 137, 138–40
Ryan, Pat, 195

safe environment, 110–11
St. Albert Catholic School district, 95
Saint Lawrence River, 73n47
St. Thomas More College
(Saskatchewan), 95
San Andrés on Rights and Indigenous
Culture Agreements (1996), 140
San Cristobal Diocese, Mexico. *See*
Diocese of San Cristóbal de las
Casas
Santiago Santiago, Jorge, 7–8, 204
Santo Domingo conference (1992), 37
Sarmiento, Nicanor, 35, 39
Saskatchewan, Canada, 78–79, 86
Schreiter, Robert, 8, 53, 160, 168, 203
Schroeder, Roger, 8
Scott, Duncan Campbell, 61, 185

Second Vatican Council, 14, 14n6, 32,
65n25, 138, 142, 171
"Seeking Freedom" (Santiago), 137,
137n5
self-esteem (*qamasa*), 24
self-forgiveness, 212
seminary experience, 122–25
Sensoy, Özlem, 191
Seven Laws, Lakota, 157
Seven Sacred Mountains, 157–58
sexual abuse, 49, 66, 70, 75, 81
shared experiences outcomes, 84
Shining Path Maoist-inspired terrorists,
39
Shoal Lake 40 First Nation, 46–47
Simpson, George, 85
Sinclair, Murray, 49, 188
Sing over a Young Girl
(*Isnatiawicalowanpi*), 159
Sioux, government name, 162
social relationship, 25
sociocultural imaginary of *Buen Vivir*,
38–41, 38n16
Sollicitudo Rei Socialis (John Paul II,
Pope), 62n14
Solomon, Eva, 7, 45, 83, 83n6, 203, 206,
211–12
Spirit (Ruah), 24
spirit, soul (*ajayu*), 24
spiritual violence, 64
spirituality, renewal of, 207–9
Standing Bear, Luther, 199
Standing Committee on Indigenous
Affairs (SCIA), 50–51
Standing Rock Reservation, North
Dakota, 9, 73n47, 194–95
Stang, Dorothy, 197, 213
Star Boy (*Wicahpi Hoksila*), 158
"Statement of the Government of
Canada on Indian Policy
(1969)," 87
Steinhauer, Mike, 83
Stone Boy (*Inyan Hoksila*) story, 157–58
Stone Mountain (*Inyan Kaga*), 158
stories, importance of, 88–89, 111
structural sin, 62, 62n14
submissiveness, alternative to, 144
suffering, 71, 71n44

Sullivan, Lawrence, 201–2
"Summer Amerindian Leadership"
    program, 83
Sun Dance (Wiwayang Wacipi), 154–55,
    158
SVD (Divine Word Missionaries), 160,
    166
Sweat Lodge (*Inipi*), 159
symbols and gestures, in dialogue,
    109–10
systematic understanding of encounters,
    34–36

Takes War Bonnet, Ray, 156, 161
"Tale of Two Brothers" myth, 30–31
Tatanka Tatiopa (Buffalo Gap), 158
Teilhard de Chardin, Pierre, 197–98
Tekakwitha, Kateri, Saint, 70, 74n53,
    95, 96
teología india (Indigenous theology
    movement), 6, 141, 145
teología india maya (Indigenous
    theology), 8
terra nullius, 49–51, 90–91, 91n14, 179
"The Passion to Serve the People"
    (Santiago), 137
Theological Pastoral Congress (2000),
    144
Theological Pastoral Congress (2010),
    142
theology
    accompaniment, role in, 147
    contextual theology, 171–72
    defined, 112
    mission as, 112, 166–72
"theology of cultures," 137
Third Diocesan Synod (1995–99), 145
Throwing of the Ball (*Topkaholyapi*),
    159
Tokahe (the first man) story, 157–58
Tomichá Charupá, Roberto, 6, 13, 33,
    203, 205, 206–7
Topkaholyapi (Throwing of the Ball),
    159
toxic waste, 195–97
Traditionalist, Christian tradition and,
    155–56
Tran, Peter Tam, 166

transcultural affirmation, 13
transcultural content, 13, 14–16
Treaty of Chicago (1833), 45
tremendum et fascinans, 19–20
Trinitarian Mystery, 18, 19
Trinity, 16, 20, 20n35, 26, 139, 168
truth, expression of, 15
Truth and Reconciliation Commission
    of Canada (TRC)
    apologies, 66, 88
    Calls to Action, 49, 66–68, 92–96
    challenges in reconciliation, 68–70
    church's responsibilities, 62–66
    composition of, 89
    cultural genocide, 59–60
    future prospects, 75–77
    introduction of, 56–57
    launching of, 57n3
    multiple generations impacts,
        57–59, 75n56
    reconciliation, 72–74, 189
    reflections on, 7, 49
    Residential School impact, 70–71
    settler willingness toward
        reconciliation, 74–75
    state responsibilities, 60–62
    testimonies, 186
Truth and Reconciliation process report,
    Guatemala, 38, 39
Turner, Victor, 31
Twelve-Step Pilgrimages program, 94
Two Crow, Mr., 155
Two Persons, One Cause (film), 213

United Nations Declaration of Human
    Rights (1947), 39
United Nations Declaration on the
    Rights of Indigenous Peoples of
    2007 (UNDRIP), 39, 49–51, 67,
    89, 94, 190, 205
United Nations Human Development
    Index, 187
United States of America. *See* Lakota
    Nation
Uni-Triune Mystery, 20, 26
universe (cosmos), 17
universe story, 198

Valencia Parisaca, Narciso, 194, 202
Vallejos, Luis, 36
values, 26, 74, 75n55, 105, 133
Vancouver, "City of Reconciliation," 97
Vanier, Jean, 82
Vatican Council II, 14, 16, 65n25, 138–
    39, 142, 171
    See also Second Vatican Council
Velásquez, Alberto, 123
Vera López, Raúl, 136
Vision Quest (*Hanbleceyapi*), 159
"voice of voiceless," 37
vulnerability, 116

wacante ognaka (generosity), 157
wacintanka (fortitude), 157
Wakinyan Hohpe (Harney Peak), 158
Walk a New Path: From Hurt to Healing
    (Lavoie), 82
wampum belt, Mi'kmaw symbol, 178
Wanagi Wicauhapi (Keeping a Ghost),
    159
war of extermination, 141
waunsilayapi (kindness), 157
wayuonihan (respect), 157
werken (messenger), 101, 101n2
White Buffalo Calf Woman Society, 163
White Lance, Daniel, 151
White Lance, Francis, 8, 151, 161, 164–
    65, 171, 172, 206
White Lance, John, 151
white privilege, 92
    See also racism
Whitecap, Susan, 79

Who Leads the Leaders? (booklet), 83
Wicahpi Hinhpaya Win (Falling Star
    Girl), 158
Wicahpi Hoksila (Star Boy), 158
Wiebe, Rudy, 165
Wind Cave (*Pte Oti Kinapapi*), 158
Winka (non-Mapuche people), 109
wisdom (*woksape*), 157
wisdom, communal, 198–99
wisdom/knowledge (*Kimün*), 112
Wiwayang Wacipi (Sun Dance), 154–55,
    158
woksape (wisdom), 157
women
    recognition of, 143
    women's movements, 141
Wood, Thomas, 181
Woods, Bill, 34–35
woohitika (courage), 157
World Bank, 195
World Popular Movements (2015), 197
World Social Forums, 40
"Worship Without Walls" (Lavoie), 82
Wounded Knee Massacre (1890), 151,
    162
wounds, healing of, 205–7
wowahala (humbleness), 157

Yellow Hawk, Gilbert, 153, 154
Yoneyama, Lisa, 200
Yugra, Cristobal, 195

Zachary-Deom, Christine, 56n1

CPSIA information can be obtained
at www.ICGtesting.com
Printed in the USA
LVHW091940290319
612383LV00002B/12/P

9 781532 631115